The Eightballers

John Stanaway & Bob Rocker

The Eightballers: Eyes of the Fifth Air Force

The 8th Photo Reconnaissance Squadron in WWII

John Stanaway and Bob Rocker

Schiffer Military History
Atglen, PA

Acknowledgments

The acknowledgments for the 8PRS are these generous people:

Ben Armstrong, Connie Bailey, Dick Bailey, Allen Blum, Woodrow Cobb, Mrs. Aden Davis, Curtis Dell, Jim Dieffenderfer, Moe Dmochowski, Byron Dobbs, Tom Farmer, Bill Gailfus, Mrs. Marvin Gardner, Len Headley, Bill Hilliard, Jim Kendall, Andrew Keppel, Don Kimbrough, M. F. Kirby, Earl Lee, DeLasso Loos, Robert Ludtke, Jim McEwan, M. Melman, Harold Moffat, Vince Murphy, John Neilson, Roy Reid, Frank Reindl, Hector Rodgers, Norb Ruff, Roger Sheldon, Dick Shipway, Harold Southard, Clark Sykes, Vic Tatelman, Herbert Thomas, C. Thureen, Ralph Watts, James Woods, and Messrs. Bugai, Heller, Looker and Mattila.

Book Design by Ian Robertson.

Library of Congress Catalog Number: 99-61082

Printed in China.
ISBN: 0-7643-0910-2

We are interested in hearing from authors with book ideas on related topics.

Published by Schiffer Publishing Ltd.
4880 Lower Valley Road
Atglen, PA 19310
Phone: (610) 593-1777
FAX: (610) 593-2002
E-mail: Schifferbk@aol.com.
Visit our web site at: www.schifferbooks.com
Please write for a free catalog.
This book may be purchased from the publisher.
Please include $3.95 postage.
Try your bookstore first.

In Europe, Schiffer books are distributed by:
Bushwood Books
6 Marksbury Road
Kew Gardens
Surrey TW9 4JF
England
Phone: 44 (0)181 392-8585
FAX: 44 (0)181 392-9876
E-mail: Bushwd@aol.com.

Try your bookstore first.

Contents

	Introduction	6
	8th Photogrpahic Recon Squadron Begins	7
Chapter 1	8th Photo Squadron Diary 1942	8
Chapter 2	8th Photo Squadron Diary 1943	39
Chapter 3	Operational Summary 1944-45	101
	Escape and Evasion: The Eight Month Ordeal of Fred Hargesheimer	102
	Color Gallery	145
Appendices		
	Appendix I	160
	Appendix II	161
	Appendix III	164

Introduction

Happenstance played a large part when we started working on this project. John Stanaway had decided to do something on the photo reconnaissance version of the P-38 Lightning (F-4 and F-5) when he learned that his old friend and Pacific air war research whiz, Bob Rocker, had contacted sources in the target unit (the 8th Photo Reconnaissance Squadron) who possessed hundreds of heretofore unseen photos of aircraft, personnel, and famous locations in New Guinea and the Philippines. In addition, the photos were mainly of professional quality from the very cameras used in combat. Other photos were personal examples taken by pilots and crews who had an edge in composing and producing fine pictures.

In addition, the story of the 8th is unique and distinguished enough to provide quite a narrative. The diary portion of the text was probably never meant to be widely published, evidenced by its many personal references and rambling jokes that were the bane of at least one 8th PhS commander who deferred from the digressions around the solid history of the squadron. However, the feel of the period is conveyed by the exuberance of at least three writers in the Intelligence Section who were responsible for recording the story of the 8th Photo Squadron from the middle of 1942 until the unit was absorbed into the 6th Photo Reconnaissance Group late in 1943.

The diary itself reveals the problems that every photo reconnaissance unit faced during that part of the war. There were the problems of shortages of pilots and serviceable aircraft. Then there was the weather that seemed to go bad every time the 8th had enough planes and pilots to schedule missions. When a pilot got his Lightning over the target in acceptably clear weather it seemed that the camera would fog or break down and turn a dangerous mission into futility.

The writer of the diary sometimes makes bland jokes about the danger of flak or fighters, or of the ever-present fear of becoming lost over the forbidding landscape of New Guinea or other equally uninviting islands in the area. Some pilots were lost and made it back through the jungles to survive for another bout with the need for pictures of the Southwest Pacific. Other pilots just disappeared into the void as part of the payment for keeping Headquarters supplied with photographic intelligence.

The photos in this pictorial history were, for the most part, taken by the 8th PhS itself, thereby providing a quality survey of the unit's history. Virtually all of the pictures are presented for the first time and provide a unique record of a great photo unit. The reader will have a complete view of the troubles and triumphs of photo recon crews battling various obstacles in their determination to complete the mission.

8th Photographic Recon Squadron Begins February - July 1942

The 8th Photo Recon Squadron started its existence with a War Department letter dated 23 December 1941 that authorized personnel and equipment. At first only three officers and twenty- eight men formed the cadre after the squadron officially became organized on February 1, 1942. Nine more officers from the 4th Mapping Squadron joined their comrades on 7 March 1942, and forty additional volunteer enlisted men from the 102nd Observation Squadron moved from Morrow Field to March Field, California.

Additional personnel were added and three flights were formed (A, B, and C). Because of the war emergency in the Pacific, "A" Flight was hastily moved out to Australia aboard the S.S. *President Coolidge* on March 19, 1942. The 8th PhS was in the war zone at Melbourne Australia by April 7, 1942. Leading the flight with no more than four F-4 Lightning aircraft was 1Lt. Karl L. "Pop" Polifika, who practically singlehandedly flew the 8th Squadron's first operational flights in late April and early May 1942.

Polifka joined the Army Air Forces in the late 1930s after leaving the construction business in Oregon. He had come from a Russian-Czech family, which background gave him a solid dislike of the Axis point of view. He learned the photo reconnaissance occupation well and became one of the great American reconnaissance aces. After commanding the 8th Squadron until November 1942 he was reassigned to Europe to photograph the despised Third Reich.

While flying over the Pacific he learned the valuable arts of improvisiation to secure badly needed photos of the advancing Japanese. He began to take photos as early as April to become a legend in the effort to halt the Japanese offensive. In general, he is credited with heavy contributions in photographic intelligence regarding the Japanese fleet before the resulting battle in the Coral Sea.

One of the reported events that led to his high reputation was the acquisition of a B-24 bomber and crew in April to photograph the gathering fleet at Rabaul. He is credited with a number of apocryphal feats, such as outrunning pursuing Zeros over the Japanese ships nearing the Coral Sea when one of the engines on his F-4 was shot out. One of the feats attributed to Polifka is the downing of a Zero with his unarmed F-4. Another 8th pilot was officially credited with downing a Japanese fighter, and the story may have become confused with Polifika.

However, Polifka was an extraordinary pilot with many attributed acts of skill and daring to his record. The legendary Col. Boyd "Buzz" Wagner worked with the versatile Polifka to plan ways of using their meager resources to plot out Japanese positions and intentions. Polifka was so intent on his missions that he sometimes overlooked the danger that always maintained its presence. Once, Polifka accidently shut off his oxygen supply at high altitude and woke up forty-three minutes later at 3,000 feet upside down in a valley between 10,000 foot mountains about 170 miles south of New Britain. He quickly righted his F-4 and flew back home, but for months he was jibed for his excellent series of photos detailing sky and clouds that his activated cameras shot, one every forty-five seconds for almost forty-five minutes.

On May 2, 1942, Polifka and "A" Flight arrived at Townsville, which finally gave the F-4s a reasonable base on the northern coast of Australia. "B" and "C" Flights arrived at Melbourne on July 16 aboard the S.S. *Matsonia* and joined their sister flight at Townsville on July 27, 1942, to complete the 8th PhS in the combat zone.

An advance party of three officers and eighty enlisted men left for Port Moresby on September 5, and a few weeks later the entire squadron was together and operating from Schwimmer Drome, north of Port Moresby. The squadron flew from Schwimmer until January 5, 1944, when it moved to Durand Strip. From July 16, 1942, until February 23, 1943, the 8th PhS operated as part of the 19th Bomb Group, even though the 19th BG departed for the continental United States late in 1942. For much of its early combat history the 8th Photo Squadron operated virtually alone under the control of Fifth Bomber Command. Most of the aerial photographic intelligence was gathered from the efforts of the squadron, and the 8th pioneered the methods and procedures later employed by the Reconnaissance units of the Fifth Air Force. The heart of the 8th Photo Reconnaissance story lies in its own operational diary that covers the period from late July 1942 until the end of 1943 when the squadron became part of the 6th Photo Reconnaissance Group.

1

8th Photo Squadron Diary 1942

Monday, July 27

The Eighth Photo Squadron has come of age today with the arrival of 19 officers and 133 enlisted men. What with the new men from the 435th Bomb Squadron and our own fledging group, we now total 32 officers and 230 enlisted men. These new stateside chaps look like smart boys, and although they perhaps lack a little in experience, they will rapidly pick up and absorb the pearls of wisdom dropped by us veterans and soon will be a terrific fighting aggregation. Allow me a moment of repose while I stroke this long white beard.

Lt. Paul Staller, by all reports, did a magnificent job of herding the group across that wide blue sea and looks in pretty good shape considering the responsibility. It is rumored, however, that he heaved more than a faint sigh of relief when Capt. Polifka, the bemustached commanding officer, met the group in Melbourne.

Just to show the boys that they were here for business, Lt. Newton met the train and grabbed off "Hap" Hazzard as co-pilot for the flight to Charters Towers where B-17 #126666 is to be overhauled. Forgetting that Hap was just in from the States, Newton said, "Get the superchargers." And so on takeoff Hazzard proceeded to pull them back one by one. That is one of the reasons a man seems to age quickly over here. Hazzard was aptly named.

Capt. Polifka completed a photo mission of Bundaberg and vicinity.

Tuesday, July 28

To aid the Squadron in its training program, the Nips visited Townsville with air raid No. 2 at 0221. One serial 43 (Kawanishi H6K "Mavis") Flying Boat was picked up in the searchlight and engaged by A/A (antiaircraft). The Jap jettisoned his bombs five miles NW of Garbutt field and then disappeared. Six P-39s were airborne, but couldn't seem to locate the enemy.

Capt. Polifka departed for Port Moresby in P-38 "2325" at 0930 for photo missions from that base. He reached Port Moresby at 1150.

The following named officers were appointed to the Squadron jobs listed below, effective this date:

Captain Weidner	Squadron Executive
Lt. Savage	Flight "A" Commander
Lt. Staller	Flight "B" Commander
Lt. Surles	Flight "C" Commander
Lt. Thomas	Squadron Engineering

First commander of the 8th Photo Rcn Squadron. Karl Polifka took the squadron to New Guinea and practically flew a singlehanded show for the first few weeks before the rest of the squadron made it to Port Moresby in July 1942. Polifka went on to the Mediterranean later in the war and became a legend in photo reconnaissance. He was killed in action in Korea. (Delasso Loos via Rocker)

F4 #25 at Garbutt Field in Townsville, Australia. April 1942. (Jim McEwan)

8PRS F-4s at Garbutt Field. (Hector Rodgers)

Lt. Rogers	Squadron Operations
Lt. Vestal	Squadron Adjutant
Lt. Search	Squadron Supply
Lt. Leonhardt	Squadron Communications
Lt. Cobb	Squadron Chemical Warfare
Lt. Olson	Squadron Intelligence
W.O.Schrader	Sq. Tech. and Admin. Insp.

Wednesday, July 29

Raid No. 3 was endured this cold morning. One serial 43 Flying Boat came over at 0027 and dropped from six to eight bombs in Cleveland Bay west of Magnetic Island. There were no casualties and no damage was done. Four fighters were airborne and two intercepted. The passes were made at 21,000 feet, and the enemy's tail was observed alight but later extinguished. Five more passes were made and hits scored.

Lt. Post, A. L. was appointed Squadron Armament Officer, effective this date.

Friday, July 31

Remember those new B-17s we were promised? Well, 2458, better known as "Old 58," was turned over to us today, and it still has the old remote turret. Another headache for the Armament Section.

Harlan Olson briefing John Kneeskern beneath F4 "Limping Lizzie" at 14-Mile. (Jim Sills)

Herbert Thomas at 14-Mile. (Thomas)

F-4 under repair at 14-Mile Strip. (Mrs. Marvin Gardner)

Harold Moffatt and groundcrew under F-5A #90 "Sheila" at 14-Mile, probably in 1943. (Moffatt)

Taking advantage of a brief breathing spell from our arduous duties, the officers and men opposed each other in a softball game. Why is it the officers, those hand-picked specimens of physical manhood, supposedly possessing the ultimate in coordination and reaction time, can never beat the enlisted men? The EMs didn't even need that last half inning.

August 1,2,3,4

Not much happening these days. The new ships down in Melbourne aren't ready yet, and our old beat-up jobs are out of commission, so most of the men are getting set in their jobs, with occasional excursions to the countryside to find out what makes Australia tick.

Surles, Newton, and Reid have been giving B-17 transition time to Staller, Thomas, Roerig, Gorton, and Rogers.

Jim McEwan next to a Fairey Battle that lost power and crashlanded at Garbutt Field. (McEwan)

Fred Hargesheimer was one of the top photo pilots in New Guinea before he fell to a Ki-45 "Nick" fighter early in June 1943 over New Britain. He was one of the first to tackle the formidable Rabaul run. (Loos)

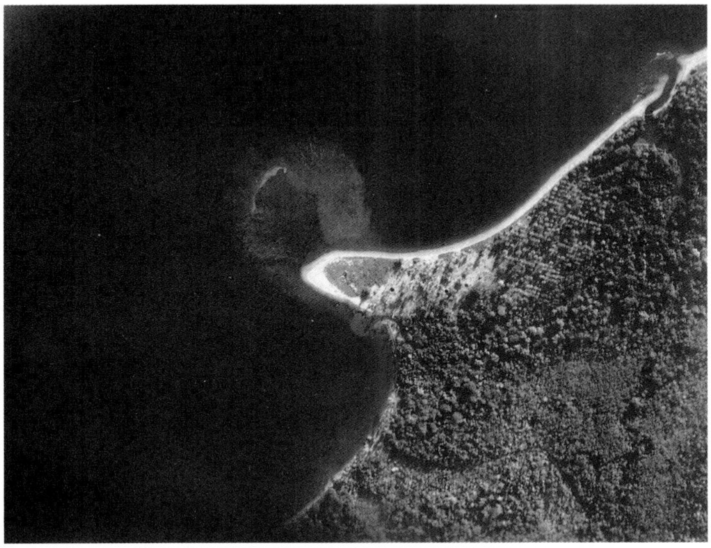

Sananada Point. Site of the Japanese landing at Buna in July 1942. (Melman)

Friday, August 7

Lieutenants Newton, Rogers, Surles, and Thomas and crew in "Old 58" departed for Horn Island carrying enlisted personnel and supplies for the photographic laboratory. They arrived Horn Island at 1330 and departed for Townsville at 1500. Because of darkness and bad weather, it was impossible to distinguish position along coast and they were forced to climb above the weather to avoid the danger of mountains. Since Townsville could not be seen the ship was flown to Charters Towers (which was) also closed in. They returned to Garbutt Field. The same thing could have been done earlier had the radio operator been more familiar with the green code book. All operators are forewarned.

Monday, August 10

Lts. Gardner and Foster returned from D.S. (detached Service) with 435th Recon Squadron. They each have a mission to Rabaul and to Buka in the log books—B-17 time.

Lt. Savage in ship 12123 returned from Port Moresby at 1715/K having successfully completed photographic missions from that base.

Thursday, August 13

Lt. Paul Staller in ship 2125 left Townsville at 1045 for Port Moresby via Horn Island. He reached Horn Island ok and took off from there at 1700. He is now long overdue at Port Moresby and they have no word from him there.

Lt. Newton with a makeshift crew left this morning in "58" for a mapping mission of the Darwin area. With Art Post as navigator, Fred Hargesheimer as bombardier, and Air Commodore Hewitt as a passenger, he will have his hands full.

Friday, August 14

We have received no word from Paul Staller, and a thorough check of the New Guinea airdromes has been made without results.

Harlan Olson, 8th PRS Intelligence Officer and one of several writers of the squadron diary. (Loos)

8th Photo Squadron sign, probably at one of the Port Moresby fields. (Hilliard)

8PRS F-4 at 7-Mile in September 1942. (via Rocker)

Jim McEwan, 8PRS B-17, B-25 and F-7 photographer and gunner, photographed in September 1942.

We must therefore assume that either his engines or navigation instruments failed him and must list him as "Missing In Action."

Paul did a swell job of bringing "B" Flight across, accepting and carrying out in fine fashion the responsibility entrusted him. It is a serious blow to the (8th Photo) Squadron to lose a man of Paul's caliber, and we pray that he is down safely in the jungle and can make his way back.

Sunday, August 16

A big promotion day in the Squadron. Surles is a big dog now with Captain's bars. Roerig, Sowers, and Rogers are strutting along with First Lt. bars. Congratulations, one and all.

Newton returned from Darwin today, and except for landing at the wrong field and a slight and very excusable hole in the photo mosaic, they performed very creditably. We apologize for calling it a makeshift crew.

Monday, August 17

Reid and his crew on returning to Moresby from a photo mission of the Buna-Sananada area picked up an air raid warning from Moresby and came on to Townsville. The Jap's habit of raiding Moresby every day ending in a seven is still in force.

Monday, August 24

"Doc" Savage, after completing his photo mission around Brisbane, took off for Townsville at 1320 today. Tired and worn from the strenuous duties of the photo pilot, he tacked onto a B26 coming in this direction, thereby dispensing with the difficult task of navigation. Everything was going nicely, and Doc was having a wonderful time sticking his wingtip into one side and then the other of the B-26 cockpit. Presently the '26 peeled off and landed, and Doc in his best stateside manner did likewise. Everything 100% except for one thing—the field was at Bowen. Only the best of the Air Corps is here, Doc. We had to put the other fellows somewhere else.

#56 "Limping Lizzie" taxiing by F-4 #17 at 14-Mile. (McEwan)

"Alas De Mort" at one of the Port Moresby strips. (Bugai)

8PRS F-5 #02 at 14-Mile. (via Rocker)

Turnbull Strip, Milne Bay under construction. (Woodrow Cobb)

Turnbull Strip, Milne Bay at the eastern end of New Guinea. (Thomas)

Melbourne to Townsville in July 1942. (Hilliard)

Top Left: **8th Photo Lab, Townsville, Australia, in December 1942. (Hilliard)** *Top Right (Clockwise):* **Flightline and native village at Milne Bay late in 1942. The Japanese made their last thrust into eastern New Guinea at the end of 1942 and were pressed back north of Buna by the beginning of 1943. The 8th PRS mapped the entire area in spite of difficulties with equipment, weather, and shortage of pilots.**

P-39 landing at Milne Bay and primitive living conditions in the sweltering palm groves at the end of 1942. (via Rocker)

22nd Bomb Group B-26, just leaving after a run over Lae. The Markham River is on the left and the Butubum River is on the far right. Lae is in the midst of the bomb bursts at the center. Lae was the first Japanese target after the Allied landing at Buna in December 1942, and the 8th PRS made numerous reconnaissance runs over the dangerous base. (via Rocker)

Wednesday, August 26

Capt. Polifka went into the hospital today with an infected foot. His is a bad case of athlete's foot. Others are now forewarned.

Friday, August 28

Savage, Gardner, Thomas, and Hargesheimer left for Melbourne today to pick up our new F-4s. At least that is the official purpose of the mission. Pretty good town, Melbourne. I sometimes wish I were a member of the exalted truck driver clan.

Saturday, August 29

We got our C.O. back from the hospital today. Except for a slight limp, he seems to have thrived on the attention of the nurses.

Thursday, September 3

Savage wheeled in from Melbourne with Gardner and a Capt. Warden flying on his wing. We now have F-4s 2139, 2130, and 2177. Soon we'll look like a squadron.

Friday, September 4

Thomas and Hargesheimer brought ships 2156 and 2098 up from Melbourne.

All of the squadron equipment is now packed, and the boys are just waiting to climb aboard the boat and head for Maple, Port Moresby, to the uninitiated.

Saturday, September 5

Capt. Surles and crew had lousy luck on their photo mission of the Port Moresby-Buna trail. This is the trail down which those

Lt. Colonel Boyd "Buzz" Wagner, one of the first American air heroes of the war and a spark plug to the Allied aerial operations in the first year of the war. He and Polifka worked well together to obtain maximum efficiency with the limited sources available to the 8th Photo Squadron. (Ralph Watts)

8PRS F-5A at Townsville undergoing work on its cameras. (Cobb)

SSW view of Port Moresby with harbor at upper right and 8th PRS photo lab in the center of photo near road. (Hilliard)

Southeast view of the same area with photo lab again in the center of photo. (Hilliard)

Nipponese are advancing on Moresby. Photographs of it are getting pretty vital, and yet we can't get the weather to fly it. Surles returned to Moresby, picked up Lt. Humiston and crew, and reached Townsville at 1720.

We are seeing the last of the B-17 as an Eighth Photo aircraft. Air Force today transferred the B-17s to the 435th Bomb Squadron. Capt. Polifka gave the three crew commanders, Capt. Surles, Lt. Humiston, and Lt. Newton their choice of flying personnel, and we are certainly losing some good men. All the best, gentlemen, we hate to see you go.

Eighty-five enlisted men and three officers boarded the boat for Port Moresby today. The rest of the Squadron is either flying up or remaining in the photo lab here in Townsville. We are now headed for the Nips and the Jungle. Is that .45 oiled?

Operations are getting very confused these days. We are to operate from Moresby's Seven-Mile strip until our camp at Laloki

19th BG B-17, #12417. The 8th PRS was attached to the 19th until after the bomb group left the theater. (Thomas)

7-Mile Strip known as Jackson Drome with B-17s of either 19th or 43rd Bomb Group in the revetments. (via Rocker/National Archives Fred Pernell)

Port Moresby town on October 24, 1942. (Hilliard)

"Limping Lizzie" at 14-Mile. (Via Rocker)

Drome is prepared. In line with this, Lt. Reid flew pilots Morton, Foster, and Gardner, and crew chiefs Nielson and Meech from Townsville to Moresby. Tomorrow other pilots will fly F-4s up there. Somehow or other, we will finally have everybody in Moresby and commence to function.

Monday, September 7

Lt. Newton flew the weather and his right hand man, Sgt Hammond, up to Moresby where they are to set up Operations and Intelligence and carry on until the rest of the squadron arrives. The site of operations is to be 14-Mile, or properly Laloki Drome, in honor of the river rushing past the field. May I comment on the occasion?

We were unceremoniously dumped at 7 Mile, complete with filing cases and other impediments, and then Newton took off for Townsville again. Morton, Foster, and Gardner met us finally, and being in something of a tailspin, I was more than ordinarily overjoyed to see them. They had one of the trucks, so we threw our stuff aboard and went up to Arcadia.

We had no more than sat down to dinner when the air raid siren screamed, so we charged up the hill to our slit trench. Soon 26 medium bombers of Nipponese origin unloaded their bomb bays on 7-Mile Drome. This was our first taste of daylight bombing, and we were properly scared. After the raid everybody went down to look at the damage. There we are sitting in Operations, what was left of it, when a delayed action bomb goes off. Everybody hit the

8th PRS enlisted: Back row Ernest Young, Walter Undsey, Cpl Peterson, Wesley McClimans, John Yourman, Paul Merril, Max O'Connell, Jack Parrish, Gerald Grover, Howard Rose, Robert Edwards, Thomas Nulty, J. C.. Robertson. Middle row: Fred Nelson, William Babcock, Victor Heldenbrand, Albert Bruer, Harry Abrams, Baird Obermann, Aaron Teicher, Jack Hallack, Carl Barkved. Front row: Clark Terry, James Woods, Hector Rodgers, Morris Levine, Thomas Leonard, Joseph La Scala, Antone Camillo, Angelo Guerrieri, James Thursby, Robert Pear, Stanley LaFeen (Hilliard)

F4 at Garbutt Strip. (Hilliard)

dirt at once, and they ended up stacked about three deep. A few pieces of metal flew around, but mostly dirt and nobody got hurt. This is almost war.

The camp site is just as bad as one might expect. We set up tents last night and started out putting them in the woods where they couldn't be seen from the air. The idea was all right, but the mosquitoes presented too many arguments, so after the first tent (was erected) we set the rest in the clearing. Olson is carrying about 100 bites to the rear of each knee and didn't sleep last night, but the tents are up. The first lesson of the jungle is, "Don't wear shorts."

Capt. Polifka, Lt. Savage, and Lt. Rennels flew three of the F-4s into Seven-Mile today.

Wednesday, September 9

We learned today of Capt. Polifka's much belated promotion to Major. If we had something with which to celebrate we could throw a big one.

Those eighty-five men finally arrived on the *SWARTENHONDT* (so aptly translated "The Black Dog"), and I've never seen such a disgruntled bunch. The ship was filthy, the food inedible, and the weather torrid. They were taken off by lighter and were really happy to hit Mother Earth again. The boat won't be unloaded for about a week, so we'll struggle along without supplies as best we can.

Camera Repair. (Hilliard)

F-5 taking off, probably from 14-Mile.

Bofors anti-aircraft near 7-Mile in October 1942. (via Rocker/National Archives Kate Flaherty)

Lt. Hargesheimer flew up from Garbutt in 2098, and Foster and Savage flew 2177 and 2139 from 7 Mile to Laloki.

Thursday, September 10

We expected to get started on our high-priority mapping project today, but Air Force had decided that we shall perform photo reconnaissance of Northeast New Guinea. Following that plan Hargesheimer took off at 0600 for a survey glance of the Buna area. He was followed at two-hour intervals by Major Polifka, Lt. Savage, Lt. Gardner, Lt. Rennels, and Major Polifka again. These were mainly orientation flights for the new pilots and nothing unusual happened in the air, but Lt. Gardner sadly but firmly bashed in the leading edge of 2139's right wing. The hard standings are set back in the trees, and there isn't much room to swing the aircraft around.

Friday, September 11

Eighth Photo's Buna reconnaissance paid real dividends today. Lt. Savage on his 0955-1255 recco spotted two Zekes flying toward Buna. Following them in, he spotted 30 more aircraft on the

A Lightning just before taking off on a mission in August 1942. (Sykes)

Camera installation in the F- 5.

#93 in flight. (Jim Sills)

drome. This he radioed to 4th Fighter Sector, and an afternoon striking force claimed destruction of eighteen. (There seems to have been, in fact, only one raid on Buna on September 12. Capt. Don Hall of the 3rd Attack Group led nine A20s with fighter escort on the first parafrag—fragmentation bombs dropped at low altitude on parachutes—mission of the war. Seventeen of twenty-two Japanese aircraft were claimed destroyed. The 8th Photo diarist was about as accurate as possible in the light of communications at the time.—Auths.)

Hargesheimer, Foster, and Major Polifka covered the same area at different times, but nothing new to report.

Three more ships arrived from Townsville with Peterson, Guerry, and Thomas at their wheels.

Saturday, September 12

A strike this morning on Buna claims the other twelve of those thirty aircraft that Savage spotted.

Rennels, Hargesheimer, and Guerry flew missions up the northeast coast to Lae. Guerry had his share of trouble. His electrical system went out, rendering useless his Autosyn instruments, props controls, and compass. But, never daunted, Guerry set his gyro com-

Bomb crater at 7-Mile in August 1942

Sgt Hector Rodgers working on the Allison engine of an 8th PRS F-4. (Jim Sills)

Pilots Watts, Weller, Gorton, and Rogers of "A" Flight and Ludtke. All were in the 8th PRS by late 1942 or early 1943. (via Rocker/ Ralph Watts)

pass by the coastline, climbed up through the overcast, and successfully returned to Laloki.

Got word that Post reached Townsville with F-4 "2140."

Sunday, September 13

We should've stood in bed today. Foster, when 30 miles west of Lae on his 10 o'clock flight, had his right supercharger blow up, fragments of which shattered his canopy and narrowly missed him. Splinters of the canopy glass lacerated his right arm. He had plenty of altitude—25,000 feet—and was able to come in, but another aircraft is now out of commission.

Guerry took the 0615-0850 recco and sighted six enemy biplanes near Lae, probably type 98, (the type O, Mitsubishi F1m "Pete" reconnaissance aircraft was the only Japanese biplane used in the area at the time), but evaded them without any trouble.

Japanese ship photographed off the north coast of New Britain on 11 September 1942. (National Archives Sharon Culley)

Monday, September 14

Tragedy is certainly dogging our boys. Lt. Peterson departed at 0610 in 2098 for dawn patrol of northeast New Guinea and nothing more was heard from him. Major Polifka, after checking the dromes, took off in search of him, but a general overcast of 5,000 feet made observation impossible.

Pete is a swell person, one of the regular guys, and he will be sorely missed. These first missions are exceedingly difficult, for the weather is always bad, and with no experience over the terrain, navigation is mostly by guess and by God. Best of luck, Pete, we shall certainly pray that you walk out.

Friday, September 18

Major Polifka took off at 1040K for a recon and photo mission of Buna and the Wairopi-Sananda Point Track. He returned at 1320K and reported excellent weather for photos and successfully filmed the entire track. He buzzed Buna Airdrome at 2,500 feet, and although AA was right on his tail he returned with no holes.

One enemy plane unsuccessfully bombed Moresby at 2153 tonight, the bombs dropping along the Port Moresby Road, and two or three in the jungle northeast of Laloki Drome.

F-4 somewhere in New Guinea, photographed in September 1942. (Hilliard)

F-4 #34 "Eager Beaver II" at 14-Mile strip. (Norb Ruff, 80 F.S.)

Photo lab quarters at Port Moresby, dated October 5, 1942. (Hilliard)

Port Moresby harbor, lab and quarters on October 5, 1942. (Hilliard)

Saturday, September 19

Lt. Rennels departed in 2130 at 0915 and lost the cockpit canopy on takeoff, but was able to maintain his altitude and landed at 0925. He departed again at 0950, and when 15 miles east of Salamaua spotted six Zeros headed toward Lae. Since his right engine would pull but 25 inches of mercury, he listened to reason and returned to this base.

Major Polifka departed at 1030 in ship 2123 and successfully completed a photographic mission of Cape Nelson and vicinity and returned to this base at 1300.

Major Polifka, or "Pop," as he is known to the boys, was overcome by heat exhaustion and overwork and was taken to the hospital tonight. Lt. Stark reports that he will be strictly ok in a few days and will be flying again within a week or two.

We underwent another raid tonight at 2005, but the enemy planes were unsuccessful as usual, dropping their bombs in the woods northeast of Laloki.

Monday, September 21

Lt. Hargesheimer departed in ship 2177 this morning at 0910 for a photographic mission of Lae and the northeast coast of New Guinea. He accomplished same, filming Lae, Salamaua, Buna and vicinity, and the Sananada-Wairopa Track. He returned to Laloki, but the 1200 air raid warning sent him out to sea, and he returned to the drome at 1335.

Lt. Guerry, today's alert pilot, took off at 1205 upon notice of a Red Alert to shadow the 23 bombers said to be approaching Moresby. The bombers never came over. Lt. Guerry was unable to locate them, and hence returned to the drome at 1330.

Henry Mathes by 8th PRS nose, #81. (Don I. Kimbrough)

Port Moresby, October 24, 1942. (Hilliard)

"What were we fighting for?" 8th PRS F5A-10 with a reminder. (Kimbrough)

MacArthur at 7-Mile Field on October 2, 1942. (Hilliard)

Wednesday, September 30

Lt. Guerry departed in ship 2140 at 1200. The interior of New Guinea was socked in, but he found a narrow strip of the coast to be clear and returned with numerous photos. Lae, Salamaua, Buna, and Wanigela airdromes show no activity; considerable supplies were noted at Mubo, and a possible supply dump (was noted) southeast of Wanigela Drome. He also photographed some of the track from Sananamda Pt. and Seven Miles of the Kumisi River. He landed at 1515.

The 38th (Bomb Group) of B-25s is now located here with us. Still without ground personnel, they are messing with us. Very eager group which shows the advantages of personnel fresh from the States. How quickly one loses that eagerness.

Friday, October 2

Major Polifka completed a four-hour photo mission and picked up pictures of the following spots: Buna, Sananamda Pt., Cape Nelson, Wanigela Mission, Wairopi Bridge, and a mapping strip from Marshall Lagoon to Moresby. He reports that both the trestle and suspension bridges at Wairopi are useless.

Monday, October 5

Gardner picked up photographs of both Lae and Buna this morning, but all the other areas were socked in. Savage flew a local

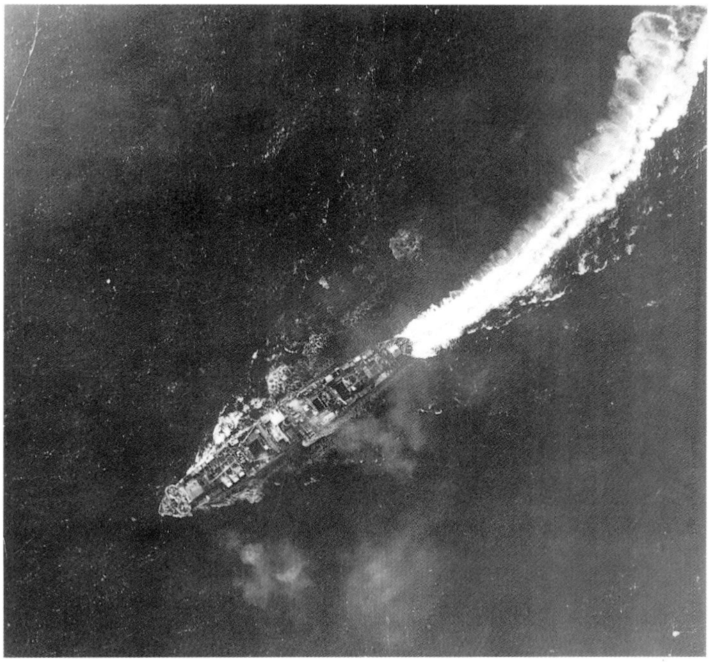

Japanese transport photographed 20 miles north of Buna on October 4, 1942. (Hilliard)

mapping strip from Laloki to Efogi covering our supply road to the troops pushing the Nips back down the other side of the range.

The Japs are evidently getting more supplies into Buna, for Major Polifka found seven new barges at Sananandа Pt. Morton couldn't pick up any photos at Lae or Buna because of complete cloud cover.

Wednesday, October 7

I don't know how you fellows are faring up there in the main camp, but I'd like to point out the hazardous manner in which we are living down here on the line.

Every night after we have climbed into our rather damp sacks, the wallabies pay the nearby grass a visit. Now that in itself may be just a normal habit for nature's little creatures, but with the Japs just over the hill, the rustling of the grass and that odd thumping of the tail becomes a whole patrol of Japs moving in on our little tent. The result is a group of very trigger-happy tentmates.

Well, last night, about an hour after turning in, we suddenly heard something crashing through the bush. Up jumped our automatic weapons man, Roerig, with gun cocked and flashlight in hand.... A moment of silence, and then a tremendous Bronx cheer or suitable substitute rent the air. You guessed it. G.I.

Thomas reached the straddle trench.

Friday, October 9

Foster flew 2130 to the following places with photographic success. Lae, Buna, Salamaua, and a mapping strip of the Yodda River.

Thomas picked up lots of mapping for us on a three-hour afternoon hop. They are: Track from Wanigela to Pongani via the Illia River to Futore, the Musa River to Dove, and thence through Beaps and Boitiva to Pongani. That's quite a set of names.

I haven't previously mentioned that sterling group of four, Kneeskern, Lessner, Loos, and Sykes, because until now they haven't been doing any flying. However, in response to their frequent complaints about the lack of publicity, and the entry of one of the clan into a F-4 cockpit, I shall now correct that slight in part.

Lieutenant Sykes, with our usual cross wind worrying him, took his first hop in a P-38 today. Naturally, he did a magnificent

8th PRS Officers near 14-Mile: Front Row: Raymond Starr, Fred Rennels, John Stark, John Foster, Harlan Olson, Alexander Guerry, Henry Leonhardt. Middle Row: Waymoth Vestal, Murphey, Davis, Clark Sykes, Moffat, Southard, Gingerich, Kenneth Murphy. Back Row: Woodrow Cobb, Grigg, DeLasso Loos, George Hamlin, Bill Fairbank, LeGrand Kneeskern, Homer Taylor.

Another group of 8th PRS enlisted serving in 1942-43. (Bugai)

job, but for the benefit of future hot pilots, I am listing a few of the mistakes. First, he forgot to close the windows; second, he took off with props in manual: and last, he spilled the flaps before gaining sufficient altitude. This sounds pretty bad, but remember, the important thing is that with all these errors he got her up and down without injury to himself or the precious aircraft.

May the author mention, in passing, that he is now 1st Lt. Olson.

Saturday, October 10

Loos underwent the second initiation of the clan in F-4 2139 today. With Sykes proffering advice from all sides, Loos pulled her off and landed in fine fashion. A very neat job.

Gardner went to Buna, Salamaua, and picked up a mapping strip from Lae to Hanishe Harbor. We salute you.

Monday, October 12

Long John Kneeskern took his first ride in a P-38 today and survived the experience remarkably well. A little green about the gills, perhaps, but a smooth take-off and landing proved him the master of his fate.

No combat missions went out today.

Tuesday, October 13

Only two of the boys got busy today. Rennels from 1015 to 1315 flew tri-met strips from Aban to Namoodie, thence up the Kumusi River to Wairopi, and finally one from the junction of the Mamama and Kumusi Rivers to Myola lakes.

Guerry covered both Lae and Salamaua with a string of photos.

Friday, October 16

Lissner, without a trace of trouble, took a F-4 off this afternoon, flew around for a time, and then landed. Very nicely done for the first time in a hot aircraft. Nice going, fellow.

Reid, in the 8th Photo Vacation Liner, departed these parts for more seasonable climes. He was framed the honor of carrying the first leave-bound men and officers to Sydney. Now that it's actually happened, all the rest of the squadron are waiting with tongues a-hangin' for their turn.

Thomas flew a mosaic of the Cape Vogel area.

The flightline at one of the Port Moresby strips. (Cobb)

8th PRS Photo lab near 14-Mile.

Philip Lissner was killed in a crash on the New Guinea coast on November 28, 1942. (Sykes)

Tuesday, October 20

Post was in the air at 1100, wended his way to Misima Island, snapped the trimet pix, and returned to our little home. So accustomed is he to that Sydney and Brisbane per diem that immediately upon landing he filed a request for same on today's hop.

Two Jap planes got over the area tonight, and searchlights had them right in the beam, but no hits. It would certainly be nice to have something to cheer.

Photos of the LaeSalamaua area taken on November 26, 1942. (National Archives via: Rocker)

Zero recovered near Buna late in 1942. The tail marking identifies it as part of the crack Lae unit (National Archives via Rocker)

Thursday, October 22

Doc Savage got off at 1115 and picked up trimet strips of the Markham Valley and obliques of Lae and Salamaua.

Gardner took a strip from Hopoi to Lae and another down the coast from Lae to Morobe. Excellent pictures to please our 648th Engineer friends.

Moresby underwent raid #85 this evening. A (medium bomber) dropped four bombs on 7-Mile and two more on Ward's Drome. About the time it got over 7-Mile, the 3.7 AA gun immediately back of the camp opened up with a thunder resembling a bomb burst. Everybody—and I mean just that—made mad rushes for the slit trenches. And a good thing, too, for in a few minutes schrapnel from the Moresby guns started falling like rain. No damage to personnel or equipment.

Sunday, October 25

Post scored again today on his trip to New Britain. Finding the area clear at ten o'clock, he photographed Rooke and Tolokwin Islands, and picked up a strip along the Finschhafen coast.

Gardner sallied forth on the Squadron's longest mission to date: A mapping trip to Wewak. Going by way of Madang, he snapped cameras from Madang to Wewak, excepting only those areas too cloud-covered for successful mapping.

Raid #(86) burst upon us at 1950 this evening, but only a few bombs were dropped on the harbor, and damage was nil.

Wednesday, October 28

Gardner went off to the northern islands this morning. About Finschhafen he bumped into a front and picked up fifteen minutes of undesired (flight on) instruments. Finding things even worse then, he did a one-eighty and returned home.

Morton was airborne at 1010 to pick up that elusive mosaic of Rorona and Ward's Drome. He flew it, but not for posterity, as the cameras failed to function. Morton blames Camera Repair and CR blames Morton. Ho hum!

Thursday, October 29

Post took another shot at Ward's Drome. The cameras were not turned on, however, so we are still trying to get pictures of the local area.

Friday, October 30

Kneeskern on his first mission with cameras flew over and picked off with no trouble whatsoever the Ward's Drome mosaic. It is highly satisfactory and, in view of the fact that it has been missed four times by our so-called veterans, it seems in order to decree tomorrow as "Salaam to Kneeskern Day."

Sunday, November 1

Hargesheimer took the dawn flight to Lae this morning and on the way out had a (lot) of trouble. The report obtained from him while still excited is somewhat confusing, but the following approximates the truth. Hargey was skillfully flying (on) instruments when suddenly one supercharger cut out, and at the same time the other engine ran away. This placed the excited one on his back, and after losing seven thousand feet he righted the aircraft. Since the weather was bad he returned to base.

Monday, November 2

The long expected finally happened today. The B-26s went out on an unsuccessful bombing mission, and in addition ran into some Zeros. Unknown to the crew of the first B-26, a tire had been shot out in the battle, and when it hit the runway they veered off to the left and piled up in front of Operations. Five minutes later another B-26 was coming in to land, but was cut out of the pattern. In attempting to go around he ran out of gas and had to dead stick it into the field west of the drome.

There were no serious injuries in either plane, but some of the crew members had to be helped out. "Doc" Stark, our medical officer, despite the presence of fuzed bombs aboard, fearlessly set himself to the task of getting the men out. For this extraordinary

Ward's Drome photographed on November 22, 1942. (National Archives via M.F. Kirby)

bravery in the face of danger, he has been recommended for the Soldier's Medal.

Wednesday, November 4

Guerry ran a recco of the shipping lanes from Cape Nelson to Finschhafen and thence to Lae, Salamaua, and down the coast to Buna in search of a reported enemy convoy of two transports, two destroyers, and one cruiser. He reported nil sightings except for the old wrecked transport on Salamaua Isthmus, which was in its usual position.

Company C, 128th Infantry Bn., came out of the hills to engage us in a baseball game. The Eighth Photo officers trimmed their officers 8-3, but the rough tough infantry boys manhandled our EMs to the tune of 8-0.

Reid, Chief of the Joy Ship 458, returned to New Guinea with several vacation-spent passengers. Savage returned with lagging step, but Rennels remained in Sydney to recuperate from Sydney. He has a bad case of dysentery.

Sunday, November 8

The Squadron observed the Sabbath as a day of rest and performed no missions today. All was not idle, however, for we did play a couple of ball games with the 101st AA gang from Mosquito Hollow. The Eighth's officers performed nobly, winning by a score of 8-6. The EMs did not fare so well despite the speedball pitching of Sgt. Meech, for they went down in defeat 6-0. They can't seem to hit the old apple.

Tuesday, November 10

Art Post set out for Buna at 1040 to get a mapping strip from Dobodura to Bofu. In his desire to win the low altitude contest he went down to 2,600 feet. If this tendencey to burrow continues, by Christmas our P-38s will be taking deep sea photos of New Guinea fish.

Oh, to be a B-17 pilot. Reid wired in today the "58" was laid up in Brisbane for an engine change and could they get per diem while the were waiting. I recommend sending them a case of Corn William.

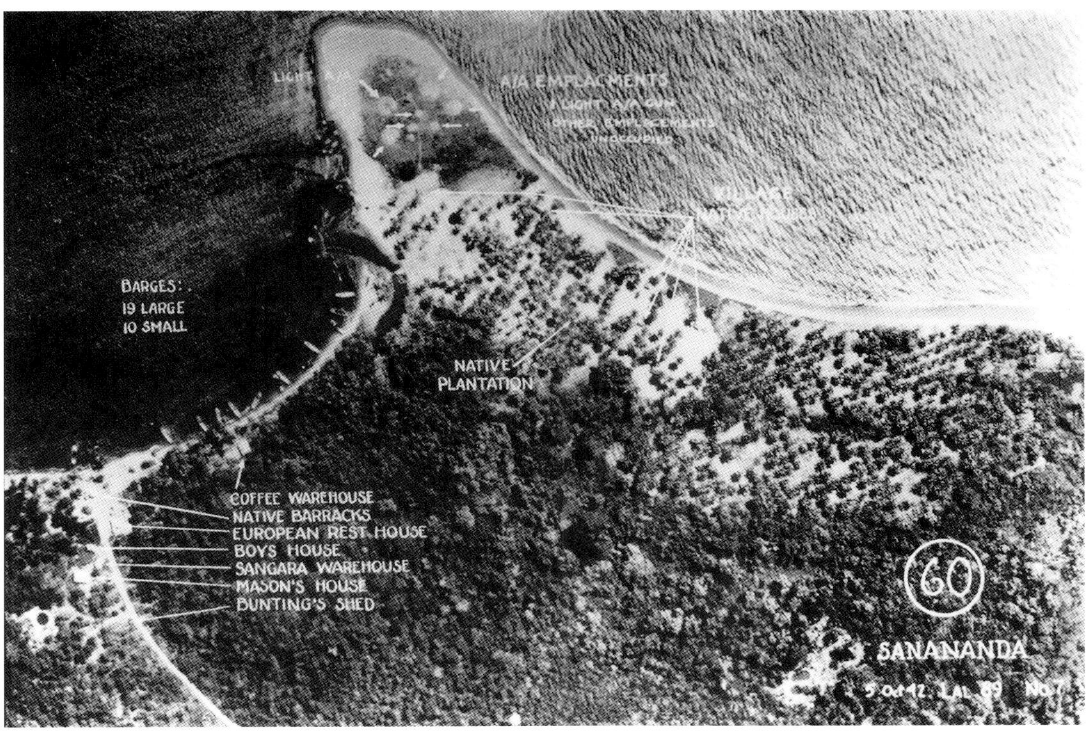

Original landing area of the Japanese Buna invasion at Sananda Point in July 1942. Note invasion barges along upper left coastline. (National Archives Dale Connelly)

Milne Bay. Gurney Strip is visible at right center. (National Archives via Jack Fellows.)

In an effort to supplement our long range mapping program we requested a B-17 and crew from bomber command. Last night Lt. Rogers and Lt. Watts with their crews arrived with 12666 to fulfill that request. However, Rogers, being slated to return to the States, declined any lone B-17 recco flights over Rabaul or Kavieng, so after many harsh words he departed for Townsville. That eleiminates half of the missions, at least.

The big news today is that Pop Polifka is to return to the States. He goes to Brisbane tomorrow and thence homeward. Naturally, we threw a big party to wish him luck and to celebrate his good fortune.

Big "Doc" Savage is now acting C. O., which is doing pretty well for a First Lieutenant. Let's go, Doc. We are ready for work.

Friday, November 13

Watts and crew spent nine hours trying to get photos of Kavieng and vicinity, but no satifactory pictures could be obtained. However, their visual reconnaissance of the area was the first received in several months and therefore of considerable value.

Many promotions today: Reid made Captain, and those hardworking, high-flying Second Lieutenants Foster, Guerry, Hargesheimer, Post, and Rennels are sporting Firsts.

Monday, November 16

Lt. Savage's new regime went into effect today. Lt. Thomas has taken over Operations, and Lt. Post is now the Engineering Officer. Lt. Guerry is temporarily acting S-2, while Olson is on his much-needed leave. Lts. Hargesheimer, Rennels, and Foster are Flight Commanders, and Lts. Guerry, Gardner, and Morton are Deputy flight commanders. With the average of one flyable plane to a flight, the duties do not promise to be too exacting of our time and efforts.

Rain descended upon us today in a never-ending torrent, and it begins to appear as though our camp site will soon be untenable. Native stories have it that the water is frequently four or five feet deep on Laloki Drome. Now schemes for putting pontoons on the ships or of abandoning them altogether are being proposed. Pilots and mechanics favor the latter, for that appears to be the only method for getting new aircraft.

Tuesday, November 17

In the early morning hours the air raid siren screamed out the warning that the Nips were overhead. The officers and men gave it the reception practiced of late: Turn over and go back to sleep. Considering the overcast, rain, and mosquitos, it seemed more dangerous out than in.

The new regime made a gallant start by sending Hargesheimer to Wau and getting Post briefed for a trip to the mountains. Unfortunately, Hargey was back within an hour reporting a runaway supercharger and bad weather over the mountains. This ended the day for Eighth Photo operations.

A delightful show, "Anne of Windy Poplars," starring Anne Shirley, did much to brighten the dampened spirits of the men. Promise of a show every fifth night in the future was enthusiastically received.

Wednesday, November 18

Today was noteworthy mainly because little rain fell. As this was to be only a temporary letup, a party of hardy pioneers crossed the river in search of a new camp site on higher ground. Despite this, lack of raincloud formations prevented any missions and stopped all flying, except Post's daily test hop.

Encouraging news arrived from the Solomons regarding the shellacking the Jap Navy has been taking there. News from New Guinea Forces reported our troops within ten miles of Buna, but reported Jap warships approaching the coast from two directions. All this indicates that excitement can be expected from that quarter promptly.

Thursday, November 19

In the early morning hours, Lts. Thomas and Gardner boarded a flying boat for Melbourne, there to study the problems and techniques of the 648th Engineers. The officers looked forward to their trip, not only because of the valuable knowledge they expected to gain, but because they need a rest. You see, Lts. Thomas and Gardner had not been down south for four days!

Lt. Guerry has taken over Thomas' position as Operations Officer, and rather than bring in any new radical changes, Lt. Guerry is trying to maintain continuity of policy. In line with this, no missions were flown.

Our claims for a new spot for our camp were filed and approved. It will be on the other side of the river, and moving starts as soon as the trucks can cross in sufficient numbers.

Hallelulia and Praise Be! The new regime took off and went into action with full vim and vigor. Despairing of ever again finding mission weather in New Guinea, the triumvirate Lts. Savage, Post, and Guerry (C.O.,E.O.,O.O.) decided on a series of local flights. Their announcement at noon that there would be several (i.e., more than one) during the afternoon was greeted by remarks of disbelief and amazement. Realizing that great men and ideas are often met with laughter, the trio kept to their determination, and by evening there had been five flights in the air. Not one, but five! Lts. Loos, Post, Guerry, Foster, and Rennels were the lucky pilots. Most pathetic note of the day was Lt. Foster trying vainly to take off in the first flight with Lts. Post and Guerry, and having to return to the line with a burned out generator.

Joy reigned in the camp at suppertime when $23,000 in back pay was distributed among the men in the organization. The Sydney drain has been so great that hardly a farthing remained in camp, and the great influx of folding money was used to pay off back debts and to store up for future trips to the south. Corp. Jones of the Cook Shack received his usual treatment from the Finance Dept. He has yet to be paid for his first day in the Army.

The successful day was brought to a close by a movie under the somewhat hazy light of a beautiful tropical moon. "Too Many Girls" was the title of the picture, and though it was most entertaining, it did remind the felows that there are too DAMN few girls around these parts. In fact, no white ones at all, except some of the native girls that are getting whiter each day.

Saturday, November 21

Moving day today! At dawn's first light the vanguard of the Eighth Photo Squadron started the trek to the new campsite across the river. Choice locations were sought by the early arrivals, and there was much switching about. Periodically, large grass fires sprang up, as the novices such as Lts. Murphy and Bizzel attempted to clear off a little patch for their tent. A couple of particularly large conflagrations jumped over the hill and down into the Negro camp, where one poor individual lost all his clothes, as they were drying on the line.

B-17s of the 19th Bomb Group, the administrative unit over the 8th PRS for part of 1942.

Pugnacious 8-Ball insignia that came to signify the 8th PRS during 1940.

All was bustle and turmoil at Operations and Engineering as it appeared that two missions would be sent out. Off went Lt. Rennels to the local strip, but as he went down the runway the clouds dropped from 6,000 to 2,000. He landed several times a few minutes later.

A move in the old camp area brought the day to a close. "Room Service" was the title, and the Marx Brothers the stars. Afterwards the men split up in two groups—those moved and those to be—and went their separate ways, but with a common purpose: to win the evening battle with the mosquito force so predominantly occupying our camp these days.

Monday, November 22

The first mission in eleven days went forth today, and there was great rejoicing, although it was only a local flight. Lt. Foster shot a mosaic of the Moresby-Laloki area. Camera repair had developed a novel and ingenious hook-up by which the camera switch and intervalometer operated the charting camera. The pilot was not let in on the secret, however. Poor Lt. Foster, baffled by the confusing and uncontrollable lights, still got his picture. Lt. Foster always carries through. Moving from the old to the new camp site continued with no more serious hishaps than wear and tear on people's nerves. Apparently, the lesson about playing with fire had been well learned, for there were no large fires. The hash slingers served their first beans at the new location.

As the sun dropped behind gorgeous, multi-hued, red, pink, and blue clouds in the west, the tropical full moon climbed over the stately mounts in the east. Soon there were not even scud to mar the splendor of the moon, the stars, and the vast blue sky. The Loloki River was liquid silver, and the weaving trees seemed touched with gold. The thoughts of the Eighth Photo'ers drifted far afield, to Melbourne, New York, and more recently, Sydney. Such reveries could not long be continued outside in all the beauty of the New

Alex Guerry by F-4 serial 41-2123 "FAINTING FLOOZIE II." (Roy Reid)

Guinea night, for the mosquitoes were abroad, too, and (were) even more ferocious than the Japs.

Tuesday, November 23

Our first combat mission in twelve days was ordered today, and Lt. Post did a beautiful job on it. Into Lae he went twice at 8,500 to 10,000 feet, despite two attempts at interception by Zekes. Through bad weather he continued to Buna and ran a strip at 2,000 feet before buzzing Soputa at 1,000 feet.

B-17 "458" finally returned from the South with another group of overdue vacationers. Capt. Reid had remained in Brisbane because of an alleged rash, and a very pleasant Lt. O'Donnell had brought the plane back, much to the whole Squadron's appreciation. Lt. Fairbank was sincerely welcomed back by all personnel. Lt. Rennels retired to the Moresby hospital at 17-Mile. Thus, 8th Photo officers were scattered from Melbourne to inland of Laloki in various states of indisposition, all the way from Dengue to the D.T.s. The remaining pilots are carrying on without undue difficulty.

Wednesday, November 24

The Sydney Sleeper, this time Townsville bound with a lab crew exchange, was unable to get off at dawn because of a bad No.1 engine. Discussion of an engine change here met with the general disapproval of the wishes of the men to get South, and of the desire to keep intact Capt. Reid's record of never having an engine change north of Brisbane. 18 spark plugs were installed instead, and an afternoon take-off attempted. This time the hydraulic system went out, disheartening crew and passengers.

Shortly after lunch Lt. Vestal went over to pick up the 14 natives. The boons were installed at the line and given the afternoon to get settled. A hurry-up call came in from Major Hipps at 2:30 for a shot of Lae, and the Zekes reported there. Lt. Guerry departed hastily in "2177". He was back in 45 minutes, reporting the right engine cutting out completely at regular intervals above 10,000 feet. Inspection showed a shorted-out fuel boost pump.

The Japs visited us twice during the evening without casualties or damage, although the full moon made this whole area a clear target. On the first raid, the hospital zone was bombed, but only one man was injured.

Wednesday, November 25

Readers will wonder at the balled up dates. Due to the fact that this theater is far down the list in priority, we did not have, up until the present time, a current 1942 calendar. One just arrived, and we are now in agreement with the Solar System.

Today was one of the biggest in the brief history of Eighth Photo Squadron. Three ships were sent out on combat missions, and all three photographed their targets. Lt. Guerry darted off early for Lae and ran into bad weather, drifting light stratus at several altitudes. He took two strips of Lae at 22,000 (feet) and then suddenly remembered a pressing operational detail at Laloki when he sighted three Zekes coming up underneath him. (He came home to take care of his operations duty.)

Lt. Foster hurried his lunch period to take 2130 down to Milne Bay. The weather was very good as a whole. He ran several strips at 22,000. Lt. Post received a special call from Major Marchant (John Marchant of 8th Fighter Group Headquarters) to hurry over and take pictures of Buna and Gona. One strip was taken over Buna. Two big booms reached his ears at one time, but he knew not what caused the noise. Possible artillery fire. He went in over Gona at 3,500, and not observing any supply dropping, he hastily improvised a three-strip mosaic. Lt. Loos completed the day's flying with a successful test hop. The Operations native hut is taking shape surprisingly fast.

"Along the Rio Grande" with Tim Holt and other western stars was shown in the Eighth Photo area, under the capable hand of W/O Ray Starr and Camera Repair Section.

Thursday, November 26

Thanksgiving Day in Laloki! No turkey for the Democrats and no chicken for the Republicans, and still a lot of things to gripe about, but still a lot to be thankful for—not the least of which is the new spirit of the Squadron and the ways of getting things done that have arisen under our new C. O.

The flying line was all a-bustle again today as two more combat missions went out and returned with pictures. That makes five in a row and establishes a new record. Lt. Guerry again went to Lae, and in addition to a strip of that drome, he also photographed Malahang and Hopoi and then ran two strips Wau to Bulolo, one of the Waira River Valley, and one of Ioma. He reported no attempted interception and no ack ack.

Lt. Post departed for the Markham Valley as soon as Lt. Guerry returned. He tri-metrogoned this objective and a strip Wau-Salamaua and obliqued Hopoi-Lae. The wary Lae Zekes all remained on the ground.

Lt. Ken Murphy (thin Murphy) went up twice today to get a local five-strip mosaic and completed it the second time.

Lt. Hargesheimer returned from the trip to Melbourne this afternoon with tales of wine, women, and work.

Lt. Gardner and Lt. Thomas were reported on the way up from Brisbane with the two '38s that came over with the Murphys.

Friday, November 28

Tragic day! Lt. Phillip D. Lissner took off at 0200 in "2123" and crashed fatally almost immediately thereafter near 12-Mile Drome. Nothing definite could be established as to the cause, except that he apparently had trouble with the right engine and feathered the prop. The plane burned almost completely with the pilot in it. Lt. Lissner was the fourth 8th Photo pilot, the third "B" flight man, to lose his life in this theatre.

Lt. Guerry took off in the morning and supposedly took 570 6" shots of the ranges, Tufi, Buna area for mapping purposes. When he returned he discovered that not a picture had run through. After much clamouring, shouting, and cursing, the pilot and camera repair split the blame 50-50. This was later amended to include only the pilot.

Lt. Loos went down the coast in the morning for a 6" strip of the shore line. He ran all the pictures he was supposed to and returned with much valuable material, we hope.

Sunday, November 29

Headquarters requested a special mission to Lae and Gona, and the Engineering Department hustled, bustled, and worked all morning to get a ship ready to go. Finally, when hope had been abandoned, Lt. Post got F-4 "2177" into the air successfully and completed the mission. The mighty men of Moresby seemed pleased again by the deeds of the 8th Photo Squadron.

Lt. Thomas arrived at noon from the mainland in a replacement ship, F-4 "2220." The ship, which somebody back in the States was kind enough to send us, was one of the old model ships and had been used for training back home. It is in such bad shape that a 100-hour inspection is needed immediately.

The Sydoruk Sleeper Special, assigned to sending soldiers to Sydney, after an early morning test hop took off for Townsville and returned the same day. What a quick trip for the old bus.

It has been a long time out of Sydney, though, so back for the next venture.

We were overwhelmed with good food today. The powers-to-be decided that this Thanksgiving Sunday we should eat in style, and that we did. Roast beef was served for lunch, and steak for dinner. There were potatoes, hot biscuits, cake, and such delicacies added to the menu. The gang enjoyed the delicious food, but all were wise enough to realize that we'd eat stew for a week as a result.

After dinner, Chaplain Cockran, Base Chaplain, held services in front of the mess hall. Cpl. Ross played the piano for the hymns. This was the first time a Chaplain had visited the camp since we left the States, and the occasion was appreciated by many. This is another evidence of the interest and activity of our Special Services Officer, Lt. Guerry.

The very full day was brought to a close with a picture show in the camp area. Rain chased a few of the spectators away, but the faithful who remained were soon rewarded by the show being completed under a starlit sky.

Monday, November 30

The day started with a BANG as the ack ack blasted away at the Nips' early morning raid on Seven-Mile.

The Squadron Journal was subjected to wide inspection and some criticism by various members of the organization to the policy of the present editor, Lt. Guerry, and S/Sgt Hammond (Squadron Roustabout Clerk). Lt. Thomas was the chief objector, and the source of his dissatisfaction lay in his not getting enough personal mention. We now take the occasion to express the highest personal esteem for Lt. Thomas and the greatest admiration for his inherent ability. As Lt. Foster has so aptly said, "We have been only a kind of 'Lame Duck' Operations Officer," and the changes for the better that have occurred of late were suggested by Lt. Thomas before he left. We regret that Lt. Thomas has not received more mention lately, but we would be very glad to drop completely out of the picture ourselves for a time if it were possible to spend over three weeks out of four in the South. Lt. Savage objected to the "Pseudo-Literary and Adolescent Style" of late. I reckon we do the bestest we all can with what light we have. We would like to mention Lt. Savage's name pleasantly once more today as a matter of good policy. We must always remember to name the C. O. in a complimentary fashion whenever possible which, of course, will not be hard to do.

Lt. Gardner arrived today with sad stories of missed connections and forced landings, and of how hard it is to get from Wards Drome to Laloki.

Lt. Hargesheimer went a-missioning at noon, but couldn't find any decent photographic weather. He took a few shots and then brought his misbehaving plane home.

The funeral services for Lt. Lissner were held in the afternoon at Murray Barracks. Almost the entire Squadron attended, and full military honors were paid by the men and officers to their deceased comrade who had given his life for his country.

Captain Reid, with crew and another group of Sydney-bent members of the squadron, plus a few outsiders, took off at the crack of dawn for the trip to civilization.

Tuesday, December 1.

Lt. Savage's new regime gave way to Lt. Thomas' order of things as Lts. Savage, Foster, and Loos departed for Melbourne, and Lt. Thomas became acting C.O. The three wayfarers seemed delighted to be on their way to the Battle of the South, and the newest C.O. entered on his duties with vim and determination.

Lt. Gardner started for New Britain, but was back in two hours reporting supercharger trouble. Inspection of the plane showed faulty exhaust stacks.

There were two missions ready to go out immediately, but no planes were available. There was general gloom and sadness throughout the departments on the line.

Wednesday, December 2

Lt. Guerry started the day off at the line by climbing into a plane with numerous maps and pertinent data, and starting for the other side to "see what he could see." Despite a fair amount of clouds, he did a mosaic of the Buna area and ran a strip from Oro Bay and another from Tufi. When he returned he reported the right engine almost cutting out on the left mag(neto), and the ship had to be grounded. As a result, none were available for an urgent Lae and Salamaua mission.

A telegram arrived early in the morning bringing word that B-17 "458" had been forced down at Rockhampton. Captain Reid dropped the men off there and proceeded to Brisbane on three engines. What a time the Sydney Sleeper is having.

A few of the men from "A" Flight, who had transferred with the B-17s "2627" and "2666," returned to the Squadron to have a little visit. It was through this visit that we learned the present whereabouts of "2627" again, and we have an eye on it.

Thursday, December 3

Today was a gloomy day in the Eighth Photo area as all ships were grounded and (there was) good weather overhead. Despite the efforts of the Engineering Officer, the crew chiefs, and the mechanics, all that could be had were hopes that a ship might be ready tomorrow.

Best remark of the day, Lt. Thomas', "Well, we might not be getting anything done, but we are working like hell!"

News from the Buna area continued to be about the same. A few Japs are holding a little bit of land around Buna, and we can't seem to dislodge them. Four destroyers steamed down from Rabaul to Buna and back without our bombers ever doing more than scaring them a bit.

Friday, December 4

We tried again today, but it availed us little. About 9 o'clock the good news that a ship would be ready shortly came into the anxious waiting in Operations. Joyfully, Lt. Post got ready to go to the target, but when he got there the clouds had just rolled in. Back he came and off went Lt. Guerry, closely followed by Lt. Gardner in another ship that had suddenly become ready. Both pilots were back in an hour with engine trouble, and no other flights were possible during the day.

The old Gona wreck was reported again today, this time as a Jap cruiser off Buna. Out went the B-17s to bomb, and one didn't come back. Plenty expensive carelessness.

Saturday, December 5

Lt. Hargesheimer slipped into the air early this morning before the clouds realized he was coming and mosaiced Moresby area again. First reports from the lab hinted that it was a beautiful job, and everybody downtown wanted a copy.

Lt. Gardner started Lae from Ward and had quite an exciting day of it. At 25,000 feet above Finschhafen his ozygen gave out, and he nearly passed out before he could get down below the oxygen belt. There he had to pursue a route home to avoid mountains, clouds, and Jap hot spots. When he finally got back to Laloki, his landing brought him the new nickname "Dirt Track" Gardner.

An excellent flow of improvements that had been progressing daily for the last two weeks under SSgt "Hardworking" Hammond neared completion today to the pleasure of everybody in the Intelligence Office. Neatly filed maps, orderly files, an up-to-date Squadron Diary, and a nearly complete set of Pilot Mission Reports gave evidence of all the recent labor.

Sunday, December 6

A very excellent mission by Lt. Hargesheimer was pushed into the background by the first "piggy back" F-4 ride in the Squadron. #37, with the radio equipment out and another seat built in, was turned into a two-place job. Lt. Post loaded T/Sgt Baker in the ship and away they went, climbing, diving, and buzzing. The fact that nearly everything, from an inoperative air speed indicator to rough engines, was wrong with the airplane didn't keep Baker from having a marvelous time.

Lt. Hargesheimer went out to Lae and vicinity and passed the Lae Drome up because of a very rough engine. After pondering the kidding he might get if the ship returned without pictures, he hazarded a pass at the drome. Away he headed for Salamaua, and then, thinking perhaps he had missed the airport, he turned back and photographed the drome again.

Lt. Vince Murphy almost stole the spotlight from both Lts. Post and Hargesheimer, and gained many a nickname all the way from "Wrong Field" to "Corrigan." He took off on a local flight, and after a few minutes aloft he did a glorious job of buzzing and landing on the wrong field. As he passed the tower he suddenly realized he was not at Laloki, but in a strange land of B-25s. He waved politely at the befuddled man in the tower and then whipped the ship about and took off in the direction from which he had just landed. Let's hope he doesn't drop in at Lae someday by mistake.

Monday, December 7

All day long we expected a raid and, no doubt, the Japs did, too, for it was a stand off for the two big bases of Rabaul and Moresby. Still, the war must go on, and did, for the two opposing air forces are said to have engaged by the numbers over Buna today. (Five squadrons of fighters from the 8th, 35th, and 49th Fighter Groups engaged formations of Zeros and Vals, claiming seventeen shot down. Japanese Navy sources admit the loss of two bombers, a fighter, and a reconnaissance seaplane.—Auths.)

"458" returned after a long absence with the usual glib excuse of, "We had an engine change in Brisbane." Amazing how many things can go wrong when the ship gets South. Still, she was a welcome sight, for she was loaded with plenty of PX supplies, and it's rumored some beer. Doc Stack also returned, and once again the boys fear for their lives as the jungle quack goes to work.

Eighth Photo celebrated the year of war by flying no missions whatsoever. The usual reason, of course, no planes available.

Tuesday, December 8

Old "458" actually soared off the field this morning, instead of the stagger, for there were only a last pitiful few of the Eighth Photo stalwarts to depart for the dingy dens of iniquity. Lt. Guerry, after an arduous three weeks of combined Intelligence and Operations, was carried aboard the plane and whispered gallantly that he'd be back. Personally, we doubt if we know Sydney, and we do.

Hargesheimer brought home the bacon today. Namely, six strips of the Owen Stanleys southeast of Myola Lakes.

The P-39 and P-40 boys, in the worst ships in the world (they say), tangled with the Japs yesterday over Buna. Final score: Americans 19, Japs 0. Five Vals, six Bettys, and eight Zeros took the count in the fracas. Today not a Zero showed its sun over Buna. Not a bad retaliation for the same date last year.

Cold beer for all the boys tonight, and while the W.C.T.U. might not approve, let it suffice to say that nobody missed the beer formation.

Wednesday, December 9

Another day, another dollar, and no missions completed. Lt. Gardner got off early for Cape Gloucester, but "2130" refused to run, so he returned within a half-hour. "2156" is ready for tomorrow and will save the face of the Eighth Photo.

Father Weidner honored us with a visit this afternoon, and his new job as Asst. A-2, Fifth Air Force, hasn't sugared his tongue any. Nobody evaded a tongue-lashing, so he must like the position.

Much mail arrived, and the war is forgotten for once. The Squadron tonight looks back to the far-a-way, but ne'er forgotten, USA. Thank God for mail from home, and to hell with all who fail to write us. No excuse will ever suffice.

Thursday, December 10

Ace pilot, erstwhile C.O. Operations Officer and Engineering Officer, H. C. Thomas, brought 'em back alive today. Three 24" strips of Buna coast and the reefs off shore. "Modest Herb" says they are absolutely the best, but the writer waits to see. If they are, we are once again in good favor at Hq, for this stuff is red hot.

General Walker today decreed that the Eighth Photo would not lose any of its valuable personnel, thereby handing one staff officer one very wet towel. The transfer was out of the Townsville lab and would have resulted in the usual SNAFU. Happy landings to the General!

Friday, December 11

The war, as far as the Air Force is concerned is at a standstill. Small sorties are being thrown at Buna, but nothing worthy of note.

Sgt James Woods of Camera Repair in the cockpit of a F-4. (Woods)

Bombing there has become very difficult, as the enemy has so little territory that the danger of hitting our own troops prevents any large-scale efforts.

V. E. Murphy (Wrong Field) executed his first mission for Eighth Photo today and came through with flying colors. Weather prevented any mapping, but he reddoed Lae, Salamaua, and Lababia Island with the 24" camera, and between the jobs entertained the Nippos with lazy eights. Pretty cocky for a first mission, but we like 'em that way.

Saturday, December 12

Eighth Photo once again sets the pace in the aeronautical world. Today, for the first time in history, two men did enter, take off, and fly into enemy territory in a P-38. Lt. Hargesheimer, with Lt. Olson back-seat driving, flew three photographic strips in the vicinity of Buna. The only thing to mar the performance was the small matter of a sheared pin in the vertical camera. No pictures were therefore obtained, but you can't have everything.

I wonder who buzzed the camp today? Strictly against orders.

Sunday, December 13

The latest additions to the Squadron, Lt. Moffat, and Flying Sergeants Churchill, Rigsby, and Ludtke, arrived at our jungle home last night. We now have 19 pilots for 7 airplanes, one of which is in commission. The only way to get flying pay now is to get four hours a month in the Sydney Hotel elevators. A good idea, but for some reason not approved by the C.O.

Monday, December 14

Eighth Photo held rifle inspection this morning and, surprisingly enough, the guns for the most part were clean. Aside from the inspecting officer, Lt. Olson, knocking a few guns to the ground, it went off quite well.

Learned this morning that the Japs landed 3,000 troops at the mouths of the Kumusi and Mambare Rivers last night. That undoubtedly accounts for the raid of last evening in which a few bombs were dropped at Ward's Drome, though no damage resulted.

Buna, supposedly a quick and simple job, has become a very difficult nut to crack and, with the arrival of last night's troops, becomes steadily worse.

Wednesday, December 16

Gather roun' Chillun', for Eighth Photo has woven a gossamer thread of gold midst all the gloom. This is a tale about a sterling but oft forgotten group of men, the airplane mechanics. With the oldest and most delicate ships in the entire SWPA (Southwest Pacific Area) they successfully put in the air four ships out of seven, and two others ready to go if needed. On top of that, four of those ships completed nine missions without a sputter.

Lt. Savage initiated Capt. Board into the Piggy Back club with a trip to Buna and a successful filming of the Waytutu Point-Cape Sudest mosaic. Lt. Loos brought pictures of the southeast New Guinea coast. Lts. Hargesheimer and Thomas got up all the same to practice formation flying, and Lt. K.J. (Shapeless) Murphy shot off to Lae and Lababia in a faultless endeavor to get the extra stew, but he too was unable to get a camera on the island before it disappeared. We are unable to give any authentic proof of the phenomena connected with this mystery, for we have only the word of the pilots. More of this at some later date.

A new paragraph to deal with the episode of the three new pilots, Moffat, Rigsby, and Ludtke, who departed this afternoon to photo the coast and get the feel of an airplane again. No sooner had they gotten away from the field that the much-talked about Guber winds descended upon us. Narrow in scope, they are nonetheless terrific, with a 70-mile gale and a deluge of water. The field was completely socked in.

Upon return, the pilots couldn't see the mountains, let alone the landing strip, so they wisely set down on the first available field. Lt. Moffat and SSgt Ludtke at Three-Mile and SSgt Rigsby at Five-Mile. They will return here in the morning. Those of us here on the ground received the full force of the Guber and observed its ravages. Lt. Savage is claiming damages for his tent which previously set on a high hill. After the flow it was located somewhere down the hill and all contents were much soaked. A tree was blown down at headquarters with no casualties, and the line is inundated with water, but Eighth Photo continues as though nothing had happened.

Thursday, December 17

"Glammer Pants" Kneeskern headed east today for Milne Bay. Weather prevented much work but, never daunted, he started back up the coast and, sure enough, some of the clouds had blown off the coast and he secured some good strips from Marshall Lagoon to Hood Point and Amazon to Gadaiso. Meanwhile, Hargesheimer was photographing all over the place at Cape Gloucester. This represented the eighth attempt to secure pictures of the vicinity and seemed to be the charm, for all the shots were good.

Lest I forget, Bill Fairbank is a new member of the Piggy Back Club as of today. "Ace" Thomas took him over to Buna in old "37" and put the plane through the paces. One slow roll, one 450 mph drive, and one assortment of turns and stalls convinced Fairbank that this is a young man's game and not for steady engineers, but he still has a new glint in his eyes, so perhaps there is still some hope for him.

Friday, December 18

Lt. Moffat and Lt. Hargesheimer went pursuiter on us yesterday with almost dire results. Seeing the little P-39s taking off in formation, they set their jaws and determined not to be outdone. All commenced well, but suddenly Hargesheimer's propwash caught Moffat, and he was all but helpless in the face of it. Do what he might, she just didn't want to fly on an even keel, and one wing and then the other dipped for the ground, but at last he staggered off and they proceeded on their search for a transport said to be on one engine losing altitude out to sea. Fifty miles out from Moresby the 8th Photo Sea Search Flight spotted what appeared to be some sort of wreckage which looked like a giant pineapple. No trace of survivors. With this startling bit of news they returned to Schwimmer. This satisfied nobody, so Lt. Hargescheimer took off again, this time with fighter escort. Skillfully navigating the seaways, he once again located the large pineapple. Peeling off with a vengeance, they went down for a look, but it was nothing but a palm tree floating about in the ocean. No Japs strapped to it, and no submarine under it, so a disappointed Hargescheimer once more returned to his jungle home.

Sunday, December 19

The jungle quacks grabbed their needles last night and proceeded to inoculate the entire Squadron for Bubonic Plague, cholera, and a refresher of tetanus. The first man almost got a cattle serum for tuberculosis, but someone stopped the quacks in time, reminding them they were no longer following their civilian trade.

Today everybody was so out of sorts and possessed of such sore arms that all operations were called off for the day, and the Squadron hit the sack to lick their wounds.

We did collect the ground crews together and gave a short talk on the situation and our part in it. Capt. Board expounded on the enemy's activity and probably strategy. Lt. Olson explained the importance of Eighth Photo on reconnaissance, and Lt. Fairbank the mapping program. It is our hope that the mechanics now relize how important their ships are and their work is in keeping them flying.

Sunday, December 20

Don't forget, boys, the extra stew is still in the offing for the lucky man to shoot Lababia. V. E. Murphy is the latest victim of the mystery isle. He claims that he had it, but the camera sweated so much that the pictures wouldn't come up. Seems that the gremlins have reached this front and are there to stay.

All in all, the day was none too good. Kneeskern went Kakodaway and found nothing but clouds. He cut a few doughnuts and came home. Savage piggy-backed an Engineer Captain, but ran into the same difficulty—weather. And so down the roster. Moffat and SSgt Churchill hit the Milne Bay trail only to return again. Seems the tropic rains have got us.

Sgt Woods with a broken wheel from the squadron's B-26. (Woods)

Monday, December 21

Old John G. (Rummy) Foster rejoined us today. He almost made the trip yesterday, but got within 40 miles of the coast and was forced to turn back because of a violent tropical storm. Something of a record, 5 hr. and 15 min. of flying, and there still remained 216 gallons in the tanks. He made it today, arriving at 1415 with ship "2217," a new ship to the squadron, but nevertheless a F-4 of the same undependable quality.

A good show at the camp tonight. "House of Seven Gables," with delovely Margaret Lindsay. Twenty years is too long to wait!

Tuesday, December 22

P.O.G. Gardner whipped the Lae and Salamaua problem nicely today, getting the runways directly under his 24" photo, and that, coupled with excellent light and haze condition, rendered the first photographs we have seen in many moons. Enlargements are being made and will undoubtedly produce excellent results. Ken Murphy, the one known as Shapeless, took a gander at Milne Bay clouds and forthwith hurried home.

"Glammer Pants" Kneeskern, our Asst. I.O., ran into more of the same Kakoda-way and returned. Not such a good day, either.

The G.F.U. HQ solution to the night bombing problem failed to do the trick tonight. Ack-ack was silenced, and a P-38 was sent up to intercept. Unfortunately, they failed to nab Nippo in the searchlight. Hence the P-38 zoomed and dove to no avail, the opponents being at the other end of the sky. A good idea, but needing better coordination.

Wednesday, December 23

Moffat did the Lae hitch today and got us some nice stuff. We haven't found a suitable sobriquet for him yet, so he shall be carried ignominiously as "Moffat" until such time as he either goes to the head of the class or joins the G.F.U.s. Our time will come, never fear.

V. E. Murphy flew around the bends in the Mambare River today and brought us a strip from Kokoda to the coast. Somewhere probably resides a baby-blue dry tank, for Murphy returned minus one. Probably find some native paddling down stream with it one of these days.

Thursday, December 24

John G. (we got 'em better) Foster flew over the blue Pacific chanting "Anchors Aweigh" today, but ran into a tropical front. He promptly decided the check points were not so good and wisely returned home.

Our pride and joy, Kneeskern, got religion in a big way. He not so wisely found the same front Foster hit and pushed on through. Pardon me, I don't mean through, just into. From there on the plane flew Kneeskern. Five hours after departure he was still among the missing. Whereupon C.O. Savage held his left you-know-what, you-know-where, and sure enough, the glamour boy showed up much the worse for wear. With bloodshot eyes and a very blank stare he climbed out of "56" and was led by the hand to Operations. He shows signs of recovering, however, so we shall, no doubt, have to turn him down to size again in a couple of days.

SSgt Ludtke went over to the other side, but was faced by bad weather and had to return. Better luck next time, Sgt.

Lest we forget, Ken Murphy went the limit today on the Cook's tour of northern New Guinea. He photographed the coastline between Madang and Wewak and, after 5 hr. and 20 min., set her back down here with 75 gal left in the tanks. Let it suffice that he was a mighty tired boy tonight.

Christmas Eve and Eight Photo celebrates with a lousy movie "Zanzibar."

It is rumored that a few of the officers got hold of firewater and had the Eighth Photo Indian doing a war dance before the night was over. The midday appearance of a certain Engineer lends considerable credence to the rumor.

Friday, December 25

Christmas Day, and our thoughts wind homeward. Still, the war continues and we must hold up our end, so we dispatched several missions Japward.

SSgt Rigsby photoed Lae and Salamaua. SSgt Ludtke flew trimet strips around the Warie River.

The cooks really outdid themselves for our benefit today. Shrimp cocktail, baked Virginia ham, mashed potatoes, fruit salad, pumpkin pie, and iced tea graced the table. What a feast! The usual table banter was missing as everyone was busy gorging. A rare pleasure, and therefore treated with proper respect. After that feed Merry Christmas was more than just two words.

Saturday, December 26

Gardner took up where Foster left off and headed across the seas to Gasmata. As usual it was clouded up, and he was forced to return pictureless. What a thankless task this photographic. "Powerhouse" Murphy ran the monotony haul of Lae and Salamaua. They don't bother us anymore, for even the ack-ack was silent today. What a beautiful type of monotony! Just keep those fingers crossed, boys.

You have heard everything now if you listen to this recital of woe. December 8th, "2458" departed Sydney-ward. December 18th, we received wire, "Held up by weather Brisbane." Lord only knows where they were the intervening days. December 20th, they left Townsville with Foster on the wing and got another forty miles off Moresby, met a tropical front, and then returned to Townsville. December 21st comes a wire, "Held up for wingtip repair. Will arrive Wednesday." December 23rd, a wire, "Ship laid up for general overhaul. Have advised Lt. Guerry to take first available transportation." Now we learn that they are taking "58" away for combat use. Nothing but abuse we are getting. The lot of a photo squadron!

Wednesday, December 30

It has just now come to the attention of this raconteur the abysmal depths to which the Medical Department has fallen. Rumor has it, working in a Persian seraglio has had a dire influence on their conduct. Whatever it may be, we have it from generally unimpeachable sources that the doctor, not being a normal person, did not contract the habit in the normal way. His is a passion for needling others. In fact, he will inject the wrong person just to have an excuse to needle a person a second time. How about that Cobb? All others take heed.

'Tis moving day for the Eighth Photo Operations and Intelligence. The natives put the finishing touches on the big beautiful hut, and we proceeded to inhabit the place. People in the States might question the finishing touches, for the roof leaks and the floor has innumerable holes, but to us it's big and beautiful. It is just the same as people at home who think water comes from a tap when we know it comes from a river and must be hauled eight miles. Strictly in the point of view.

SSgt Rigsby held four aces in the Lae, Salamaua, Malahang deal. He completely whipped all past performances and returned with some neat little prints. His Salamaua strip is so good that we have decided to lay a mosaic. How's that for showing the old H.P.s of the Squadron.

Thursday, December 31

Happy New Year's Eve Day to Everyone. But not for Everyone. P.O.G. Gardner had a bad day. First, he departed for Lae and upon reaching altitude discovered a small hole in his oxygen mask. Armed with a new mask, and that is all he was armed with, P. O. G. set forth again and this time got to the target, but not alone. Somehow three Zeros were finding the same place at the same time. With the pictures tucked neatly away in the camera, Gardner waved adieu and took out. Last seen, the Zeros were flying backwards.

Aviation engineers building revetments at 14-Mile. (Woods)

V.E. Murphy proves the old adage of try, try, again. Conqueror of the Tufi area, he now has earned the rating of cameraman. First, he has the correct overlap, 65% by measurement; second, he continued the strips to the coast; and third, he landed at the right drome. What a day!

2

8th Photo Squadron Diary 1943

Friday, January 1

Just to start the New Year off right, 8th Photo records no missions for the day. There are various excuses proferred by differnet members of the Squadron, but the only correct one is the presence of an all-day rain. This writer will not attempt to set forth what could have been the order of the day had the weather been good, but will let it suffice that a good time was had by all last evening and a good rest today.

Saturday, January 2

Mother told me it would be like this, but, fool that I was, I didn't believe her. By this I'm referring to the tropics and its rainy season. For the last three days we have been inundated, flooded out, and steeped in the residue of cumulus clouds. It is generally believed that the combined efforts in the realm of witchcraft by horticulturalist Hargesheimer and Gardner have brought all this upon us. Our answer is Aussie Captain Doug Board, who has gone South to pick up some ABOS who we shall set to pointing bones at the above evil two. "An eye for an eye, a tooth for a tooth, and witchcraft for witchcraft," is our motto.

This morning before our very eyes was enacted the least successful melodrama yet to result from World War II. Entitled, "Who'll Do It, Whodunit?" It brought for the first time to the New Guinea stage that charming ingenue, Lieutenant Thomas.

...Scene two shows Lt. Thomas in his blue F-4, on instruments, climbing through the overcast, blithely singing, "Deep in the heart of Texas." Finally, he emerges from the mist and soars over the snowy cloud banks. But here, having built us up to a climax, the play sadly lets us down, for the great leader finds Lae overcast and returns sorrowfully to Schimmer Drome. He then sinks into the permanent depressions in the cushions, and within two minutes is once more back in his usual coma.

Scene three shows Lt. Olson at the phone making excuses on the mission's failure with little or no success. FINIS.

Sunday, January 3

Yesterday was too much for your writer, and the missions to Buna and Lae today were unsuccessful, so this day's operations pass unnoticed and unsung. We have, however, amidst our happy little throng a new, but not unexpected, Captain. It is our C.O., one F. S. Savage, who received his long overdue promotion. Let us not forget to "Hit a Brace, you Misters," occasionally.

B-17E #41-2627, "RFD TOJO," sent to the 8th PRS from 43rd Bomb Group to facilitate long range missions during 1942 and 1943. (8th PRS)

RFD Tojo on the ground at 14-Mile. (Frank Reindl)

Jackson Strip (7-Mile) with B-24s on the ground (probably 90th Bomb Group) early to middle 1943. (National Archives Mary Ilario)

Monday, January 4

Lts. Guerry and Post, having recovered from that New Guinea disease, Lackanooky, were returned to the Squadron today. Unfortunately, while South recovering from the one disease, they contracted another, the German malady, Assadragin, but our revered medical officer, Lt. Stark, says that a good Papuan rest cure is the finest treatment in the world. Speedy recovery, gents.

Capt. Savage carried Lt. Olson over to Buna again today and flew a strip of the track from Sananda to Soputa, but clouds interfered about halfway to spoil the success of the trip. It wasn't wasted time, however, for the Intelligence Officer is now even more intelligent, if that is possible.

Lt. Moffat, the industrious and able pilot of the 8th Photo, proved once again that through a knowledge of the airplane and cameras, one will obtain success in his work. He brought back some excellent pictures of Lae and Salamaua taken at 12,000 ft. While we don't recommend that altitude as a steady diet, we can endorse the flying, which results in the target being in the center of the picture. Take note, gentlemen, that you are being out-worked and outflown.

Tuesday, January 5

Lt. Foster, satisfying the request for large-scale photos of the track, flew at 7,000 ft. with the 24 inch camera on runaway from

A B-l 7 adorned with the 8-ball logo. (M. Melman)

8th PRS parachute packer. (Reindl)

Coffee time for senior NCOs. One master sergeant wants no mistake made about the matter (Reindl)

Camera repairmen and aerial photographers of the 8th PRS. Frank Reindl is in the front row at far left (Reindl)

Sananda to Soputa. We have learned another lesson from this flight, namely, that the 25 inch camera below 10,000 ft. does not provide sufficient overlap for good photo strips.

Lt. Guerry, getting back to shape in easy stages, photoed Koki Mission from 5,000 ft. and then returned to terra firma. It should be mentioned here, as we cannot escape noting personally day and night, that Lt. Guerry has not returned empty-handed from the metropolis of the South. He brought with him assorted musical instruments, namely, a trumpet, a saxaphone, a bass viol, clarinet, complete set of bass and trap drums, and the guts of the piano. This, gentlemen, accounts for the various and sundry noises issuing from a number of the tents about the camp. Should we complain from time to time, don't think for a moment that we unmusical members of the organization have no appreciation of the finer things in life. It's just that our souls are not as yet attuned to the patient endeavours of the true artist.

Thursday, January 7

The war once again claims the services of the 8th Photo Squadron. HARK! HARK! for the enemy advances. News has just reached us that a convoy is en route from Gasmata and is now headed for Finschhafen. We shall send a ship off at dawn to ascertain its position and probable destination, now thought to be Lae.

Friday, January 8

Sgt. Rigsby headed out at dawn seeking the enemy. Reaching Lae, he located three transports and four warships, taking pictures of the same. He picked up considerable ack-ack, but undaunted, remained in the area until his search was completed. He proceeded there from down the coast, noting no activity at Salamaua, but found at Buna Mission one cargo ship of 2,000 tons, 3 pinnaces, and six barges. Thence to home.

Lt. V. E. Murphy, out on a mapping mission, also did a neat bit of reconnaissance. Having flown a strip from Bulldog to Wau, he proceeded to Salamaua to Mubo. But wait—what is that headed this way? Investigation proceeds, and it seems to be a 5,000 ton cargo and a destroyer midway between Lae and Salamaua, headed for Salamaua. That determined, he flew the Salamaua-Mubo strip, the Mambare River strips, and then headed for home. Alas, the left oblique on "2220" failed to work, but all is not lost, for the verticals are good, though thin.

"Rummy" Foster took the afternoon recco and found pretty much the same deal at Lae, but weather was so bad at Salamaua that good observation was impossible. He noted a possible U/I ship off Burning Point, but clouds prevented any photography.

Saturday, January 9

This is as good a time as any to complain about the treatment this front is getting from the States. Today another of the B-26s cracked up on take-off. The plane almost had flying speed when the nose tire blew out. The pilot tried to pull up the wheels, but the nose-wheel refused to come up.

F1m Petes at Kavieng, New Ireland. (Hilliard)

Harlan Olson and pilot Herb Thomas reviewing aerial photos at 14-Mile. (Thomas)

Instead, it tore up the metal runway and finally swerved the plane off the runway where it crashed, the nose-wheel coming up through the bottom and severely, if not fatally, injuring the turret gunner's back. The B-26s are receiving a lot of unjust criticism because they are cracking up so often, but it must be remembered, these are 1940 planes flying combat. Because the U.S. considers this front secondary, the finest B-26 pilots and crews are losing their lives. This is true throughout our forces here. We ourselves have the only F-4s flying combat. No dive or torpedo bombers have been supplied this front. While this sector may be only secondary, it still must be fought and cannot be fought correctly with present equipment.

Gardner went to Milne Bay to pick up the mapping strips of the reefs between Milne Bay and Louisade Archipelago. Bad weather once again prevents success. May history record our trials and tribulations.

Sunday, January 10

Today was another tragic day, which adds weight to the above statements. A B-26 taking off for the South with fourteen aboard going on leave failed at 100 ft. and crashed near the west end of Twelve-Mile Strip. Bursting into flame immediately, only those thrown out of the ship by the explosion had a chance to live, and several of those finally died. Of the fourteen, seven will survive. Our own medical officer, Lt. Stark, with P.F.Cs Ratcliffe and Sills and Pvt. Vinson of Operations, were there to assist with the rescue. Their eagerness to aid those unfortunates, despite danger from the fire, speaks well for their courage and valor. This is the fourth B-26 crash where Lt. Stark performed his duty in the face of definite personal danger.

Monday, January 11

Our old B-17 "12627" is once again with us, but without a crew. We are at last to be given a chance to get the long range mapping stuff. Said to be in condition for missions, we now find it to be due for a 100-hour inspection, the gun barrels and belts rusted to the point of inefficiency. The ship is filthy from stem to stern. No self-respecting crew would claim ownership of such an airplane. The linemen, aided by Lt. Moffat, are busy cleaning it up to get it ready for some of the hottest missions to be flown in this war. Make it a good job, men.

Lts. Stark and Thomas are no longer among the rank and file. Gentlemen, may I present Captains Stark and Thomas. Treat them easy, boys, or they'll rack you back to the seventh chin. We are glad to see it, Captains, and await your every order.

"Sparks" Hargesheimer finally heckled (Bomber Command) into action, and 8th Photo is now broadcasting with a complete transmitter and receiving set. We can now maintain contact with our ships. If we can wrangle serviceable transmitters and receivers for the planes, we will really be a red-hot outfit. Hargey also ran the Lae job, but failed to photograph because of the old boogey, weather.

Tuesday, January 12

Action! Cameras! Our B-17 crew has shown up, and we can soon commence operations. Captain Barnes will be pilot, and Lt. Guerry will be (winner of the toss, too bad, Foster) assisting from the right side. The ship will operate from Seven-Mile and will be briefed there by Lt. Olsen. All is ready except the weather. When it breaks, we function on a great scale. "Bring 'em back alive Barnes" is the watchword.

"Tobacco Road" Loos is bemoaning his fate these days. Today for the third time in a row he came back without pictures. You can quit wailing, Loos, because we all know it can't be helped. Such is the fate of a photo pilot. So be it. Amen.

Tony Troiano, 8th PRS motor pool sergeant at 14-Mile. (Jim McEwan)

Wednesday, January 13

Art "They're All Mine" Post let his running mate, Alex Guerry, have an airplane to visit Lae, but aside from that allowed no one to play in his backyard. Art, of course, put a plane through the paces locally for the benefit of the Koki Mission nurses, but the rest of the day was strictly rest period.

Friday, January 15

Capt. Barnes got the B-17 off the ground today, with Lt. Guerry pulling the superchargers and OLSON whipping the Bomb Sight, but after an hour they decided the engines were too rough to continue, so returned to Jackson. We know why the 43rd Bomb Group released old "2627." It is no longer serviceable, so they came to the conclusion that the 8th Photo really did need an airplane and generously GAVE it to us. If Bom Com proceeds according to schedule we will soon be landing at Lae and photographing A/A postions with a C-3 camera. Today they asked for Lae at 10,000 ft. with the 24 inch. Nice work if you can get it, and SSgt Rigsby did.

"Reaction Time" Ludtke is beating his head against the wall, for his cameras failed again with his attempt at the Louisiade Archipelago job. V. E. Murphy had better luck and returned with four strips of the Fall River Area.

Saturday, January 16

Barnes, Guerry, Olson, and TSgt Reindel finally completed a mission in the B-17, but with little to show for it. They rode all the way to Bougainville just to look at the clouds and then headed for New Britain. A short strip resulted at Jacquinot Bay, but fuel shortage made it imperative that they return to Seven Mile. Five hours on oxygen and slight results. Poor reward.

A new fad has hit the Squadron. Someone made the mistake of receiving a jigsaw puzzle for Christmas. The results—Foster and Gardner taking all bets that they can put it together in 35 minutes. The writer is happy to announce that they lost.

Hargey went toward Milne Bay, but returned on account of engine trouble.

Loos went from Bulldog to Wau and secured the best pictures of the week, but the obliques failed so we will have to run it over again. This strip is definitely the home of all the Gremlins of New Guinea, but having run them to their lair, we still can find no way to destroy them.

Tuesday, January 19

Capt. Barnes, Rummy Foster, and I.O. Olson took off for Rabaul at 0530 and returned at 0730 because the navigator was ill. Off again at 0830 with Olson handling the navigation. They flew for two and a half hours on instruments and then let down through a series of overcast. At 2,000 ft. they broke out into the clear right over the convoy. A few bursts of A/A soon decided them that this was not the accepted place and method of locating convoys, so they hightailed it for New Ireland. Land Ho at 1130, but what strange country is this? Ask the navigator, but, of course, he didn't know.

Carl Prince, 8PRS Crew Chief. (Bugal)

Prince and his crew under a F-4. (Bugal)

F-5A #77 under repair at 14-Mile. (Reindl)

F-4 #56, serial 41-2156, "Limping Lizzie." Camera installation provided for both vertical and oblique photography.

Oh well, there is a lighthouse they can strafe, and strafe it they did. They then sailed onward to Blanche Bay when suddenly they discovered 15 Zeros overhead. But the good Lord protects the ignorant. The Zekes after peeling off changed their minds and chandeled away, and the B-17 made tracks for the clouds. The rest of the day passed uneventfully, and we still have an airplane. SSgt Nulty flew around Buna photographing the dromes and vicinity. It is pleasant whipping about that area without worrying about A/A.

The famed William Fairbank, a liaison intelligence officer to the 8th PRS who did much valuable work, and who was mercilessly kidded in the squadron diary, standing next to "Limping Lizzie." (Ludtke)

Wednesday, January 20

Murphy has lost his color now that he is an accomplished Photo Pilot. No mistakes, no publicity. He now whips out the strips one after another with proper side lap, cameras turned on, and intervalometer set. Today he flew a mosaic of Port Moresby, not to mention the mosaic he flew at Port Harvey to Boga without an error. How prosaic!

Alex did the Bulldog to Wau job. The photos hold considerable cloud, so we are still flying that strip. P.O.G. got us a few pictures of the Milne Bay area. I wonder how many feet of film we have of that place now. It isn't that important.

Friday, January 22

Churchill had no luck today because of the bad weather that always haunts the Finschhafen area, but it hasn't carried over to his crap shooting any, for he's still lining his pocket.

Cecil H. Rigsby (nice name that) went to Milne Bay, photoed three strips and returned via coast of Hood Point. Notice how dull and commonplace that is. Let's go Hollywood and see how it sounds. It is dawn on the 22nd of January 1943. The mechanics of the 8th Photo Squadron are on the flight line checking the airplanes before they take off on their perilous combat missions. With the motors ticking, the great "Lightnings," America's greatest, speediest airplanes are quivering, alive, and anxious to get on with the day's work. But the pilots must wait until the clouds lift and the sun rises higher in the heavens. At nine o'clock Rigsby, alert , handsome young pilot, typical of America's fast growing Air Force, climbs into the cockpit. He taxies to the end of the runway and there checks each functional part as knowingly as a jockey feeling out his mount. Everything is ok, so Rigsby squares off on the runway and slowly pushes the throttles forward. There is a high pitch hum as the superchargers cut in and the plane starts slowly down the runway, gathering speed to the roar of the two powerful motors. The plane rises easily up from the Drome and soon disappears through a hole in the clouds.

We now join the pilot as he soars over the white flooor of clouds. He's busy now checking all the gauges to be sure nothing is amiss, computing his time and distance to be sure of his navigation, and just flying the airplane. Soon, through the hole in a cloud he sees the coastline below him and a known reef reassures him of his location. He then sets his course for Milne Bay, the target for the day. At 11 o'clock the target is sighted. Locating the points to be photographed, the pilot sets himself to the job at hand. This is the most difficult flying in the world, for the altitude cannot change and the airplane must be level at all times, but these pilots are specifically trained for their tasks. With the regularity of clockwork he runs one, two, then three strips. His mission is completed, the terrain below recorded on film more accurately than the human eye could ever attain. With the knowledge of a job well done, Rigsby points the nose of "Opisonya" homeward and lightheartedly looks forward to the lunch awaiting him.

At 1330, as instinctively as a homing pigeon, he flies across the home drome, circles the field, and sets her down. Just another part of a day's work done. Smoothly and competently these pilots fly their missions, day after day, assuring America of final victory.

Vince Murphy by the fuel drums that made the return to Port Moresby possible for "Limping Lizzie." (Murphy)

Saturday, January 23

TSgt Scott flew as photographer with a 90th Bomb B-24. Supposedly just a quiet little recco, it turned to quite a fracas. First, the pilot hated the idea of returning with the bombs, so he headed for Rabaul and unloaded his eggs on a cruiser. Somehow the Nips resented it, and 20 of Lakunai's 150 Zeros rose to the challenge. After 45 mins. of combat the Zeros had put only 5 holes in the '24, and the '24 had put three Zeros in the drink. Nice going, boys!

Ludtke went to Finschhafen to Madang this morning. Have him tell you about the Drome sometime. 'Nuff said.

K. J. Murphy, the shapeless one, went to the Louisade, nil results.

"Rummy" Foster went to Lae and recorded the results of a B25 strike. He had eight P-38s for top cover. Pretty classy.

Monday, January 25

Capt. Thomas to Madang—nil photos. Lt. Murphy to Soputa where he flew a mosaic (in the wrong area). Evidently this is Vincent E., but he can still do it, boys.

Capt. Savage spread himself for the boys by treating them to dinner at Moresby Officers' Club. Civilization has hit New Guinea.

For several days we have been trying to photograph a wrecked airplane sighted by the 39th Fighter in the vicinity of Wau. But each time we followed the pursuits, we have never even located Wau. Today we varied the procedure and Lt. Loos led the pursuit to Wau. Result: Photos of the wrecked ship, a B-17. This only proves what we already knew.

Hargey went to Soputa to get the mosaic of the area. Murphy's bad weather prevented photography.

March 2, 1943. Vince Murphy was flying through a 200 foot ceiling with a one mile visibility on low fuel when he decided to make a forced landing on New Guinea's Hisiu Beach. He was stuck there for two days until a repair crew came up to clear the area for takeoff. Captain Savage finally got "Limping Lizzie" into the air and back to Port Moresby. (Murphy/Thomas)

Capt. Savage takes a quick lunch while contemplating getting Lizzie off the beach and over the trees. Murphy was on a recon to Wewak when he made a good wheels up forced landing. (Murphy)

Murphy, TSgt Richard Meech, Cpl Aubrey King, and Art Post, with Lt. George Hamlin behind Post in the background celebrating Murphy's return. (Murphy)

Gardner went to Louisiade, but returned with the same old story.

Capt. Thomas, trying to look like a good fellow, offered to treat us to a meal at the Officers' Club. Not taken in, we of course refused and proceeded to stick him with the bill by the odd man method. We preserved our integrity and ate heartily to boot.

Wednesday, January 27

The band swung out tonight for the first time, and although still far from full strength, sounded mighty good to us. Corp. Peterson on the trumpet, Corp. Ross on the piano, Miller on the bass viol, Avery (from the ACK ACK) with his accordion, and Cortlett on the drums. A couple of saxes and a guitar coming up. Lead on, Guerry, and swing out, boys.

Tropical summer weather prevented photography on N.G. Ludtke tried it on the Louisade Archipelago. However, the B-17 mapped on the south coast of New Britain. The much talked about, but shied from, dreaded Eighth Photo mapping missions haven't been disastrous yet. Good luck, and keep 'em flying.

Friday, January 29

SSgt Churchill flew a Nil Photo, due to weather, mission to Lae. Capt. Thomas took our boy "Dusty Dan" Daniels for a piggyback ride in "Hellapoppin Hepcat." Both pilot and passenger saw black. Danny highly recommended installing plumbing fixtures in No. 37 immediately.

Saturday, January 30

SSgt Ludtke flew to Normandy Island, and then whipped about the Milne Bay area, picking up a strip here and there, anywhere that happened to be free of clouds.

"Shapeless" Murphy went bridge hunting this morning (New Guinea substitute for home hunting) but couldn't find a pretty baby blue one to match his airplane. He disconsolately settled for some major mapping strips from Madang to Finschafen and returned home. He is still telling people how disappointed he is in the Gogol River. "Not a respectable bridge on the whole river. It's a good river and deserves a bridge, too."

W.W. Morton hightailed home from Wau with four Zekes behind him. He already had his mapping strips tucked away, so it was a good time to find out if the P-38 could outrun the Zero. It did, but what we want to know is, "Are you sure those weren't P-40s, Mort?"

Sunday, January 31

M. G. Gardner took a strip on New Britain, not because he thought it was good photographic weather, but it just made him so damn mad to go all the way up there and then have to return with no pictures. Don't worry, POG, they weren't wasted.

Sykes went to the Purari River but returned pictureless. Kneeskern has solved the problem of how to secure perfect pictures. First you go to the Camera Repair Section and TSgt West explains all about the cameras, case drives, and pressure plates. Next, a long heart-to-heart with our exuberant engineer. Of course,

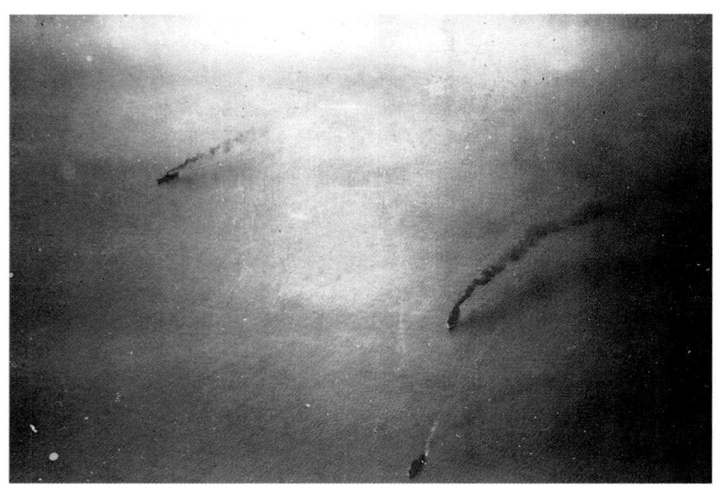

While Murphy was down on an unrelated beach the Bismarck Sea battle was fought, as witnessed by this photo of Japanese shipping on March 2, 1943. (Jim Dieffenderfer)

One of the B-25s used by 8th PRS destroyed by Japanese attack on 14-Mile, probably the April 12, 1943, raid. (Reindl)

Pilot Clark Sykes aboard F-4, serial 41-2220. (Sykes)

that is a monologue, because—well, you know Fairbank. Thus, armed with information, you sally forth on the mission and bring back the ultimate in aerial photography. There is only one thing wrong with this system. If the enemy finds you, you'll never see them, because the head is always in the cockpit computing various and sundry speeds, altitudes, angles, etc. Kneeskern, however, fearing the enemy not a whit, followed the system this morning and returned with the neatest job this week in the Wau-Salamaua area. Lest we forget, he also polished off the Bulldog-Wau strip. Praise be to Allah!

Monday, February 1

Capt. Thomas flew the mosaic of Goodenough Island, and the pictures reveal the drome there to be shaping up nicely. We only hope that F-4s will never grace that runway. Can you imagine being stationed there and referring to New Guinea as the mainland? It's bad luck even to think about it.

After reading Hargesheimer's report, I cannot decide whether he is a member of the 8th Photo Squadron or the 8th Communications Unit. The photos may be good, but "the CW was wonderful" is the gist of the report. It is nice to see Hargesheimer happy, anyway.

Tuesday, February 2

Churchill to New Britain, Ludtke to Lae, nil photos due to weather.

Wednesday, February 3

Our Commanding Officer, Capt. Frank S. Savage, took off in "Baker's Bastard" today heading for Cape Gloucester. He flew a strip heading for Cape Bredown to Bulu River and then took operational pictures of Lae. On his return we find that he tried to photograph the well-known Jacobsen's farm in preference to Lae Drome—a complete miss!

Lt. K. J. Murphy then set out for Lae, and being very determined, did take pictures of the Drome from 13,500'.

Lt. Post decided that his time needed a bit of building up today, and as a result took off on two test hops—just another hour, Post.

Friday, February 5

Our representative from Victoria, Texas, Lt. Loos, took the Lae run today. The Nips must've known he was from Texas, as they laid in some pretty close ones. The A/A aroused the Texas in him, and he carried out his mission is spite of the Nips' accurate shooting.

POG Gardner found more airdromes today than I knew were in the area. Dromes of Moresby, Milne Bay, and Buna were all covered by Gardner.

The following photos are of members of the 8th PRS who served in the squadron during 1943. Most of the aircrew are mentioned in the diary in reference to reconnaissance missions which were either frustrated by mechanical or weather problems or were completed with commendable results and little apparent glowing comment from higher headquarters. *Above:* Jim McEwan, gunner and cameraman, and Larry Costigan, orderly room clerk. (McEwan)

Raymond Stromer, (probably) Carl Prince, Aden Davis and Tom Lane at 14-Mile in May 1943 (Mrs. Aden Davis)

Bart Morely, a pilot of the 8th PRS. (Murphy)

Lt. Hargesheimer tried a little mapping over New Britain, but the weather forced him to turn to his alternate, the D'Entrecasteaux Group (some name—try it sometime). He flew several strips and then returned to base.

Sunday, February 6

SSgt Churchill proceeded to the D'Entrecasteaux Group for the usual purpose—picture taking. In this he was successful, but then the trouble commenced. The writer will not attempt to translate or interpret the meaning of such words as "ammeter showed over 100 amps, and voltage exceeded 30," but merely repeats it for intelligencia (and communications). Suffice to say that it means something was wrong, so Churchill set her down at Turnbull Drome. There they replaced the voltage regulator, and once again he was in the air and on the way home. May the writer suggest that should any similar disturbance occur, the pilot will find the Trobriand Islands a pleasant haven of rest, contentment, and entertaining, anyway.

Norm Scott, one of the aerial photo men, doing the laundry. (McEwan)

Sunday, February 7

Another joy ride for "Shapeless" Murphy today. After photographing Nadzab Drome and a few huts at Bukembare he returned to Schwimmer. He reported several fires in the Markham and Ramu Valley, probably Aussie pickets having a spot of tea.

SSgt Ludtke went to New Britain and flew two strips. A very good job indeed. Weather prevented photography of other areas.

The first casualty of the enlisted ranks of the squadron was SSgt Stephen Humenchick. He was on a B-24 of the 90th Group, flying as an aerial photographer. It crashed shortly after takeoff, and all the crew (were) killed.

Monday, February 8

Today we were nothing but "engine time boys." Kneeskern went all the way to the Sepik River, but could not photograph on account of weather. Photos nil. Time: four hours.

Capt. Thomas proceeded to New Britain and picked up two of those much-needed New Britain strips. Time: three and one half hours.

Lt. Morton covered most of the New Guinea Island today. Madang, Bena-Bena, Markham, Watut River, and Ramu Valley were just a few of the many interesting spots in his itinerary. After photographing these he returned home. Time: four and one half hours.

Capt. Barnes and his boys, Lts. Guerry and Fairbank and Capt. Olson, took a trip to Manus Island today. Despite the heavy overcast and showers, they were successful in getting four strips to completely cover the Island. Olson very skillfully maneuvered the ship onto the proper flight lines for the first three strips. Then, against his better judgment, he let Fairbank, "The Wingless Wonder," guide the fourth strip. (Unfortunately) the fourth strip is nothing but clouds. Fairbank will try to explain this by saying that the weather is at fault, but don't be taken in, for the other three flight lines are superb. And don't think that was the only department that Fairbank failed so miserably in today. On the way home the 2nd Lieutenant

Herb Thomas (Loos)

DeLasso Loos (Loos)

(Fairbank, of course, being the only shavetail on the plane) climbed up behind the pilots. When Guerry bravely asked him, "Wanna Fly," he was all eagerness. "Hold 135," instructed Guerry as he climbed behind the wheel, knees noticeably shaking. Looking in bewilderment at the maze of instruments in front of him, Fairbank timidly queried, "What by?" Noticing that the gas gauge was just then at 140, Guerry pointed helpfully to that. In relief the "Engineer" settled down to show the boys how constant a course he could hold: Two lazy eights, a loop, and a slow roll later, he decided something must be wrong.

Tuesday, February 9

Three attempted missions today, and three reports of nil photos. Lt. Loos tried Talasea; Gardner, the Markham Valley; and Sykes tried Karkar, Bagabag, and Long Island. All pilots returned downhearted, complaining to a very great extent about the New Guinea weather.

Thursday, February 11

The weather looked very bad to everyone except "Eager Beaver" Olson. He took one look at Kneeskern and ordered him off for Wewak. Kneeskern, doing only as he could when a superior officer gives him an order, hobbled mournfully out to his ship, "Baker's Bastard," with only one thought in mind—if Olson says good weather, it has to be good! Kneeskern returns in an hour and a half to tell the I.O. what a damn poor judge of weather he is. What the hell—he does as good or better than the Met Section.

Friday, February 12

8th Photo put out a solo mission today. Lt. Morton handling the "Daily Mail."

Saturday, February 13

We wonder if the Nips call a red alert as "Photo Joe" makes the daily run over Lae, Salamaua, and Malahang. Lt. Kneeskern called their raid today. Capt. Savage, in search of a back-door water route,

Marvin Gardner (Mrs. Vivian Gardner)

Cecil H. Rigsby. (Loos)

Norman Churchill. (Loos)

Clark Sykes. (Loos)

Legrand Kneeskern. (Loos)

Kenneth Murphy. (Loos)

Arthur Post. (Loos)

Fred Rennels. (Loos)

Marvin Gardner. (Loos)

followed the Purari River to the headwaters, thence over to the Markham Valley.

S-3's Asst., Lt. Murphy, brought back the nil report today.

Capt. Barnes, in the "RFD Tojo" with his ace crew (Fairbank stayed home), flew to Wewak and disturbed a Nip convoy anchored there. Ack-ack gave them the only excitement of the day. The islands in the Dampier-Vitiaz straits were mapped, but will have to be flown over. The cloud disperser is still not effective. The engineers are reportedly developing one, but...

Sunday, February 14

(Mission to Rabaul was a difficult one, with one or more engines of B-17 no. "27" stopping. No good pictures were taken.—Auths.)

Lts. Loos and Gardner were weathered out of photos, but Lt. Hargesheimer picked a winner and brought home the Daily Mail (Lae). A little mapping also was thrown in just to prove his ability. Of course, the real object of the mission was a radio check. I might add, in passing, it worked.

Wednesday, February 17

I sometimes wonder why we are over here, and today is one of those times. We were so completely socked in that not an engine turned over.

The old Army game of hurry-up-and-wait is still in effect. Our two new officers, Lts. Blackard and Southard, were rushed to the west coast, boarded a plane, and were whisked to Australia. There they rushed aboard another plane and came to New Guinea. Now, amongst a squadron overloaded with "Eager Beaver" pilots, they must sit on their "cuffs" until they have been trained in our type of work. Their special mission turns out to be just the usual replacement. Sorry, boys, but that's the way it is.

Thursday, February 18

Another two officers in the fold today. Lt. Davis will assist Post on the engineering end, and Lt. Garcelon, Statistical Officer, will take over many of the Headquarters' duties. Best of luck, and a hearty welcome to the Squadron.

Friday, February 19

Yesterday, Lt. Post, in his usual thorough manner, placed on the bulletin board an analysis of a mission to Rabaul in a F-4. Today, he departed at 1104K and returned at 1510K. Although Rabaul was socked in and no pictures available, the mission was indeed a success. Weather was difficult and had to be avoided as much as possible, which added many miles to the mission, yet he returned with 120 gallons in the tanks—a healthy margin. The Rabaul hop will now be incorporated as a regular 8th Photo haul.

The islands in the Dampier Straits, now a daily run, were attempted by POG Gardner. He is leaving them for someone else to try tomorrow.

Sunday, February 21

The weather has been nothing but bad, with continual rain for the last four days. Laloki River has reached a new high and is washing out the road just east of the bridge. Orders have been issued to evacuate the Drome at once, and we are moving all flyable ships to 12-Mile. 39th Fighter is going to 17-Mile, and 9th Fighter to 7-Mile. The long-feared flooding is at last upon us.

"Tobacco Road" Loos went up to Karkar and Bagabag Island and then returned to Schwimmer only to find the big evacuation under way. He wasn't about to be left behind, so took off again and slipped over to 12-Mile.

Pilot Harold Moffatt and F-5A Sheila, 14-Mile strip. (Loos)

Pilot Clark Sykes. (Rocker)

Monday, February 22

Those folks back in the States think this is Washington's Birthday, but all of us at Laloki think this should be changed to Slit Trench Day, for today shows an epochal evolution of the human mind.

Many moons ago 8th Photo moved from one side of the river to the other. Even then we were old and hard-bitten New Guineaites. Much time spent in slit trenches and listening to air-raid sirens had bred contempt for the Nipo raids, so, upon reaching the new home, a few hardy souls started digging trenches, but soon laid aside the spade and lamented that the ground was too hard and rocky to bother with. And, anyway, you can go to the top of the hill and the bombs won't have much chance of hitting you.

Now, last night, the Nipponese chose Laloki as the target of opportunity and opened their bomb bays at the ungodly hour of 2 A.M. Ten bombs were dropped in a string from the runway to the 9th Fighter camp, a mere 100 yards from our camp. Came the dawn and there on every side were 8th Photo men diligently throwing rock and clay with reckless abandon. Tonight finds the area a veritable maze of trenches, and now and then an occasional yell rends the air as another luckless chap sprawls into the lower levels of mud and water.

As to the raid itself, for some reason nobody reached the haven of safety at the top of the hill. Hargesheimer and Sowers landed under Fairbank's jeep, and Guerry, always thinking of his better half, went under the jeep feet first and left his head sticking out. I wish I had a picture of the three of them taking a shower by the lister bag at that dismal time. Olson hit the dirt beside his bed with the sheet still wrapped around him. Post, the great mechanical genius, just stayed in bed and kept asking what S.O.B. was driving a freight train past his bed.

The bombs straddled the runway, just missing on each side. Two bombs landed in the gasoline dump, but hit only the piles of empties and threw dirt on the full drums. Just to prove that even a flood had its better points, the planes which might have been damaged were the ones evacuated to 12-Mile. Damage nil; casualties—oil on the cheeks of Guerry.

Operationally speaking, the Shapeless One went to Malahang, the Powerhouse went to the Ramu Valley, and Moffat went to Rabaul. I have stated that casually, as I hope that misssion can be as successful in the future as the Lae-Salamaua milk run, but it was today a very outstanding event. Harold brought us the first pictures of Rabaul ever taken by any member of our present organization. For months we have fought against sending (P-38s) because of the length and navigational difficulties, but the high moguls have ordered us out, and it seems that our pilots will solve it with their usual efficiency. The pictures are excellent K-18 shots of the harbor and township.

Tuesday, February 23

(SSgt Rigsby encountered antiaircraft fire) on second and third runs over Wewak, becoming quite heavy and accurate on third run. Upon completion of the third run over the target he noted six Zekes coming up, so he proceeded to get out of there by diving to 15,000' and setting his throttles ahead. After having flown at 250 MPH for

Vince Murphy in the cockpit of a F-4 (P-38) photo plane. (Murphy)

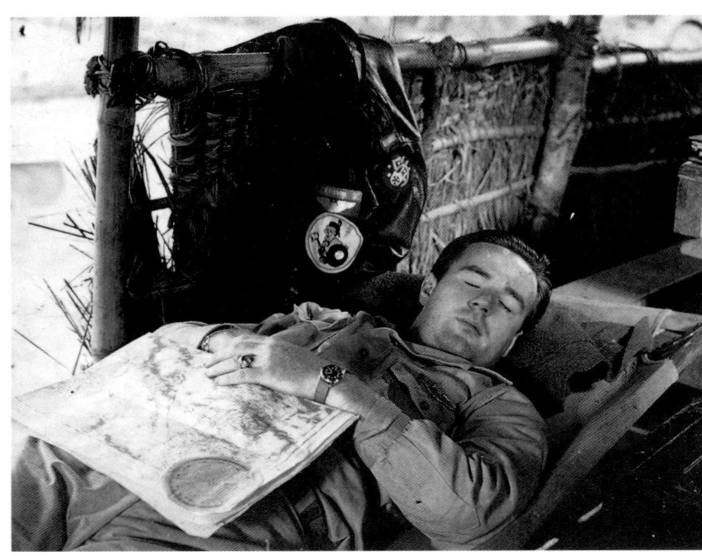

"Sleeping Beauty" Vince Murphy. (Murphy)

John G. Foster. (Rocker)

about 10 minutes (during which time he sent a message back to base), he heard a click, click, and upon spinning his head rearwards found a Zeke spitting lead at his tail. With simultaneous motions he shoved the throttles and stick full forward. That "Lightning" is ok at 47" and 3,000 RPM. When he pulled out at slightly above ground level there weren't any Zekes in his immediate neighborhood. To be on the safe side he hedge-hopped through the Valley several minutes before climbing to get back over the Hump and to "Home Sweet Home." Upon landing and examining the plane, "Dotin' Donna" was found to have one drop tank missing, a rip in the flap, bullet holes in both props, a bullet hole in the wing, and a crease in the fairing beside the supercharger where another slug had ricocheted off. A check on the fuel supply tells us he had about twenty gallons of petrol left. Rigsby's pictures are excellent. Bomber Command admitted it, so it must be so.

"Oxy" Nulty pulled a fade while making an altitude test and photo mission of Lae area in "RFD Tokio." Capt. Barnes dove from 26,000 ft. to 11,000 ft. to revive Photo Joe. He brought him back ok, but the poor fellow is so weak he couldn't beat his way out of a powder room. By the way, the pictures were satisfactory, "Wild Bill" Fairbank being Director of Photography.

Rennels, of Texas, flew around Mubo area taking pictures of the tracks for Fifth AF. He came through with a wonderful set of pictures, too. Good man, this Texan.

Lt. Blackard on a training mission to Milne Bay in "Lackagas 37" was forced down at the emergency strip at Hood Point due to rough weather and short fuel supply. After sweating him out, Capt. Savage went in search and found him there and ok.

What a day this has been—always something new, something different, anything for a thrill.

Thursday, February 25

Another day of labor for the fellows unfortunate enough to get caught on the ground or in the camp area. All day the phone operations rang, "Send so and so to the Officers' Club, we need a few more men." Gravel is heavy, and shovel handles breed blisters. All this is going to warrant something in the line of a "big one" some Saturday Eve. In the line of business—Moffat actually got some mapping in the Ramu Valley. "27" went out, but No. 1 engine trouble forced a return with no photos. Loos took Wewak and brought back a sighting report of AKs and destroyers. He also sighted two Zekes, but saw them soon enough to keep his distance. He, too, pushed throttles and stick forward and found the F-4 quite a lively ship. Ack Ack was encountered at Madang.

Saturday, February 27

Lt. Morton headed for Wewak but returned due to engine trouble. Lt. Gardner then tried the same ship on the same mission.

Vince Murphy flew 85 photo missions and was awarded the Distinguished Flying Cross with Oak Leaf cluster and the Air Medal. (Rocker)

Cameraman and gunner Frank Reindl. (Rocker)

Woodrow Cobb. (Rocker)

8th PRS sign. (Bugai via Rocker)

After spending much time skirting around, over and under clouds, he decided it was no use and came home.

"Drag" Kneeskern went to Ramu Valley. After buzzing the clouds and blowing them out of the way, he obtained two flight lines. Good job, too, says here.

The "High Altitude Boys" took off in their "Boeing Baby" today. They climb to an altitude of over six miles, then bitch because they get no interception. Mapping was completed, nevertheless.

Sunday, February 28

Lt. Post turned in a masterful job today. One pass was made over Wewak at 27,000 feet. Clouds then obscured the area, so down he came to 16,000, where he made his second pass despite heavy Ack Ack.

Last night was the official opening of the Officers' Club. The results of our past weeks' labors has at last borne fruit. "Ore" was bartender, and handed out the Juice with gusto and bravo.

Capt. Savage handed "Junior" Sowers his Captaincy and POG, and Morton each were complimented upon their new white bars.

Monday, March 1

Lt. Loos combed the jungle in the Baroi River area in search of and photographed the Romilly sawmill for the ever-curious Fifth AF. "Tobacco Road" is a very happy lad now that Texan Sykes, "The Sydney Kid," brought back a goodly supply of "El Ropo's."

C. W. Fred Hargesheimer made an extensive tour of New Guinea, photographing Wewak, Bena Bena (later identified as Kianantu), and Lae at 8,000 feet, and Salamaua at 7,000'. To really top it all he shot some pictures of Yule Island with one motor feathered. There is no vibration in the pictures, so it has been recommended that a one-engine F-4 be developed—another new problem for modification pit. With the ever-increasing complexity of the job there may be some specialist who will make Sergeant yet.

General Kennedy's B-17 on the 7-Mile strip. (Rocker)

Tuesday, March 2

This is March 2nd, and the busiest March 2nd 8th Photo has ever seen. Capt. Savage led out and returned home with a bad weather report from the Markham area. This is some kind of a record, as he is the only one of today's expeditions to return to base. What a wandering crowd this is. Prodigal, no less.

"Powerhouse" Murphy, originality-plus, landed on the beach at Hisiu, wheels down. It was an outstanding feat of aviation, and one which cannot be commended too highly. He not only risked soft sand with bad weather, but had to wedge his landing gear between driftwood on the beach. After landing safely he taxied above the high-tide line, then radioed we sweater-outers as to his location.

"Shapeless" Murphy took a quickie to Lae in search of and to verify the sighting of a ship in that area—the Malahang Wreck, no less. Inclement weather prevented his return to this side, so he dropped in on the Dobodura strip. We sweater-outers were very much relieved when the message finally came informing us of his whereabouts.

The "H. A. Boys" landed at 7-Mile with their previous load of mapping photos of Bougainville, plus K-18 shots of various points of importance. Beautiful stuff, but taken from six miles closer to Heaven than they will ever get, anyway.

Our activities were minor, however, comparatively, as all combat aircraft in the area were socked at a Jap convoy in the Bismarok Sea, and the results were good.

Wednesday, March 3

Air activity went to the limit today, and the Japs took a whipping that makes history, and we make the news. The entire convoy of 20 ships headed for Lae was destroyed by our fliers. Many were transports, heavily loaded with Nips. The sharks had a field day, and the sea ran red. A salvage team consisting of Capt. Savage, Lt. Post, TSgt Meach, and Cpl King braved the briny deep in a crash boat to inspect "Powerhouse" Murphy's stranded F4. They made a safe but miserable trip. Some almost died, and others wished they could.

Allen Blum doin the wash outside his tent at Port Moresby. (Rocker)

Thursday, March 4

The last of the prodigals returned this morning. Capt. Savage jumped "Leaping Lizzy" off the beach and brought her home. Lt. Moffat got in a few good licks in the absence of "T. H." Post. Two test hops more than Post's record. Good break. "Sewanne" Guerry shot 7-Mile landings with the able assistance of everybody else who wanted to fly.

Friday, March 5

The "Fearless Fortress F. U." headed for New Ireland today and got within shouting distance, when they turned back. Something about an engine going out (The Old Bromide).

Looks like "Another Hour Post" has found some compatriots. They are really blasting away at the medal racks.

Our long-lost lad, "Powerhouse" Murphy showed up today looking very healthy and red at the face. He was dragging Post behind him, that being the way to get Post away from the natives and per diem at Hisiu.

Top Row, standing L to R: T/Sgt Emil Thieus, Capt Jay Zeamer, Lt. Hank Dyminski, Lt. Joseph Sarnaski. Kneeling L to R: T/Sgt Willie Vaughan, S/Sgt George Kendrick, Sgt Johnnie Able, Sgt. Herb Pugh. (Rocker)

Lt. Holton and Lt. Clark, tent members of Allen Blum, outside their tent in Port Moresby. (Rocker)

8PRS F-5A #02, Nadzab, New Guinea. (Rocker)

Alex Guerry, Bill Fairbank, and Ben Armstrong. (Rocker)

Many interesting tales of native life and the usual revelation of the white man being out-traded by the ignorant black. Later in the day Murphy's healthy redness turned to unsightly scales, and he began losing his face here and there. Nothing serious, of course, in Murphy's case.

Saturday, March 6

Now I ask you, is this any way to fight a war? For the last two days we have been sending out airplanes looking for sawmills.

Sawmills are all right in their own way; in fact, we have been known to bribe sawmill foremen from time to time, but when our granchildren ask, "What did you do in the war," it is going to be embarrassing to fling out the chest and say, "Oh! Looked for sawmills." Moffat, however, with an "orders is orders" complex, ferreted out a small mill around Romilly and photographed the same. Maybe we can get back to the war again.

Lest we forget, the light touch of the fairer sex has al tong last caressed the portals of the Officers' Club. Guerry, twisting the morals as usual, propounds the theory, "Lips that touch liquor will often touch mine." So the new singer for the band found herself consuming large quantities of the stuff under the heavy encouragement of Fairbank and Guerry, the cads. Is it Guerry paying Fairbank, or

William Morton. (Sykes)

Fred Rennels. (Sykes)

Robert Ludtke. (Sykes)

is it Fairbank on his own? Whatever it is, there was Fairbank on his hands and knees (stop those unkind thoughts) learning to Hula. What price, Guerry? Sad to relate Fairbank does not hula, and Guerry still has a drawn look on his face. Keep the flag a-flying.

Sunday, March 7

"El Capitan" Savage gave the renovated and soon-to-be christened "Photo Joe" its first chance to preen itself in front of all the admiring females of his harem. "Dotin' Donna" and "Poutin' Peggy" sighed once and have since refused to budge. Donna, demanding her regular physical check-up under the ever watchful eye of "Nick" of Yonkers (not Texas, as a name like that might suggest, but New York) in Kennedy's Klassy Klub. The jungle technicians brought forth a new motor for "Poutin' Peggy." "Photo Joe" then went on to Rabaul in 3 hr. and 45 min., just to further establish himself as cock-of-the-walk. Some very "nice" pictures of the harbor resulted.

Morton, after all these months of questionable identity, emerged from behind the brush and was forthwith sent to represent us in the Markham Valley. He successfully purchased a series of K-18 prints of the river Markham and the drome Malahang from the Nips and returned to the home office.

Monday, March 8

Churchill, having finished Anne Morrow Lindberg's "North to the Orient," set out in his little blue "Photo Joe," armed with film and "K" rations, to outdo the famous pair. Needless to say, he was refused gas at Wewak, so the expedition turned back discouraged, but not a total loss. The film has recorded for posterity the scientific data so assiduously collected, and, though not Orient, there is something oriental about the whole thing.

Sykes in his own words has this recorded in his mission to Dobodura: "Took off, proceeded to target, took pictures and returned to base." Enough said? I don't think so. How about a little more details, boys?

POG took off, had engine trouble, landed at 30-Mile on account weather and then returned to Schwimmer. Markham Valley still remains to be photographed.

Tuesday, March 9

Bom Com's Lehe, like a landlubber telling a seadog about squalls, misinformed 8th Photo Squadron how K-18 photos should look and what ours are. We only can hope that he has seen Ludke's pictures of Lae today. The flight line may not be the best, but the cameras know their business and well. In the future, please send self-appointed experts to Intelligence, and we will straighten them out on a thing or two.

Cominch Fotoron Eight had a meeting this morning, and the new regime is on. Lts. Olson and Murphy, damn fools, encouraged and abetted the new training program of which you are now being forewarned. We hope you will find it interesting, but interesting or not, you will be there, as the C.O. has given his full approval. Come on and get those gold stars after your name, and drink deeply at the Fountain of Knowledge. Processing will begin in a few days. Prepare yourselves. Capt. Thomas, who desires that henceforth all shall

Weymouth Vestal. (Sykes)

Cecil Rigsby. (Sykes)

LeGrand Kneeskern. (Sykes)

Dewey Aucoin and Kay Klages, Homer Taylor, Woodrow Cobb, and William Southard.

refrain from referring to him as a ground officer (a word to the wise is sufficient), fell into the evil clutches of the Embarcadero St. Wharf Rat and consented to carry him on a mission. Thus, having accomplished the first act in the spider and the fly, Fairbank armed himself with a K-20 camera and they set out today for Milne Bay. Thomas, although hampered by one Fifth Column, was successful in securing photos of the Duboyne Islands and returned to Milne Bay. Fairbank, having photographed all our vital airdrome defenses in that area, is now hounding everybody for rides to our other ramparts of defense. I ask you, in the interest of the war effort, to aid me in burying him under his precious maps where he so rightly belongs.

Lt. Post, having gotten away from the drudgery of test hopping for a day, was at last given a combat mission. He proceeded to Wau, Malahang, and Lae, took pictures, and returned home in his usual workmanlike manner. Orchids for a change, Post.

"Powerhouse" to the Markham, a strip flown and returned.

Thursday, March 11

Rennels to Rabaul was the morning cry, but this yielded nil photos account of weather so we're backing "Honest John" (that's Kneeskern, if you are having trouble) for tomorrow's trip.

Major Woodward, Capt. Dunstan, and Capt. Board procured seven of the Australian Sisters, and 8th Photo provided innumerable escorts, to initiate the Officers' Club into the formal party spirit. Champagne flowed freely, and the singing became more riotous as the evening progressed, but everything remained under control throughout. Fairbank, piqued because his date was taken over by brother Hamlin, did the gentlemanly thing and annointed the two with champagne from time to time during the evening. Foster claims an assist.

Saturday, March 13

Lt. Gardner brought back operational photos of Lae and Salamaua, and Sykes on return from a nil photo-mapping job, slipped in beneath POG to expose the leader of his film. Fortunate that we had the Gardner photos, as Sykes' camera didn't function. Turned on...?

Monday, March 15

Rigsby did a bit of K-18'ing for the AAF. Good stuff, but we don't like it—everyone expects us to map the island with a K-18 now.

Today we have a "new low" in recco as Moffat drops to 50 ft. to have a look-see. He left the area upon the arrival of two Zekes. The shipping was an eyeful—"biggest cargo ship I've ever seen," says "L.A." Moffat.

Tuesday, March 16

Capt. Savage put out a bit of mapping. At least he took photos for Fairbank. They turned out to be a half-acre island in the Solomon Sea.

Lt. Morton took off this morning for the Ramu Valley. Our last word was the terse message, "Over Range." We have heard no further. Other aircraft reported bad weather thoughout the entire Owen

Refueling at Marilinan in September 1943. 8PRS F-4 serial 41-2130.

F-4 making passes at B-17. (Sykes)

Stanley area. We shall search all areas tomorrow and are manning the radio all night. All that can be done will be done. This is a tough country, and we expect losses, but we must increase our caution.

Lt. J. J. Murphy flew to Dobodura—another C. M.

Wednesday, March 17

This is a 'elluvah thing—Legrande (Drag) Kneeskern didn't get pictures when he went out to Markham.

Search missions were carried out, but nil sightings made of Lt. Morton's ship. We'll continue to look, but it's a big island and a small airplane.

POG carried out a 13-minute flight toward Milne Bay area.

Thursday, March 18

"Angus McDonald" Rennels got himself the cheapest drunk of the year today. While he was cavorting about at 28,000 ft. his oxygen mask came apart. The last thing he remembers clearly was turning on the cameras for his run across Wewak Drome. He next found himself at 17,000 ft. and some 20 miles south of Wewak. Evidently, his instincts are all right, for the cameras were turned off and the plane (was) well under control. The flight strip was not the best, but better than you would expect from an inebriated pilot.

Foster, coming in for his share of glory, slipped in and out of Rabaul and brought us the best pictures yet secured. The Japs must not have been expecting us, for they forgot to hang "Old Faithful" over Vunakanau. Foster noted large fires east of Rapopo runway, a gentle reminder of last night's raid.

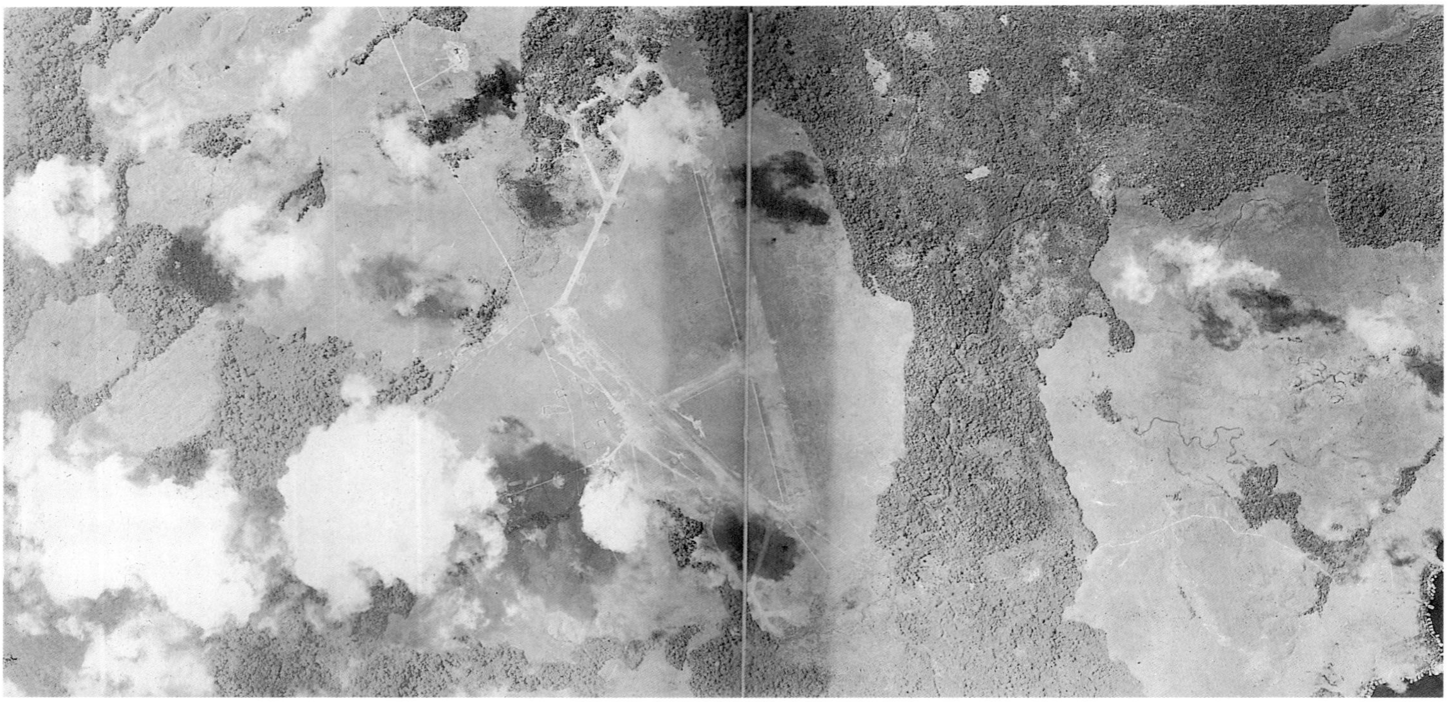

One of the photos taken on the first reconnaissance to Hollandia flown by Allen Blum on September 6, 1943. Somehow Blum got the prize mission and found perfectly clear weather at the target, earning a promotion for getting fine coverage of the area.

Col. Berkowitz and Col. Dunbar have arrived from the south for their first look at New Guinea. A good survey of the area and they will return to their respective posts. We are indeed glad to have their responsive ears to pour our troubles into.

Friday, March 19

Powerhouse at Wau, Sykes to Woodlark, and Ludke to the Markham, with bad weather and nil sightings the only reseults.

Major Prenti(ce), CO of the 39th Fighter Squadron, gave us an excellent insight into the pursuit side of the Far East War. Since having been equipped with P-38s, the Squadron has accounted for 90 confirmed enemy aircraft against four of their own. It makes our trouble seem less important to hear those of other units.

D. G. Board, Capt. A.I.L.A., propounded on the phone at the laxity of each operator along the line—calling, "Hello. Hello. Who is this? Capt.Board here—that you, Jeff—you thea'h. Oh, bugger it. Hello, hello, you thea'h? Oh, what is the matter with this phone? Don't cut me off—I'm trying to get N. G. F. G-3. Hello, Checker, did you get Domino? Well, give 'em another ring. I'm going to get to the bottom of this—I'll have it out with that bloke yet, by hell. Oh, Jeff, guess we were cut off momentarily. Well, I'll give you the guts of it in a hurry this time. No, there were no sightings. He didn't get any photos. You there? Yes, yes, I'll give you a ring later with that other." And so goes the war.

Saturday, March 20

"Honest John" Kneeskern's Communication Section and Lt. J. G. Foster's code are somewhat at odds with each other. First we pick up a message from Foster saying, "Landed Salamaua. Out of gas!" This was received with considerable question by all concerned. Frantically the communication boys called the expert on voice and CW, and the only answer—"Your code stinks." Honest John refers HPJG to proverb of Fox and Holes. Need I add that Foster did not land at (the enemy base) Salamaua...

Moffat, after our long week of arduous effort, secured a long strip on the Ramu, but the right oblique failed again...

Pilot Robert Blackard who was lost on May 21, 1943. (Moffat)

Sunday, March 21

Tonight three new officers were inducted into 8th Photo and into the Officers Club (small matter of five pounds still outstanding). Better yet, they are not strangers to our ways and means and hence need no introduction to you at all. I hereby welcome to the diary FLIGHT OFFICERS Rigsby, Ludtke, and Churchill. Three new suckers for the (Officer of the Day) list and for the bartenders. Grab a towel and make yourself at home, boys.

Ray Starr brought with him the first issue of the 648th Engineers new publication, "Listen." Lt. Fairbank's name was conspicuous by its absence. They have once again proven themselves gentlemen. If you can't say anything good about a man, don't say anything. Thank God I'm no gentleman.

Lt. Post sallied forth at dawn to spy on the yellow ones crossing the Markham. Unfortunately, a front laying atop the ranges prevented his reaching the target. Just another hour.

POG went out for the Markham and Ramu, and Kneeskern for the Trobriands, but both were unable to reach their objectives.

Monday, March 22

Col. Perkowitz returned from his exploration of Dobodura, Buna, and Oro Bay this morning. Nothing like the great outdoors to put the glow in the cheeks and the spring in the step. We may lack a few of the Melbourne advantages, but, gentlemen, have you noticed the moon here lately? Not entirely wasted, for you can still dream.

Flight Officer Ludtke, fulfilling his still damp orders, took off for the first of his regular and frequent aerial flights with his brand-new blue and gold bar aboard. I don't know whether it was the promotion or the weather, but he grabbed off three of those D'Entrecasteaux strips that we have been seeking so long.

"Powerhouse," chattering enroute, reached New Britain and photoed two nice strips. First mission in many a moon on which we have expended all the film. This evening Murphy followed up with

F-4 #77, "Dotin' Donna," the aircraft in which Blackard was lost between Wau and Nassau Bay. His body was found a year later on September 18, 1944. The men are Harold Moffat and an RAAF airman. (Moffat)

Pilot William Southard.

an acrobatic performance in bed. Even had the thing flying backwards. Stay away from that horse's head. POG to the Ramu, Sykes to the Markham. One short strip by Lae resulted. Not a bad day, all considered.

Tuesday, March 23

Lts. Southard and Blackard returned from Melbourne last night bringing gifts and information. Information that Guerry had checked out as first pilot, and gifts consisting of cigars for the boys and a monopoly game for our entertainment. This evening, Cobb, our reserved Administrative Officer, proved himself to be a master of finance and bartender deluxe. He bought and sold, dickered and traded, until Lts. Southard, Blackard, and Garcelon retired bankrupt and disgraced. A new tycoon in the field of monopoly (is created).

The day was disappointing, to say the least. Foster detoured on account (of the) weather from New Britain to Lae and Salamaua. Churchill headed for Rabaul, flew 37,000' on instruments in an attempt to climb over the front, and finally had to turn back. Rennels got nothing on the Ramu, and Moffat picked up two strips on Normandy.

FREE BEER TOMORROW!

Wednesday, March 24

...K. J. Murphy brought back some pictures of Ramu Valley, but modestly proclaims them to be no good.

FREE BEER TOMORROW!

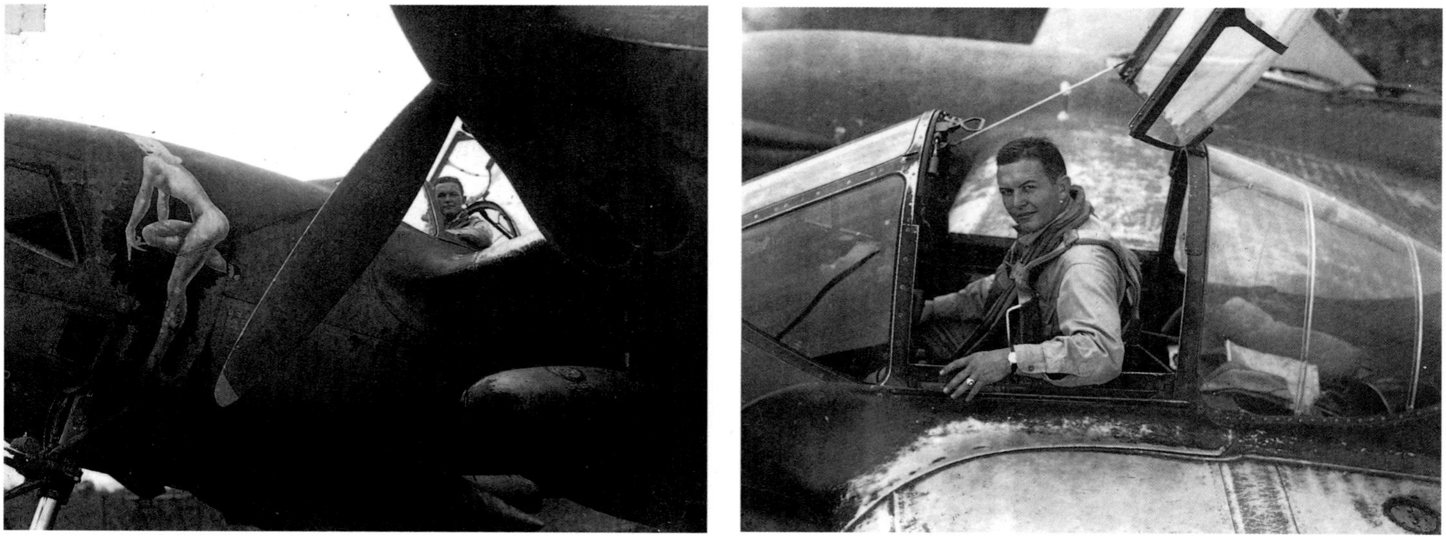

6th Photo Recon Group commander Ben Armstrong in F-5 cockpit.

Thursday, March 25

"Reaction Time" Ludtke proceeded to New Britain today to photograph his namesake, Cape Lutke, and a few other spots. It seems the Cape wasn't having same, for after 1 1/2 hours of diligent effort and an elated sense of a job well done, he returned to his home base only to find that the right oblique failed, proving that the Gremlins still hold sway...

...Sykes went to Rabaul today and found it much disinterested in his presence. Nil Ack Ack or interception, so to make the trip worthwhile, he brought us a beautiful strip from Cape Dampier to Rabaul. Rigsby to Sunshine Creek and Churchill to Bena Bena. The first took pictures from Sunshine to Markham, and the second of the dromes along the Markham.

FREE BEER TOMORROW!

Sunday, March 28

This squadron is flying too damn much. Time was when your author could concentrate on one or two missions and really give it a write up, but now just writing the by-lines is a day's work in itself.

Today we have Kneeskern to New Britain with the usual tale of weather.

POG started for Wewak, but had hydraulic trouble and returned. Churchill went off upon his return and successfully filmed the harbor and drome.

Sykes got a nice strip from Hanisch Harbor to Kohka and one not so nice from Bena Bena to Lae. Nothing wrong except weather, but that remains our biggest obstacle.

FREE BEER TOMORROW!

Monday, March 29

"Powerhouse" started out today on a mission, but ended up practicing take-off and landing. Twice he took off and twice the props ran away, so we put him back at the Intelligence desk and threw the airplane at the Engineering Section

Loos to New Britain and three strips resulted.

Moffat nil photos Zenag; Ludtke nil photos Cape Nelson.

FREE BEER TOMORROW!

Thursday, April 1

April Fools Day 'tis called, and nobody realized it better than 8th Photo. First and most important, fools, being in this God-forsaken jungle; second, for having a party last night and trying to work with hangovers this morning; and last but not least, fools for

Popular comic Joe E. Brown in the Port Moresby area late in 1943. (Al Regis)

Boram Strip under attack by the 345th Bomb Group on October 16, 1943.

being happy in the face of all the above. The Squadron has proved it can take it all with the best of them, which it is.

Clark "Butter Ball" Sykes went to Wewak today and returned with the illuminating report, "You know those bastards are trying to kill us!" Sometimes war seems to mean more here than just corn-willy and gas rationing. But to return to our hero Sykes, he reached Wewak and took one strip across the dromes. All quiet and serene, and it was a grand day to see the country, and so on up to But. After that excursion he returned to Wewak to get some more of those little pictures. Like the murderer returning to the scene, Sykes poked his nose around the corner and those boys were really waiting for him. About ten burst in front of the plane, and a brief look to the rear informed Sykes that this was no place for him. The plane being blown about must have been a deciding factor, too, for Sykes chandelled away as fast as his big and little (29-51) engines would take him. Reaching Moresby, and very happy about it, too, he found Schwimmer socked in and his hydraulic system out, but these were merely minor difficulties today, so he pumped his wheels down and landed at Ward's Drome.

Churchill went to Rabaul this morning but the place was completely covered, so he returned and made the long trek home. Three Zeros below him either didn't see him, or more than likely didn't want to see him, and continued serenely on their patrol.

Saturday, April 3

...Rennels headed out for Rabaul this morning but ran into a front south of New Britain and returned more desperate than ever.

Wewak has risen considerably in 8th Photo's estimation and will hereafter be given as wide a berth as possible. Following up Syke's experience of the other day, Drag Kneeskern played tow target for the Nip Ack Ack. Still nine down, and we hope none to go. Let's get back into the stratosphere and stay there.

Blackard hit the usual in the Zenag area and returned without!

FREE BEER TOMORROW!

Sunday, April 4

This happened to be a very eventful day in the 8-Ball Squadron. My brother-in-law, Fred Rennels, took over as Temporary Operations Officer under the new program and sent six C. M., which isn't bad for his first day. "Easy" Ludtke went to Rabaul, but I double-crossed him on the weather report, so he returned with no photos. Love-starved Moffat gave a very nice weather report from Woodlark. (I hoid the boidies sing.) POG went to Tufi and brought back three fine tri-met strips, the first today. "Paddy" Sykes flew a strip from Lake Wanum to Finschhafen. Good boy, Sykes! Olson and Kneeskern, as usual, took their day off for laundry, and Olson lost one pound to "Barney Stark, the cowboy from California." Back to the line, "High Altitude" Churchill finally photographed the coveted Zenag area. We have only been trying to fly that mosaic for two weeks now. Lt. Blackard started off the new training program with a trip to Kokada and Yodda, Wau, Bulolo, and Kerema, and on to Port Moresby. Incidentally, he was sent out at 1430 and we couldn't even see Mt. Victoria from Schwimmer. So he took pictures of Kerema. "Zoos Hat" Daniel finally straightened the pilots' roster out. It was about time, "Zooty." All in all, it was a pretty fair day for old 8-Ball.

FREE BEER TOMORROW!

Tuesday, April 6

Our team is red hot. Rennels to Rabaul and, at long last, success. Desperate Dan admits the pictures won't be any good, but they'll prove he got to Rabaul, so all is well.

Lt. K. J. Murphy went to Woodlark and, of course, got pictures. Not a long-prescribed flight line, but pictures nonetheless. Good on ye, Kenny.

Foster went to Wewak and pictures were taken. That is, as far as Foster is concerned, just pictures. He reached the target, turned on the cameras and returned home. The camera pin sheared, so no pictures resulted, but Foster remains happy.

Kneeskern photoed the Finschhafen area. He doesn't know where he flew them or how long the flight lines were. Still and all, the day was a success for 8th Photo and a failure for Bom Com.

FREE BEER TOMORROW!

8th PRS #381 on its nose. (Bugai)

Low-level mission against Rabaul on November 2, 1943. (Reindl/ Kimbrough)

Wednesday, April 7

"Powerhouse" Murphy has from time to time commented that he is through buzzing the field because everybody watches your landings. Until today I thought it was just youthful selfconsciousness, but there is considerable method in his madness. This morning he lost all three of flying's essentials at the same time: Air Speed, Altitude, and Knowledge. The result—nothing but a rough landing—and I do mean rough!...

No Beer Tomorrow! Tomorrow Never Comes!—the B-17 has returned....

All missions today were a failure. Weather.

Friday, April 9

It really happened, finally. The long-prophesied interception at Rabaul actually happened this morning. Churchill was cruising near Open Bay this morning when the dust specks on the windown began to move. Being the non-believer type, Churchill closed his eyes and then peeked through his fingers. This time there was more than a speck, and he quickly decided he must be on the wrong side of the road, so he pulled into a cloud ditch in one big hurry. On back to Gasmata went Churchill with the funeral procession behind. They got discouraged pretty quickly, however, when they saw him disappearing, and turned back to Rabaul. Churchill came back to Dobodura, gassed up, and set forth again, but this time the weather had built so that he could no longer get through.

Sunday, April 11

Moffat took his usual run to Wewak, but low overcast prevented photos on this trip. Blackard to the Markham, nil photos. "Powerhouse" took four strips on Woodlark. "De Lousy" took a nice mapping strip on New Britain.

Today is a very eventful day for 8th Photo. "666" with Josh Barnes at the wheel, assisted by Capt. Thomas, Sup, and S. F. C. Guerry took off for New Ireland. After photographing Kavieng dromes, they were intercepted at 13,000' by ten Zekes. The Zekes made three passes before the lower turret went out of operation. Immediately Josh took the ship to 200' where 16 more passes were made from several postitions on the clock. Expended shell after shell into the Zekes as they made their passes. Two were seen to crash into the water, and another went off in flames. Three were hit by tracers from our guns. The attacks lasted twenty minutes. None of the crew were injured, and the plane was damaged only slightly, other than having the hydraulic system shot out. Capt. Olson, Lt. Guerry, and the rest of the crew "entertained" themselves at the various gun stations, while "Sup" was copiloting. Everyone agreed that it was a beautiful sight to see Zekes peel off and head straight into the water. The plane went completely out of sight immediately. The crew will be recommended for the D.F.C., and they well deserve it. Incidentally, these boys have the distinction of claiming the first Nip aircraft for 8th Photo. A word of praise should be given to Private La Rosh for his excellent marksmanship. He has been given official credit for the destruction of these two Zekes. Our hats off to the crew and may they have continued success.

Unloading fat cat supplies. (Martha Cobb)

Monday, April 12

"Hargey," eager as a beaver, ready as a Teddy, and wanting to get pictures of Rabaul so he can be recommended, took off and returned with a nice mapping strip of New Britain and Rabaul and vicinity. "Gremlin" Rennels went to Wewak, but returned due to interception by two enemy aircraft. That Wewak trip certainly has become hot. "Photo Joe" Kneeskern brought back some mapping strips along the coast in the vicinity of Saidor. We haven't finished Woodlark yet, so Rummy Foster picked up a few more strips there. Every little bit helps on this mammoth job.

"Hell hath no fury like a woman scorned," quoth the bard, but personally I'll take the scorned woman in preference to the hell we had today. 45 bombers and 60 fighters was our quota for the day. They approached from the northwest, and God knows where our fighters were. They droned overhead, and we hit the dirt. Everything let loose. 30 to 40 bombs hit between us and the B25s, with the latter catching most of the damage. Two B-25s were hit by daisy cutters and went up in flames. Another was riddled by schrapnel but did not burn. Two of our own aircraft were hit, but not very seriously. Never again will 8th Photo laugh at the air raids. Sgt Kaplan, unaware of the danger from the skies, was driving a truck near the 13th Bomb when the eggs started to drop. A piece of schrapnel caught him in the shoulder and cut through his arm. Our own "Doc" Stark says he'll be o.k. shortly. We all wish him godspeed on the recovery trail. The hospital awarded Sgt. Kaplan the Purple Heart.

Tuesday, April 13

If it is O.K. with everybody, I will merely mention the passing of the day, for after yesterday and the day before, anything said would be anti-climatic. There was an alert, however, but the Nips failed to do more than get on our nerves.

The Squadron was absorbed with the digging of slit trenches and the usual pursuit of photographs. The first a success, and the latter a dismal failure, with the exception of Southard's strips over Woodlark.

Wednesday, April 14

The day started out quietly, as all days start, but ten o'clock found us in our usual sweat. First the phone call telling us to disperse our planes as the Nips were enroute. After an hour of waiting we relaxed and radioed the ships an all clear. The siren started again. That kept us away from our dinner, but proved to be a false alarm. So-o-o we trooped down to the mess hall and proceeded to shovel in the unpalatable chow. Yep, you are right—it started wailing again, so back to the slit trenches and hill tops, and this time to watch some 150 fighters take the air, or as one J. G. Foster puts it, three D.F.C.s worth of fighters with an Air Medal thrown in. Fortunately, the raid went to Milne Bay, and we were spared for another day.

Murphy, the squat one, found cloudless skies and zephyr breezes over Woodlark, and was so surprised he couldn't figure out where to start, but finally deciphered his mind and rolled out strip after strip. Now we only have to tie the whole thing together and the whole job is complete.

Loos and Moffat went to Wewak and Hansa Bay today but didn't see their targets because of clouds. Both returned during the alert, but cold, tired and disppointed, they said, "To Hell with the Nips," and landed.

Friday, April 16

Churchill finally got to Rabaul and got pictures. Hargey went to Wewak and got three strips of the dromes and harbor. He also found fifteen ships on the drome. Johnny Kneeskern, getting eager for leave, returned early with nil photos due to weather. Southard to the Markham brought us a mapping strip. F/O Ludtke, and this time I don't mean Flight Officer, went to Zenag and flew a nice strip, but spotted two U/I aircraft. Damn those windows! I know I should've cleaned them before I left. Loos flew his training mission today, shooting eleven strips of the local drome.

Saturday, April 17

We had a close one today. Blackard went to Woodlark and did a beautiful job in securing thirteen offshore strips. En route home he was above an overcast, and his ETA New Guinea failed to materialize. Continued flying, produced no better results so, not knowing which direction his compass had erred, he called for the beam. When that failed to reach him he could only guess, but he did not guess indiscriminately. He noted a lengthy cloud formation to his right, and reasoning correctly, decided it was a range formation. Sure enough, he reached New Guinea around Cloudy Bay and came on in. Six hours in the air and only five minutes of gas left. This has been set forth for the guidance of others who might find themselves in a similar situation.

Sunday, April 18

Today 8th Photo's heroes (?) were presented their awards by Lt. General Kenney. Olson received the Silver Star, Foster the Purple Heart, "Doc" Stark and Sgt Fishman the Soldier's Medal. General Kenney told Olson that 8th Photo is doing a bang-up job, and he regretted that witnesses to deed were necessary, as he knew that many 8th Photo men deserved medals for their work in this theater. He reiterated that our work is not going unobserved. Now you and I realize that words do not fill the pockets or cover the breast, but those of Kenney's do show that we are not as reviled as we sometimes feel we are. Later, speaking to the whole formation, the General assured us that the area would be greatly supplemented with aircraft by the coming fall.

Monday, April 19

Lt. Southard had the milk run to Rabaul and spotted ten Zekes over the target at 10,000 ft. He got his pictures of the harbor and dromes. "Rummy" went to Wewak and reported one 8,000 ton AK and six 24,000 ton AKs in the harbor. He photographed his target, doing a nice job (in the process).

Sykes had engine trouble and returned. Rigsby went back to Woodlark to fly some tie-in strips. Let's hope we are finished with that island after this mission. F/O Ludtke went to the Markham and returned with photos of Hansa Bay area.

Tuesday, April 20

K. J. Murphy, heading for Trobriands found bad weather, but rather that come back empty-handed he photographed the two dromes on Goodenough Island. Lt. Loos took fine pictures of Nubia-Bogia, but he couldn't find Bena Bena on the way back. POG Gardner and V. E. Murphy returned with nil photo reports.

We have been overlooking a little matter, the GOOD Lt. Olson was made Captain a few days ago. Lts. Loos and Kneeskern made 1st on the 17th, so it is just one round after another.

Wednesday, April 21

"Say, Fellas, I got another letter from Linda Darnell, here it is, and please note she has given me her home address, and look what she tells me about when I get home." Hargesheimer then places the blue letter in the blue envelope and tucks it neatly next to his heart.

Flash! We quote from the A-2 Bomb Bay Review: "Linda Darnell and Sgt. So & Such eloped to Yuma, Arizona, it was revealed today. She is 20 and he is 42." Hargesheimer is now looking for another Hollywood correspondent. Thanks for the memory, Linda Darnell and Barbara Britton. Step up, gals, who's next.

Moffat to Wewak, this time somewhat above his previous 50 foot performance—27,200 ft. to be exact. Blackard was unable to reach Rabaul on account of weather. Rennels picked up a few on New Britain.

Foster finished up woodlark and headed for Trobriands, flew two overwater strips from Ferguson to Trobriands, then went to Woodlark. That finished up Woodlark, and we sincerely hope for all time.

Thursday, April 22

This morning our O.O.O.T.W. (Operations Officer of the Week) Lt. Hargesheimer, up with the dawn and turning the heat on the day's activities. Your correspondent carried along by Hargey's wake was also up and about (about dead, they claim). It bore fruit, however, for Lt. Post was off by 6 o'clock and found cloudless skies and secured pictures of Rabaul Harbor and two long mapping strips on Gazelle Peninsula. Hargesheimer himself was off by 0630, likewise knocking off one run at Nubia and another from Ramu to Saidor.

"Twenty percent go home and no more MacKay," are the best rumors of the moment. Either one would be a godsend, and the first answer to many a maiden's prayer. Perhaps I should add we hope they are still maidens and still praying.

F/O Churchill set course for New Britain and returned with a couple of mapping strips of the island. Sykes went to Wewak, but no pictures. Sykes claims the last trip there gave him that "Old Time Religion," and he didn't feel reckless enough to go in at 10,000 feet under the overcast. Hallelujah, we is in perfect agreement.

Once again New Guinea refuses to say the dry season is upon us. It started this afternoon and looks like an all-night affair of nothing but rain. We do have a good road at last, so let us be thankful. .

Friday, April 23

K. J. Murphy finally got to Rabaul today. On the way he got two fine mapping strips on New Britain. As he approached Rabaul he was intercepted by that cloud of dust on Rapopo Drome. Also, he said he didn't have any sightings, but after a talk with him he decided that Rabaul harbor had same shipping as usual—about 50 ships.

At Wewak F/O Rigsby took some fine strips. He sighted three fighters climbing to intercept him. They probably recognized him from his recent trip.

Lts. Kneeskern and Loos returned, nil photos due to weather. Capt. Olson and his ass't, Lt. V. E. Murphy, checked all missions on Woodlark and found them complete and satisfactory. The Navy and the 648th each got their prints and a beautiful coored map. We hope they appreciate this, as it is lovely.

Saturday, April 24

That new 1st Lt. who came walking into Operations today was none other than Bill Fairbank. Yes, Bill has finally staggered back after his long per diem stay on the mainland. Good to see you back, Bill.

Ludtke and Blackard returned with nil photos, due to weather. Moffat photographed Bogia and Hansa Bay. W. E. Murphy snapped Wewak, Rennels up again flew more of the rescue points on the New Britain coast.

Sunday, April 25

...Post, the new Operations Officer, sent out a batch of missions, but only Foster got photos of Wewak.

Monday, April 26

Last night we saw the long-awaited movies taken by MSgt Camillo—8th Photo in New Guinea. All that can be said of them is that Sgt Camillo should be complimented on a fine piece of photography. (There was surely some piece that was fine.)

Churchill, up to his old tricks again, had engine trouble and had to land at Mt. Hagen. Trouble always seems to cling to some people. Some very useful information was obtained on the availability of that drome.

Sykes went haywire and, unable to get high photographs, converted his F-4 into a low altitude recco ship. He followed the highway from Dagoi to Alexishafen at tree-top height, looking at the bridges and observing the road. Some people will try anything once.

"Easel" finally got to Rabaul today, but it was found that his hydraulic system had broken and sprayed oil over the lens. His pictures were useless thru no fault of "Easel 's."

Tuesday, April 27

Artie Post received his Captaincy today and immediately proceeded to "rack back" everyone in sight. "Peck of Dirt Doc" being

Wreckage of B-17 41-2627 at 14-Mile strip on December 26, 1943. Sgt. Hector Rodgers on the tail. (Jim Sills)

the closest person stood in a brace for half an hour before he was ordered to fly.

Rigsby went mad at New Britain and finished photographing rescue points.

Lt. Moffat pinpointed five targets in the Madang area. "The Thin Man" Murphy went aloft and got all dromes in the vicinity. Loos traveling the Rabaul road encountered bad weather.

Information from the lab just received informs us that condensation results from letting down to get obliques, so that gremlin will have to be eliminated.

Wednesday, April 28

Capt. Post, F/O Churchill, Lt. Sykes, Rennels took off today on missions and all returned with perfect weather reports (Weather Officer speaking), but nil photos.

Capt. Thomas, with the assistance of Lt. Foster, took off in "666" for Kavieng. Lt. Hargesheimer, after a day's preparation, did the marvelous job of navigating. Lt. Fairbank went along for the ride. Capt. Sowers was so befuddled by his cameras that he took his oxygen mask off at 30,000 feet and passed out. Luckily, Capt. Thomas had decided to let down to a lower altitude. Both pilots chalked up plenty of instrument time, but returned with nil photos.

Lt. Blackard saved the day by returning from Rabaul with a bad weather report, but photos nevertheless. Good boy, "Blackie."

Saturday, May 1

"Rummy" Foster took off for Rabaul and landed at Dobodura to wait for the weather to break. After waiting here for 6 1/2 hours, we began to sweat him out. A short time later a message came of his landing at Dobodura. He came home at 1630/K with photos of Rabaul. Rennels and Blackard reported bad WX at Wewak and Trobriand Island. "Hargey" attempted a rescue spot and a possible enemy drome.

Monday, May 3

Capt. Thomas and his B-17 crew with Bill Fairbank, Flying Engineer navigating, flew to Mt. Hagen and Wewak. In a desperate attempt to get pictures of the Yellow and Sepik rivers, Capt. Thomas put his wheels and flaps to slow "66" down to 120-130 MPH and shot his pictures from 1,600'. The photos were fine, except RAAF requested the wrong area. During the mission the tri-met cameras failed, and the crew operated the cameras by hand.

Lt. Loos, acting Operations Officer, has had bad weather to date. Rabaul has come back without photos again. Rigsby and the two Murphys did a little photography to ease the situation.

Friday, May 7

Today we hit the jackpot. K. J. Murphy, unable to reach Rabaul, returned with some fine shots of Roebuck Point, Kas Kas, and Ring Ring, the all-important rescue spots. Gasmata was photographed. Wewak mission brought home photos and a sighting report. Post tried a strip of Goodenough but the camera failed, says here. Churchill was rained out of the Markham Valley area with nil photos. Weather seems to be breaking a little, so we may expect photos more often, we hope.

Saturday, May 8

Lt. Moffat has had two trips to the Markham and has been crying for a Wewak run. He, "Many Hours" Moffat, asking to just fly again—phooey!

Loos and Blackard had nil photos of the two milk runs, Rabaul and Wewak.

B-25s of the 90th Sqdn. bombed and sank two large AKs at Madang. These are probably the same ships sighted at Wewak by Rigsby yesterday.

It won't be long now, and the 8th Photo will be in the movies. 5th Combat Camera Crew will start shooting operational scenes of 8th Photo. This activity reminds us of Camillo's movie, remember?

Sunday, May 9

Lts. Rennels and Foster returned from Rabaul and Wewak without photos again today. Hargey with pictures of the Trobriands feels that he shouldn't fly at 10,000 feet without oxygen. Post took a few pictures while he was just flying around today.

Lt. Moffat has been picked as the most photogenic pilot and will star in the 8th Photo production. He will start work on Tuesday. Ah, to be a movie star! Then again, maybe it can be worked in.

K. J. Murphy flying his training mission earned his CM by flying in the P. M. area. Tough mission?

"666" flew about the Wewak area but returned with photos of only Mt. Hagen and Oglebeng dromes. Weather prevented mapping as planned. Mapping could have been obtained as that Engineer was along again, piling up combat time, too.

Monday, May 10

Lt. Sykes got to Rabaul today...the first ship in five days. It was to his disgust, though, as it was cloud covered. He shot some

Arawe Islands viewed by 8th PRS F-5 #17. U.S. Army landed at Arawe on December 15, 1943. Main invasion was Cape Gloucester on December 26, 1943. (National Archives Kevin Morrow)

film through and some prints are usable. Sykes observed four SSF making for him. It looks like a good idea to keep our "heads out," fellows.

Rigsby finally got photos of the dromes at Goodenough Island, as well as 12" mosaic stuff of the Trobriands.

Capt. Savage recovered from the "Style on the Eye" flew to Bulldog-Wau, but heavy CU prevented photographing the strip requested.

Tuesday, May 11

Lt. Southard, acting Operations Officer, has us stepping this week. He has weather ships off at 0600/K and is endeavoring to make eager beavers out of this crowd. One is a slacker if he is not down at the line by 0700/K. It may be OK, but only for a week, we hope.

Everyone returned early today, in a hurry for another steak? Moffat, working harder than ever, was doing it for a different reason today. Publicity. He is doing a good job, too.

Col. Hutchison, former C. O. of the Air Base at Colorado Springs, visited the squadron today. Several of the pilots knew him there. What of the rumors of a new group, they now ask? Prospects look favorable, shall we say. Don't hold your breath or pack your bags yet, however, as it may be another trick.

Wednesday, May 12

Reading the mission reports where it says, "Navigator, Lt. Fairbank; Observer, Capt. Board, A.I.F.," one's first comment would be "Those Amateurs," but hold your fire, boys, as your correspondent has seen the photographs and, unfortunately, they are excellent. A 33-strip mosaic of the Trobriands with no gaps. We bow to the amateurs, as well as those war-hardened veterans, Capt. Thomas, Lt. Guerry, and SSgt Nulty.

Hargey took the weather ship out this morning and picked up a few pictures of Mt. Hagen, Nubia, and Ramu River. He filled the air with a continual stream of sparks as he tapped out the weather from every part of New Guinea. I move that Lt. Hargesheimer be given the dawn weather recco each morning.

Moffat secured the required photos of Wewak and surrounding dromes. Two planes were observed below at 5,000 ft. but failed to intercept...

Thursday, May 13

F/O Churchill and Lt Foster beat their heads together this morning. Churchill had the Markham and ran a strip from Finschhafen to Madang. At 1130/K Foster, unable to do any good in New Britain, returned to New Gunea and flew the strips between Finschhafen and Madang. All's well that ends well, however, and in this case Churchill has some pictures too far over the water and Foster had some clouds in his, so between the two we have a good strip.

The advantages of being an engineering officer seems to be in the confidence one gets in the planes. That is, if you're a good engineering officer, and Post seems to be one for he flew three strips over Vunakanau this morning. Nice going, my friends.

Friday, May 14

The B-17 crew is once again capably directed. Olson is back leading the glorified chauffeurs about by the rings in their noses, and production will begin as soon as old "627" is back in condition. This morning "666" went off to Manus Island under his leadership and picked off two mapping strips and a recco of Lorengau. We are happy that Hard Luck Hattie has been returned to the 65th Squadron, and we hold Guinea's fastest Fortress. When R.F.D. Tokio takes to the air with nose bristling with guns, and those guns under the direction of Fairbank and Olson, there will be no stopping her.

...Sgts. Daniel, Hammond, and Williams dispatched Capts. Thomas and Olson, Lts. Guerry and Fairbank in the B-17, Acting Operations Officer Southard in the weather recco...Today we went to Rabaul; for the second time his K-18 sheared a pin. It is hard enough getting to Rabaul, and then having camera trouble is adding insult to injury. (Please note, Camera Repair.) No connection to the above, but worth mentioning is F/O Rigsby's new job, Photographic Officer for S-2. When you want a real breakdown on the quality of your photos, go see Rigsby.

Ludtke did the Wewak job and brought back the works: But, Dagua, Wewak, Boram and Wewak Harbor. Sehr Gut, Herr Ludtke.

El Capitan Savage collected some K-18 at Rein Bay, but weather prevented other work and he returned home.

Loos returned from the Markham, no hits, no runs, no errors.

Saturday, May 15

No longer must we search for a suitable sobriquet for Moffat as he now added the crowning achievement to his long list of successes. Today at 2,000' he was taking off-shore obliques below Madang when he noticed some little red balls going past and some tearing noises. You are correct, the nipponese were after him. One Oscar shooting 12.7mm explosive shells had jumped from above and five o'clock. Moffat violently banked to the left and put the nose down. He leveled off at 1,000 feet doing 380 MPH with everything he had to the firewall. He pulled away, and the Nip, discouraged, turned for home. Fortunately, may we add, for a minute later the right engine cut out and Moffat limped to Dobodura on one engine. Moffat is now back from Dobodura without his trusty airplane, which will be repaired there. The newspaper reporters are crowded around Moffat, hanging onto every word. I hereby dub thee "Glamour Boy."

Sunday, May 16

Kneeskern, with sun glasses to protect his bleeding eyes, departed for Wewak this morning. Sad to report he only secured pictures of But and Dagua. When asked why he failed to get pictures under a 17,000 ft. overcast at Wewak, his eyes widened in their liquid pools of blood and his voice rose to an indignant clamor, "Ground officers wouldn't understand." And with that he walked off. Are we chagrined.

Typical New Guinea weather prevailed in all areas and Southard, Sykes, and Churchill chalked up some unsuccessful missions. Post fared a little better and collected a strip on the North coast between Madang and Finschhafen.

Tuesday, May 18

Super Salesman Foster convinced both his airplane and the weather man that today was the day to get in the photographic market. The result was virtually a corner on the New Britain business, with six strips, each a thing of beauty and a joy forever. Fairbank thanks you, Olson thanks you, and the Nips are casting harsh invective in your direction.

Blackard to the Markham Valley and four strips of that area.

Bena Bena, at least for today, immodestly forgot to clothe herself in clouds, and Blackie captured her in all her naked loveliness.

Post, acting on Foster's hurry-up radio "CAVU all over," took out for New Britain, and sure enough collected four strips up there. New Britain is no longer a thorn in our side.

P.O.G. Gardner rushed up to the Markham and got a strip from Bogadjim to Saidor.

Only Moffat to Milne Bay and Rennels to Wewak met with misfortune and returned on account of weather.

A really big day for 8th Photo. Three weeks of this sort of thing and we would head for home. Don't get your hopes up, for a day like this only occurs four times a year.

Wednesday, May 19

Guinea's irresponsible playboys, Guerry and Hargesheimer, determined to grab a first, took off this morn early, landed at Dobodura, and set forth once again. The stealth with which all this was accomplished boded no good for anyone, and sure enough they made the first trip to Kavieng and then topped that by going to Rabaul. Guerry then developed Prestone trouble and feathered one engine, landed at Buna. Hargey located a convoy north of Rabaul, headed that way, and a new drome at Keravat on the east side of Atalikiwin Bay. Suffice to say, they have been grounded.

Southard went to Wewak and photoed same. He reports two 4-5,000 ton AKs and four 500 ton AKs in the harbor.

Churchill nil photos Milne Bay. Sykes was unable to locate B-24 thought to be down near Madang.

Colonel Hutchison went to Lae and Madang to familiarize himself with this area. He picked off some low obliques of the coast below Salamaua.

Friday, May 21

Merely as a farewell gesture, Sykes went to Wewak and photoed the dromes. His pictures of Blup Blup (no, we're not blowing in our beer) were too thin to be of any real value. Nevertheless, he can go to Sydney with a clear conscience. Can he come back with the same? Lt. Blackard departed this morning at 0812 for Salamaua. We had no radio contact and hence can only surmise what may have taken place. He was to fly a strip at 23,000 feet. He would have reached Salamaua at 0900. At 0910, 41st Fighter was intercepted between Lae and Salamaua by Zeros covering a Jap raid on Wau. However, the 41st did not sight our plane in the area. That is all we know. Blackie has always seemed to travel with gremlins. Bad weather forced him down at Hood point; a bad compass placed him far off course returning from Woodlark. Each time, his good judgment saved him from misfortune. We sincerely hope that good judgment will help him once again.

Moffat went to Rabaul and returned with pictures. Gardner got four strips at Milne Bay.

Monday, May 24

Moffat did a thorough search of the Salamaua area, but found no trace of Lt. Blackard's P-38. Covered area from 7° 05'S to 7° 30'S from the coast inland to Wau.

Capt. Post is the first one of the boys to run into one of these (Japanese) twin-engine fighters. He was finishing his run over Vunakanau and did a 180 when he noticed a twin-engine fighter heading toward him. His first impression was a P-38, and evidently the Jap's was that of another Nip fighter, for they each turned to avoid the other and there was time for no more. The Nip was slate grey with a red rounder on the fuselage. Visibility was less than five miles. They passed each other at a distance of 50 yards. Imagine my surprise! (Corny, Olson, very corny.)

Foster did the Wewak job and produced.

Tuesday, May 25

Churchill nil—Kneeskern nil—Ludtke nil—the 25th of May has passed.

Friday, May 28

Why should I keep a diary when five missions fail to produce so much as one photograph? It's like writing a thesis on the processes attempted without ever reaching a successful conclusion.

Saturday, May 29

F/O Rigsby returned from photogenic Rabaul with the goods again today. 'S funny he hasn't had a camera pin shear on him for some time. Could be he has outwitted the gremlin brigade.

Then, on the other route, we have "Drag" Kneeskern coming back without photos. Ah well, there had to be weather somewhere.

"Hargey," cruising about the Markham area looking for items worthy of photoing, mapped a strip in the Saidor area. We can imagine the shout of joy which escaped from that tiny cockpit when his dearly beloved radio brought him directions to search the Hansa Bay area for a B-24. He didn't see the B-24 (which wasn't down at all), but he did sight and report a convoy in Hansa Bay—covered by twelve fighters.

The radio report was received by non-hearing ears at (Fifth Bomber Command), for they already knew of it. Just quietly may we add that Hargey's report was more accurate than that of the B-24, as the photos proved. Very nice work m'boy. Disgusting to find they didn't use the valuable information to conduct a strike.

C. O. Savage, heading for New Britain, was derailed and photoed Malahang to Hopoi instead.

Lt. Loos, victim of weather in the Milne Bay area, returned without pix.

Sunday, May 30

''Shapeless" Murphy gave up the Rabaul trip after vainly attempting an end run. He gave 'er a good go and didn't give up until he neared the D'entrecasteaux group.

F/O Ludtke photographed Wewak this day.

Lt. Gardner was turned back from Kavieng by weather.

Lt. Foster found clouds in Milne Bay area again today.

That famous B-17 2627 started out for just anywhere, landed at 7-Mile and returned to Schwimmer soon afterwards. No. 3 engine giving trouble this time.

Lt. Rennels pleased the Engineer Liaison Dept. with mapping photography. No matter how dull the day might seem, we can get pictures (a few) somewhere.

Monday, May 31

The newest long-range request is for Buka Passage, and the first to attempt the trip is Captain Savage. He landed at Goodenough Island to top his tanks before proceeding over that long stretch of water. Weather sealed him in, and after waiting for some time, he gave up and returned to the fold, safely but highly P. O.

F/O Churchill went to Milne Bay to see the clouds. He saw them and came home.

Lt. Southard came back to New Guinea when he found the Rabaul route socked in. While flitting around the Lae-Wau area, he sighted the U.S. Air Force enroute to its target. How comforting it is to know we have other aircraft in the area!

Tuesday, June 1

...P.O.G. covered the waterfront and even ventured into the mountains today. Two Bulldog-Wau strips and a series of K-18 shots along the coast, plus a few other items, left him completely devoid of film, so he had to come home.

Hargesheimer, our favorite recco pilot, carried on magnificently today. Off at 0800, he crossed the ranges and landed at Dobodura for more gas. There, they pawned off some dirty gas, and upon taking off, his right engine produced so little power that he nearly took the tower with him. He returned to Schwimmer and the trouble cleared up enroute. Landed, and off again at 1000, he proceeded to Rabaul and got his pictures. Such determination is worthy of commendation.

Loos to Wewak and vicinity with good results.

Wednesday, June 2

...K. J., wearing an aircraft-spotter armband, sallied forth to Wewak this morning. At Mt. Hagen, rumored sight of Japanese paratroops, he spotted 20 U/I on a bearing of 135°. Today we learn that Bulldog was raided at 1055. Nice going, Murph!

Another for Murph and 8th Photo! In Wewak harbor Accolade Murphy reorted 12-15 small boats, nothing over 1,000 tons. B24 on recco reported 12-15 vessels, 1,500-5,000 tons. Pictures show the largest to be 1,000 tons. We repeat, nice going!

As usual, Kneeskern returned with pictures and, as usual, didn't know where he had been.

V-Bom was over this afternoon putting engine time on the overworked airplanes. But who am I to bitch?

Higher commands, seeing the amount of work 8th Photo puts out, must think 8th Photo a Group. Today they ordered two of our planes to Dobodura for afternoon reccos. That leaves three planes in commission to handle our myriad of requests. Bigger and better headaches for Engineering.

Thursday, June 3

Always something new and different—and generally unpleasant. At 1300 today we were asked to send two aircraft and three pilots, plus the necessary maintenance and camera men to Dobodura. At 1400 Capt. Savage and Lt. Hargesheimer took off in "2214" and "3073." F/O Ludtke and the rest depart by transport in the morning. The idea is a daily recco of the North and South coasts of New Britain.

Flash! Wire received this afternoon informing Captains Savage and Thomas to report to Pilot Replacement Depot, APO 923. You all know what that means—the lucky bastards are on their way home. All is turmoil—much laughter and profanity, but Olson is over in the corner cursing his fates.

Tomorrow Operations will be a problem. Two at Dobodura and another three to take care of Buka, Wewak, and Rabaul. Where, oh where has the map program gone? Stick around, Fairbank, we'll find something for you.

I wish someone could explain to me how it happens that the noon meal is always so poor on the days when the mess officer is flying missions. Nice pictures anyway of Wewak and vicinity.

Friday, June 4

Cecil Rigsby is another of Olson's Intelligence graduates. An unsolicited statement from him tells so elequently the value of this training that I quote, for the guidance of others who might wish to elevate themselves: "...I went first to Lae and flew a difficult strip across the mountains, then to Biebeck Bay for a strip over Montagu Harbor, then up to Lolobau Island for more pictures, and last but not least, everything in the Rabaul area. Then back home to total five hours and fifty minutes. I thank you, O.I.S., I thank you."

Gentlemen, our registrar, J. Edgar Hoover Hammond, will examine your qualifications for entrance at 10000, July 4, 1943.

Saturday, June 5

Once again we face an empty chair as word comes from Dobodura that Lt. Frederic Hargesheimer has been missing since 1700 o'clock this evening. Our finest reconaissance pilot and one of the mainstays around which this quadron has been built, he will be sorely missed, first—as one of our finest friends, and second—for the work and talent of which he was so unsparing.

Hargey was flying the coastline recco of New Britain and his last radio message placed him at Open Bay. Men have come out of that area before and will again. If there is the slightest chance, Hargey is a good bet to make it. It is our fervent hope and prayer that such is the case.

"P.O.G." placed another SWPA and 8th Photo first on the record today when he completed a hazardous mission to Buka Passage in the northern Solomons. In ship 2139, he took off from Goodenough Island and made the 900 mile round trip over solid water, the first pursuit type aircraft to do reconnaissance of that area. It is with reluctance that we initiate such long missions, but we take a great deal of pride in the successful completion of these difficult tasks. Very nice job, "P.O.G."

Churchill ran the Wewak trip, and although weather socked in the Wewak drome, he was able to pick up an oblique strip along the north coast.

Sunday, June 6

...Today, after getting past Wewak's A/A and fighters, (Rigsby) was idly circling Krouprinz Harbor for a look at some barges when a Jap in a (Hamp) found him taking a nap and started flying formation with him. Probably just another recco looking for company, for not a shot was fired. Rigsby, definitely antisocial, took off for distant pastures, but in no great haste, for he couldn't get the plane, 2139, up to 300 mph, nor could he drop the tanks. Nevertheless, he evaded the Nip and headed for home. Thirty-Mile welcomed him, and not too soon, for he had 9 gallons in one main and 12 in the other.

Loos pushed on to the latest of our long-range runes—Buka. He put it down at Goodenough, coming and going, and added six and a half hours to his combat time.

Sykes had no trouble on the Rabaul job and turned in his usual businesslike job.

Monday, June 7

Lt. Guerry flew 2122 to Dobodura this morning with Olson breathing on his neck. After violent evasive tactics, they managed to avoid B-25s landing from east to west, transports landing from north to south and P-38s taking off from south to north long enough to get the plane on the ground. All seems to be well with our advanced echelon, for the enlisted men don't want to come back to civilized Port Moresby. After an excellent lunch midst tropical splendor, they set off up the coast in search of some trace of Lt. Blackard or Lt. Hargesheimer. Up the coast from Dobodura to Salamaua at 1,500 feet revealed nothing, so they returned to Port Moresby.

"P.O.G.," and in Lt Guerry's absence, "C.O.G." wheeled up to the Markham and collected K-18 of Buga and the island SW of Rooke and a couple of mapping strips on Rooke Island.

Churchill reccoed the north coast today and sighted 2 to 30 barges on the north coast of Manam Island. After seeing the pictures, I can't tell whether they are barges or not, but there is a hell of a lot of something there.

K. G. Murphy did the Rabaul try with pictures.

Clark Sykes and his friend Pauline in the front seat, Cecil Rigsby in the back during a Sydney leave in December 1943 (Sykes)

Tuesday, June 8

...(The Japanese) are intercepting us much too regularly on the Wewak run. Need I ask you to please keep thy head on a swivel?

Southard noted five Zekes attempting interception while he was over Kairiru. He advanced the throttles and took the photos of Wemot and Boram and kept going. They faded into the background, and he completed the mission.

Loos proceeded to the Markham and, as luck would have it, photographed Kainantu immediately after the Japs had bombed it. In fact, as he passed over Aiyura, he noted a twin-engined fighter 10,000 feet below him, and judging by the way the fighter was pullilng up, it is quite possible the bombing had been done by twin-engine fighters.

Rigsby, just to prove himself human, headed for Rabaul, ran into bad weather, and had to return.

Sykes took 09 to Dobodura, and Ludtke will return with 2214 tomorrow morning.

Wednesday, June 9

"Shapeless" Murphy, having lost the toss on previous occasions, finally won the turn and was given an opportunity to go to Buka. This he did with dispatch and completed the trip in six hours, including the time spent and Goodenough Isalnd. Good K-18 photos of the Buka and Machin Bay resulted.

(LeGrand) soared over the weather to reach Wewak and photograph those extremely active Jap dromes. This he did and returned, for weather prevented other work.

Gardner nil at Rabaul on account of weather.

Sykes going by way of Cape Gloucester was able to recco the north coast of New Britain, but the south coast was covered...

Thursday, June 10

I think we can say without reservation that the weather was bad from here to Rabaul. Southard made two attempts; on the first he was unable to get over the ranges, and on the second by detouring to Hood Point, he managed to reach the Solomon Sea, but then returned. V. E. Murphy took off from Dobodura for New Britain, but turned back after forty minutes of too much instrument flying.

Today (Rigsby) as usual sighted more stuff and things, such as 12 Zeros at 9,000 feet over Wewak and merchant vessels and destroyers milling about in the harbor there. He brings in the pictures, which is the highest compliment one can pay to a pilot in this business.

The '17 went out at last, this time to Dutch New Guinea. Bad weather prevailed along the coast on the north where mapping photos are so sorely needed, but they managed to get pictures from Mt. Hagen to the Sepik. Olson was so far off on his ETA that the crew missed those good Coca Colas. No cooperation from the pilots is his only, but undoubtedtly good, defense.

Friday, June 11

Ludtke successfully recorded But, Dagua, Wewak, and Boram and returned to the home base, tired...

Don DeLasso, that distinguished caballero from the Rio Grande, rode herd on the shipping at Rabaul this morning...

...Gardner couldn't repeat on Buka because of a malfunctioning compass. Definitely not the trip for compass trouble. What the hell—two out of three is a good average in any man's ball park.

Saturday, June 12

(Rigsby) flew over to Buka Passage, used 24 exposures on the passage and Machin Bay. He then took the extra trip down the island to Kahili and Ballale, having set aside 10 exposures for each....You can picture his wrath when he learned there were only 27 exposures in the K-18...

K. J. Murphy kept his record up by getting us pictures of the Wewak dromes. Two of the enemy's Zeros took off but didn't have the poop to ever get near him.

Southard ran into the ever-present weather problem south of New Britain and was forced back to his home base.

Sunday, June 13

Foster and Rennnels got back from that good Sydney leave, and we didn't waste any time getting them back to work. "Rummy," proving that he hadn't lost the touch, flipped the right switches over Rabaul and, sure enough, he got pictures. Rennels didn't have enough strength in those lax muscles to knock the weather off Wewak, so he goes pictureless for the day.

Ludtke was chased out of Goodenough by red alert, and it evidently gave him the necessary boost, for he reached the far-off isle of Buka and made his run over the passage. Then back to Goodenough. Not seeing any damage, he landed and gassed up for the homeward journey.

Sykes made the complete circuit over the New Britain recco, but couldn't find a Jap. Some day that recco will get something but be too surprised to report it. Certainly takes a lot of good engine time.

Monday, June 14

...Not only did Rigsby get (a K-18 strip along the Markham River) for me, but also operationals of Madang and Nubia and a mapping strip for Fairbank. Just like Christmas—something for everybody.

Southard couldn't reach Buka, so he picked up a strip across McLaren Pt., which is over there by Tufi.

Loos did the New Britain recco. Nil sightings.

Tuesday, June 15

The B-17 crew went to Bougainville today and again had camera trouble. Two runs over Buka Passage, one with Class L and one with infra-red, neither of which showed anything but blanks, and a mapping strip down the island on which the left oblique failed. We don't mind flying for the cause, but this no-picture deal is strictly for the outhouse.

V. E., the Murph, did the Rabaul trip for us and did it damn well. K. J. Murphy went to Ramu-Markham where he picked up a few operational photos around Madang. Ludtke couldn't get pictures after flying all the way up to Wewak...Sykes did some K-18 work on Lake Dakatund, the crocodile winter resort on the Willaumez (Talasea) Peninsula.

Wednesday, June 16

We have just received word that Capt. (Jay) Zeamer and his crew of the 65th were intercepted and badly shot up on the Bougainville mapping missions. This is undoubtedly the result of the large movement of aircraft to the Solomons for the attack on Gudalcanal today. The loss of 77 aircraft must have embittered the Nips quite a bit, for we understand the fighters pressed to close quarters.

The bombardier was killed, the navigator may die, Zeamer was badly shot up about the legs, and all the other members wounded except the co-pilot and one gunner. It is a courageous story, and we will get more details when the crew has recovered sufficiently to talk about it.

Southard got pictures of Rabaul, and the General has asked that he be recommended for the Air Medal. They picked up the movement of aircraft from New Britain to the Solomons by the absence of airplanes on the Rabaul dromes.

Foster collected photos of Wewak and returned. No fuss, no foam, but good, solid sending.

Thursday, June 17

Alexander Guerry, Jr....went to the Markham after the possible drome site pix along the Watut....he headed for home and bad weather gave him an opportunity to charm the natives at 30- Mile. This he did and, after eating a hearty repast at the D.O.'s house, he called for a transport (what, no fiddlers three?) and returned home. He claimed the engines wouldn't start, but it is my opinion that he wanted to find out whether we'd bother to pick him up. I argued against it, but others, not aware of Guerry's wiles, fell for his scheme, and he is now chortling over it. I've never been sued for libel yet.

K. J. Murphy brought home pictures of the heavily-defended airdromes at Rabaul, and L. J. Kneeskern, pix of Buka. A good day for the records.

Sunday, June 20

After only a few days a Commanding Officer and an auspicious start in the right direction, Captain Post set out for what may be his last mission. He departed for Rabaul at 815 this morning and our last radio message was received at 1015 from the vicinity of Wide Bay. As in Hargy's case, we have no inkling of the trouble but feel quite strongly that our pilots are running into a standing patrol. It is a terrific blow to the squadron as a whole, and coming so close on Lt. Hargesheimer's failure to return, it is doubly hard on the pilots.

Capt. Foster took photos of Wewak this morning. Lt. Guerry and his '17 boys twisted and turned in the Ramu Valley following the foot trails over which supplies are transported.

A report arrived today that an aircraft carrier, two AK, and a destroyer between the Trobriand Islands and Goodenough had been sighted. Either they reported the reefs and the islands west of the Trobriands or they missed the position, for Lt. Sykes could find nothing but a liberty ship and some small AKs of ours plying their way to Oro Bay.

Monday, June 21

Nil photos Rabaul, Wewak, and Buka. The only thing that saved us from failure was Lt. Guerry's "17" crew at Woodlark Island. High priority anchorage photos of Woodlark, obliques, verticals, and some experimental color photography by Lt. Powell.

Also, even though we failed to get photos, we did ascertain that the nips were not heading down for Wewak for their usual raid on the Bena Bena Valley. A negative report is better than nothing.

Tuesday, June 22

(The day was mostly negative, with Churchill and Southard flying unsuccessful sorties over Bena Bena between 0800 and 1630, Sykes to Wewak, and K.J. Murphy to Rabaul for the first fruitless reconnaissance for him in seven trips.—Auths.)

Wednesday, June 23

...Bomber Command's B-24 "Pug Nose" arrived this evening loaded down with beer, chicken, pork chops, olives, ice cream, and a hundred other delicacies which heretofore have been naught but a dream. Only the cooks are unhappy, but when they see us heave to and set in, I'm sure they'll figure it was worth it.

Our second day of patrolling for Japs yielded no results. This 043 rising is beginning to get old already, and I doubt whether relief is in sight if we cannot persuade the Nips to come down the Valley.

Foster took off today with the first of the new refrigerated film made available by Colonel Hutchison. He found Rabaul heavily overcast, and on one run was diving through the clouds at 22,000' to obtain his photos. Despite those bad photographic conditions, the prints had excellent definition and good contrast. It looks as if there is something to this fresh film idea.

Loos reached New Britain, but the weather was so bad that he came back to Schwimmer. Please note that our advanced echelon refuses to stay away from home with a party coming up. To hell with the war effort—I'm hungry.

June 24

(B Flight observed its first anniversary overseas with an evening party, celebrated with fried chicken, ice cream, and beer. Auths.)

Friday, June 25

...Captains Foster and Olson hit the line at 0600, and the missions were off before 0700. Oh, for the good old 9 o'clock days.

Lt. V. E. Murphy scored the biggest success of several months with his photographs of Rabaul...

Moffat was unsuccessful at Wewak—reported the field socked in, and then he returned to base.

Loos reached Hansa Bay, but failed to locate any Nipponese. After an hour of impatient waiting for something to happen, he returned home.

Saturday, June 26.

With Olson moved from Intelligence to Operations, Lt. Guerry has been assigned the "I" task, and the diary is now in the hands of the Tennessee Terror.

Today another name was added to our far too rapidly growing list of pilots "Missing in Action." This time it was Ken "Shapeless" Murphy, and again it was one of our best pilots. He took off for Rabaul at 0700 and was never heard from again. Opinion seems to be that he must have been jumped by fighters that were waiting for him over New Britain. "Murph" had one of the best flying records in our Squadron, and his splendid work in Operations the last few months had increased his value to the squadron. He will be sorely missed.

The "milk run" to Rabaul has cost us three of our best officers in three weeks, and even the higher-ups are beginning to realize that no squadron can afford such losses. The best answer at present seems to be fighter escort to New Britain, and Colonel Hutchison discloses he'll get it for us.

Rummy started towards Buka today, but ran into that stationary front and had to come home. A revolving (not just oscillating) compass needle was a contributing factor.

Southard made two attempts in two different ships to get Wewak but returned both times with engine trouble. Gremlins????

Sunday, June 27

Just back (we almost said "fresh") from Sydney, Rigsby and Ludtke stepped into harness again today to give our overworked pilots a rest. Taking off in formation, the two patrolled the Markham, Ramu, and Madang areas and eventually returned with engine trouble, but also with the mission completed. Highlight of the trip was when "Eagle Eye" Easel happened to glance around and found two other P-38s practically flying formation with Rigsby and him. What if they had been Zeros, Easel?

Today was a great change in the Tactical Department of Eighth Photo. So busy were the boys changing initials that a visitor might have imagined himself tangled up with Washington bureaucracy. I. O. Olson is now O. O. Olson; F. C. Guerry is now I. O. Guerry; Communications Officer Kneeskern is also F. C. Kneeskern. And, to top it all off, Capt. Gingerich, Head of the Compilation Unit, is taking Foster's place as Inspector for the Squadron. . . .

Monday, June 28

A day of rest for the good old Eighth! Col Hutchison made the amazing discovery yesterday that our pilots had an average of 46 combat missions apiece. Apparently, as a result of this, he wired General Arnold for immediate replacements and decided to conserve the energies of the rest of us by keeping us on the ground for a day.

In the afternoon, Captain Foster took off for Dobodura from where he will depart for Rabaul on the morrow with fighter escort. Good Luck, Rummy! I hope at least one of the three fighters stays with you.

Loos and Southard left this morning to make a little trip down to Sydney. Poor boys!

Tuesday, June 29

...Sykes journeyed to Wewak and covered all the dromes. Film trouble gave him some weird double exposures, but didn't destroy the value of his pictures. "Powerhouse," laden with maps, went into the Markham and made Fairbank happy with the first mapping strips in nearly two weeks.

Down to the line at nine o'clock (four hours later than usual) came Col. Hutchison, and off to Goodenough he went almost immediately. The fighters are guilty of moral terpitude (paraphrased from the original for our junior readers) on the Rabaul mission, and the Colonel is trying to straighten it out. "Rummy" didn't get off to Rabaul today, and rumors are ripe that he had been patrolling Dobodura, gun in hand, trying to corner these fighter pilots to go to New Britain with him.

Sowers returned today at long last and was congratulated by everyone on the food and beer he sent up to us. It is well for him he had sent so much or he would have been scalped for staying so long. Tell us about Southport once more, Gordon.

Wednesday, June 30

...Olson and Fairbank had the B-17 going everywhere but over the target this morning. We sent one ship out today and that returned without photos. Rigsby to a socked-in Markham was our lone effort.

Finally got the details on Foster's Rabaul trip. First the 9th Fighter chickened out of the deal, so the 80th Fighter said they would take it. An orchid to those boys, for when the C. O. asked for volunteers, every man came forward. The mission got off, but severe frontal activity forced them to return...

Thursday, July 1

The diary is once again in the hands of Capt. Olson as a result of reassignment, of duties on the Line. Lt. Guerry is Operations Officer, and Capt. Olson is back in the Intelligence saddle.

After all of the July 1st zero-weather chatter we only dispatched two missions this morning, neither of which was successful...

...Another of the boys has kissed New Guinea a fond farewell. Lt. Marvin Gardner set forth this morning on the first leg of that long-awaited journey. Within a week he will step aboard the boat with everything to look forward to—home, wife, and all of those pleasures we have almost forgotten. Good luck, POG, the rest of us will join you shortly, Or will we?

Friday, July 2

...Eight missions and eight airplanes got off the ground and, although operations and intelligence were buzzing with activity, it seemed very similar to any other day. Eighth Photo plugs along day after day, turning in the same workman-like job.

Col. Hutchison, with co-pilot Guerry and some naval commander cluttering up the airplane, rode up and down the coastline from Salamaua to Oro Bay with one naval man, Cmdr. Adair, and Olson trying to direct the plane to the proper positions, and with TSgt Tom Nulty swinging a small K-18 camera from one side to another taking oblique shots.

Brother Kneeskern went to Wewak to spy on the enemy and fortunately did spot six aircraft proceeding to Hansa Bay. He kept the wires hot for a few minutes and then tried himself for home.

Saturday, July 3

V. E. Murphy cleared the ground at 0615 this morning with the cockpit lights on in order to see the instruments. Weather prevented his reaching even Goodenough.

Guerry and Kneeskern bounced off to Madang at 1120 and then bounced back down again at 1500. They make great claims for Kneeskern's navigation, which nobody can check. But they did get there somehow, and, sighting nothing for an hour, they returned to base where they were served ice-cold Coca Cola from the Red Cross.

Sykes and Rennels took the early recco from 0707 to 1127. Their itinerary was Lae, Madang, Hansa Bay, and home. Nil sightings all areas.

Sunday, July 4

Our recco of Madang went out this morning with F/O Ludtke and Lt. Moffat covering each other. They got to Yule Island and tried to climb above the overcast but failed to get over it.

They did some good formation flying on the way back. No other missions were initiated. Moffat's first failure to reach his target.

(The officers defeated the enlisted men 3-1 in a squadron Independence day baseball game—Auths.)

Ray Starr of Camera Repair in the 8th Photo Lab. (Sykes)

Monday, July 5

...Foster and Rennels departed for Goodenough. Foster to try Rabaul again, and Rennels headed for the passage at Buka. Despite all of the skillful pilotage and defiance of weather, they finally had to take no for an answer and set down at Dobodura. Off again at 1030, they skirted thunderstorms and mountains to find Goodenough on the other side of the weather wide open and inviting them to land. Foster picked up the two-fighter cover and pointed the nose towards Rabaul. He cut over the harbor at 35, *000 feet and the fighters were a couple of thousand feet above him*...unfortunately, the cameras ran away and Foster had good pictures of Vunakanau and nothing else....Rennels hit a severe front east of Goodenough and retuned to base.

Tuesday, July 6

(Lt. Fairbank was awarded an air medal after a five hour and twenty-one minute flight in the B-17, the only engineer in the squadron to get the decoration.—Auths.)

"Powerhouse" Murphy set out with color film today and obtained the first operational color photos ever taken in this theater. Only Wewak Drome was open, but after all, Morse's first telegraph message was a short one. Results from this color work will be known tomorrow. Processing cannot begin until midnight. That is the hour of favorable humidity and temperature conditions.

The B-17 with Wayne Mueller, assistant operations officer and glider pilot, at the co-pilot's controls, obtained beautiful obliques of the Markham River area; Fairbank directing the photography and Taylor the airplane.

Wednesday, July 7

...Rigsby gave us some bad moments today. He got off early for New Britain to search for shipping someone had reported. At 0845 we received a garbled radio message stating something about DD and possibly AKs, and Olson got into his usual dither and wired all over the place. We later learned it was only one destroyer off Jaquinot Bay. Nil other missions today.

Saturday, July 10

"The Mission" was Capt. Guerry's low obliques of Lae and coastlines.

In observing Col. Hutchison's order "Don't get any holes in the B-17," Capt. Guerry didn't pick up so much as a machine gun scratch at 1200' off Lae Drome.

Churchill did Wewak operational flying and gained his objective. Photos twice in three days. Nice going, fella!

The Murphy-Markham Mapping Mission was nil due to weather again.

Sunday, July 11

Is my face red? Today I went to Madang and I had four P-38s following me like faithful dogs. I went up to Madang and flew a 30-mile strip of K-18, and when I returned to Moresby, I learned that I had failed to turn on all of the switches. And, I've been flying photo missions for almost a year. And I'm a Captain and my initials are F. L. R. Who am I?

Rigsby went to the Markham but couldn't find a single, solitary spot to photograph. So he returned home. No sightings, no pix, no nothing.

Southard and Loos went to Goodenough and then departed hence for Rabaul. The good 80th Fighter Squadron was covering them, but bad weather forced them to return. No pix, but a good idea.

Monday, July 12

Churchill went to the Markham today and really went to town. 150-foot rolls of good mapping over an area theretofore unrecorded. He covered the area between the Ramu River and Madang with two good tri-met strips.

Clark "Rolling Stone" Sykes grabbed off some beyootiful pix of Wewak, Boram, and But. In fact, Chief of Staff Colonel Cooper slapped him on the back and said, "Good work, Son." War may be for young men, but we still have to submit to the condescension of the old boys. What the hell—they have to have something to do.

The B-17 failed to produce today. With an unprecedented 12 fighters overhead, they headed for New Britain, but the weather was bad even at 500 feet, so they threw in the towel and came home.

Our good friend Grigg of Compilation got his much-desired promotion today, and your correspondent must sign off for the day to go up and join in the festivities attendant to the jump from 2nd to 1st.

Tuesday, July 13

...Five missions went out today with only one bringing back the bacon for 8th Photo. Guerry (busy man, this Guerry) with Bill Fairbanks as crew, took the B-17 EH! P-38 to Salamaua to record on film damage done by 47 B-25s and '17s. Our "PiggyBack" was just the plane for the mission. They flew 6-8000' thru a heavy barrage of ack-ack, but as usual, the marksmanship was poor. Says Fairbanks, "Whew!" Oh, yes, the pictures were good.

Moffat and Rigsby attempted the Rabaul mission but were stopped at Goodenough by rain. Landed at Dobodura returned later to Schwimmer.

Loos took a nice little ride up into the Markham but the clouds just wouldn't go away. It was the same with Ludtke and Rennels who went to Hansa Bay and Madang, respectively. Such is the life of a photo pilot.

Wednesday, July 14

...F/O Churchill held up the reputation of the 8th today by getting two mapping strips in the Markham. He had a nice run down the Snake River and found a long-sought-after area in the mountains west of Finschhafen to Mange. Fairbank is so happy about the mapping runs that he's in a dither, running around drawing flight lines all over our nice new maps. We'll have to entitle part of them as the "Churchill Series." Oh, yes, fourteen fighters were sighted on the mission, but to the joy of one pilot I know, they turned out to be those ever-cautious, high flying, rough and tough P-38s.

Thursday, July 15

Again we sent only one mission. Sykes went to the Markham with a bad-weather report in one hand and a map with those little blue flight lines in the other. Nosing down under a 19,000' overcast, he added another mapping strip to our ever increasing number. On the way home, darting in and out of the clouds with a closed field, he was forced to go in at Dobodura across the mountains. He returned later in the afternoon with only a few hundred foot ceiling. Results: one less blue flight line.

Friday, July 16

One mission went out today with the C.O., Captain Foster, and Lt. Loos piloting the planes. They were escorted by four fighters from the 39th to Madang. Photos were taken by Foster which turned out to be excellent. While maneuvering in the Madang area, the four fighters were separated from the flight. Returning to Moresby, the photo pilots encountered unusually bad weather with very low ceilings and in many places zero zero conditions. Our ships landed safely, as did two of the fighters, but the other two less-experienced fellows are missing. One was understood to have bailed out over the mountains, and the other is unreported. The (8th Photo Squadron) regrets that we have to call on the fighters for cover, but the happenings of the last few months have made it a necessity.

Sunday, July 18

Moffat and Guerry, with four fighters, went to the Madang area and obtained excellent pictures of the new road the Nips are building. It is south of Bagadjim to Yaula. Six unidentified planes were sighted in the Markham Valley. The two photo ships with the fighters pursued them, but somehow they managed to get lost in the clouds. The only time the Nips look for trouble is when they outnumber you five to one.

Rigsby secured a 6" strip across goodview Junction to the Francisco River in the Salamaua area. On the attempt at a second strip, four unidentified planes were sighted circling over the Salamaua Drome at 8,000'. He took cloud cover, gained altitude, went over to Lae, and got two strips of K-18 and down in the Markham for a low 6" tri-met strip.

Southard attempted the mission from Dobodura but was turned back by bad weather 15 minutes out.

Tuesday, July 20

Ludtke went to the Markham and brought back one of those all- important mapping runs. Of course he had the same trouble so many of the other pilots run into; he didn't know where he was. Imagine. But the important thing is the area was badly needed.

Sykes went to Madang with instructions to shoot his pictures after the raid, which he did. He went damn low over the field despite the ack-ack and turned in some nice photographyy. He remarked that it was nice to have a little company on a few of the missions.

Murphy took the search of the North and South coasts of New Britain from the other side today. He ran into bad weather but took pictures of Hoskins Peninsula and the Gasmata Drome.

Wednesday, July 21

The strip was socked in this morning, so Foster, who was to take the weather ship to Madang, went to Three-Mile and borrowed one of the fighter planes. He completed the mission, reporting the weather between here and Madang. From what I could gather, he caught up on some of his aerial gunnery by shooting at everything along the route.

Loos took the run to Wewak and covered all of the dromes in that area. It was as good a job of picture taking as I have seen, with the prints turning out excellent.

Moffat circled and flew up and down in the Markham area, but sighted no enemy planes venturing down that far.

Rigsby covered the strike on the Bogadjim area to Yaula Track by B-25s. Photos were taken, but before a complete run could be made six enemy aircraft were sighted and the run had to be discontinued. Needless to say, the fighters were on the job, bagging 19 for sure and 11 probables. Not bad for one day's hunting.

Thursday, July 22

Churchill, with fighter escort, was turned back from the Rabaul mission by frontal activity in the New Britain area.

Capt. Rennels turned in a good job by getting K-18 photos of the coastline in the Lae area and at Salamaua.

The B-17, with Capt. Guerry, Mueller doing the co-piloting, Taylor, and observer Fairbank returned from a two-day perilous mission to the Woodlark and Trobriand Islands. They had such distinguished visitors as the Chief of Staff, Colonel Cooper, and, up from the 648th Engineers, Lt. Colonel Kumpe. The boys had quite a time staying the night at Milne Bay. Very good pictures were taken of the Woodlark, Trobriand, and Goodenough strips.

On landing at Goodenough (half-way down the runway) the left brake went out. With the end of the runway coming up and fast, Guerry did a beautiful job of ground-looping, and a good time was had by all.

Murphy took the recco of the north coast of New Britain, but the south coast was covered.

Friday, July 23

Capt. Foster, who's getting to be an expert on weather, went to the Madang area, reporting the weather, cloud types, etc., enroute.

Rigsby went to the Markham Valley and took a mapping strip west of Finschhafen. Operational photos of Hansa Bay and Madang were also obtained. The heavy and medium bombers hit Bogadjim and Salamaua again today dropping the Nips a few presents weighing about 1,000 pounds. If Johnny and Mary could see the results of their scrap metal drives, I'm sure it would do their hearts good.

Sunday, July 25

...Rigsby and Churchill picked up a fair-sized convoy, four AK, 4-6,000 tons, a mine layer, and a destroyer at Hansa Bay, but for some reason the powers that be decided to leave them alone.

Murphy took pictures of Madang. He returned from the first attempt because of engine trouble but scored the second time.

Monday, July 26

...Rennels got to Wewak, but rather than photograph clouds, he returned home. Moffat grabbed some pictures of Madang, but couldn't get any pictures in the assigned area, Markham. Foster photographed Salamaua before the raid.

Sykes went out today to photograph the misses of the B-24s on Salamaua. The mission was called 207 General, and I at first thought it was named that in honor of Sykes, but it was later reported that nobody at Air Force can think of a letter between A and Z. The B-24s did a nice job today, and the "before and after photographs" showed some pleasing sights. First, there was a Lutheran Church in Salamaua, now there isn't. Those inhuman Americans. Chaptain Tojo is just another Jap to us....

Wednesday, July 28

Lt. Kneeskern...K-18'd the new drome at Tsili-Tsili (pronounced Silly Silly) and then mapped the valley and a strip up the Ramu from Bo River to Annenberg. Kneeskern must be naming his own rivers because nobody can find the Bo River on any of the maps.

"Triple X" Loos, so called because of his great love for the Dobodura missions, reached New Britain but couldn't fight his way across the Island. Hence, the long trip home without results.

9th Fighter (Squadron) ran into from 12 to 15 Oscars northwest of New Britain and neatly poured six of them into the sea, and another two probably ended up there.

On the international front the Russians are crowding the Germans around Orel, and the Allies are shooting peace feelers at the Italians now that Mussolini is definitely in discard.

Thursday, July 29

Moffat covered the B-25 raid at Salamaua, and after running five strips of the bombings, he found himself all alone, so he tried himself home.

Rigsby took operational photos of Goodenough Island for the Sixth Army. The story, the same old story, of photo, rephoto, and rephoto again.

Churchill covered the local dromes and a strip from Largon to Kareme on his training mission. This training mission sounds like a racket. Everybody has over 50 combat missions and yet they are still claiming they need training missions.

Murphy was weathered out of the Markham and Ludtke out of the New Britain area. Three B-25C-ls and one B-25G hit Cape Gloucester this morning covered by the 80th Fighter. The B-25G carries a 75mm with special recoil mechanism, and on this occasion fired ten shells at a destroyer, scoring seven hits. The pictures show beautifully dead Japs lying on the decks and gaping holes in the hull. Late reports reveal that it (was) sunk. The 80th while covering found an unsuspecting Dinah happily plugging towards Rabaul. The poor Nip never knew what hit him. Good stuff, there should be more of that.

Saturday, July 31

John Kneeskern, one of our oldest and best, is missing today. His 54th mission was to take him to Nadzab, but spotter reports indicate that the did not reach the area. Sykes and Olson searched the dromes from Kerema to Hood point but found nothing. We shall await the reports from the Watut and Wau. What can be said? John was a close friend to all of us and an important part of all our activities. A grand fellow and boon companion, he leaves a great gap in our close circle of friendship. May our hopes and prayers aid him wherever he may be.

Ludtke could not reach New Britain today on account of weather.

In this area the B-25C-1 and D-1s are hammering at Jap barge activity with considerable success. Twelve barges were strafed today and either sunk or badly damaged in the Hanisch Harbor-Finschhafen area.

In the month of July, Churchill heads the list of twelve missions, closely followed by Rennels, Guerry, Murphy, and Rigsby, each with eleven. Lots of flying!

Sunday, August 1

Eighth Photo is doing damned little work these days for several good reasons. First, the weather stinks, and secondly, we have but six pilots to cover the area.

Today Rigsby and Moffat hit the Nadzab area but couldn't find anything photogenic in nature. Loos stuck his nose on a front enroute to New Britain and promptly unstuck it again and returned home. Wise man!

Vertical photo of Simpson Harbor at Rabaul taken by 8PRS on September 11, 1943. (Sowers)

Nothing new on the international front. Main obstacle to Italian peace seems to be the presence of German troops on Italian soil.

Strafing of barges in the Finschhafen and Cape Gloucester areas by B-25 C-1s and D-1s was the only offensive action in this theater today.

Monday, August 2

Plenty of excitement this morning, but it turned out be short-lived. Foster and Southard found Rabaul in an unusual CAVU condition. They also believed they had sighted a carrier and a battle wagon in the harbor, and without hesitation radioed the information back. These later turned out to be two heavy cruisers, but the pictures were excellent, so all is forgiven. Southard unknowlingly had two Zekes four thousand feet below him, but ignorance is bliss, and the two photographers returned unscathed. Sykes and Churchill, after clearing a path through the P-47s, ran a mosaic of Salamaua and vicinity. The P-47s were there on business since they were covering a B-24 strike on the isthmus, but we take a very dim view of their choice of altitude.

Ludtke was unable to complete a recco of New Britain for a change as he found the CAVU conditions mentioned in the C. O.'s report existent in all areas.

Twenty-nine B-24s dropped one hundred tons of bombs on Lae and Salamaua today causing considerable damage to installations and, no doubt, much consternation among the Japas who came from the homeland with tales of Jap air superiority ringing in their ears. To further confound them, the 9th Fighter (Squadron) knocked down eleven Zekes and Oscars and probably destroyed some more without loss to themselves. The B-25s they were covering struck again and again at the barge activity from Lae around to Saidor. These attacks are meeting with considerable success, and the Jap is once again groping for a successful method of supplying his New Guinea garrisons.

The U. S. 15th Air Force struck at the Ploesti Oil Fields in Rumania, and it is estimated that one fifth of the facilities are destroyed

Tuesday, August 3

Moffat and Rigsby collaborated on the Wewak mission today...

Sykes covered the new Jap road from Bogadjim down the Mindjim River almost to the Ramu. The road looks wide enough for two-way traffic, and despite the countless turns should prove troublesome to our plans for cutting Lae and Salamaua off from supplies....

Saturday, August 7

Capt. Guerry, arranger and operations officer for the B-17, promoted the following rank for a little flight up the Markham Valley:

Col. Hutchison, Ass't Chief of Staff, Fifth AF

Maj. General Vassi, A.I.F., 9th Division

Brig. General Eather, A.I.F.

Lt. Colonel Robertson, A.I.F.

Substantial fighter cover accompanied the flight. Low obliques were taken of the Nadzab Drome and vicinity. A young convoy met the B-17 at Seven-Mile. The Squadron C.O., the Red Cross Canteen Service, a photographer, the general's car, the colonel's car, and the operations' car formed a train, dramatically led by a M.P.

Excitement for the day was provided when one of the fighters "butched" his landing at Schwimmer. His props tore up the runway and caused another fighter to crack up. The other fighters finally believed the tower's red light and landed elsewhere.

Monday, August 9

Lts. Southard and Sykes flew up to Yule Island in an attempt to go to Wewak. Impregnable weather sent them home. That ace B-17 crew was out getting low coastline obliques of the Hanisch Harbor area at 250 and 600 feet. The 43rd Group furnished the ship and 9th Fighter Squadron the cover.

Intelligence Section's H. P. Rigsby brought home photos as well as successfully completing the visual recco of the New Britain coastline.

Tuesday, August 10

Ludtke and Loos set out for the Nadzab area today...

Moffat proceeded to Nubia this morning with two of the fighters weaving between his booms. He noted thirty barges moving madly around in Hansa Bay and kept the wires hot for a few minutes with a much garbled message...

Southard took the same mission, only he extended it to Wewak. Same story except he counted six more barges. The tactical missions are completed....

Wednesday, August 11

The Squadron Commander and the Operations Officer, in two F5s, really did a job in the Hopoi area with K-18 cameras.

Lt. Southard took photos, but they are listed as an unidentified drome. Could it have been a mirage? His real target was Wewak. The eager 80th Fighter sent two P-38s. The watch at Wewak was resumed by Lt. Murphy, who also reccoed the coastline down to Madang.

Ludtke's late afternoon attempt to get photos of Salamaua was thwarted by a little engine trouble.

Friday, August 13

S/L "Rummy" Foster and Lt. Murphy, flying those bolts of blue lightning, were photoing the Wewak area again today.

F4s, flown by the boy from the hills of Tennessee and Iowa's corn-fed Ludtke, nibbled a little more off the Nadzab request.

Eager Beaver Rigsby, flying the New Britain recco, found favorable weather and went on in to get beautiful pictures of Rabaul. This was a good day; weather, planes, cameras, pilots, all scoring 100%, even though it is Friday the 13th.

Sunday, August 15

The great day has arrived. The RAAF pilots are ready to be checked out on a photo mission. Rennels and Southard took Squadron Leader Atherton to the Watut River area where a few photos were taken. All turned out o.k.

New Britain coastline adapts itself well to low obliques so here we go again. It being Taylor's turn to plot the course, we find Ole Olson going along for the ride. He is listed on the report as Technical Advisor, technically speaking it is probably permissible, however.

Obliques were taken and, as usual, they were most graciously received. 39th Squadon furnished a fighter escort of 16 P-38s.

Lt Murphy carried out a visual recco of New Britain in the afternoon from a high altitude.

Monday, August 16

F/O Ludtke took one of the fledglings, Lt. C. O. Taylor, to Nadzab, but returned with nil photos due to engine trouble after two attempts in four different planes.

The Fates are very kind these days. We received the biggest news of the war today when word came through that the Great Kneeskern was alive and well. The message says he has head injuries but is otherwise O.K. Navy sent a Catalina to pick him up this afternoon, but for some reason they did not return. A tremendous welcoming committee came back disappointed. A question of the moment...what are Ghouls Olson and Taylor going to do with all the effects they tucked away?

Tuesday, August 17

Well, old Honest John finally made the grade at 1600 today. What a happy day! Kneeskern is the dirtiest thing yet seen in these parts, and with no shoe on the left foot, he looks like a club foot. His head is all wrapped in gauze, but he's the same guy and claims he is as tough as nails. I guess he is to be alive all this time. The first Cat cracked up landing at Huina, and so another went up and picked him up this morning at Kerema. You will all see him soon, boys, so be patient.

The biggest Allied air move ever attempted in this area commenced this morning. The heavies struck Wewak early this morning and the B-25s moved in at 0900-0910. Loos and Farmer took photos of the four dromes at Wewak before the strike and attempted them after the strike, but only collected Wewak Drome, the film having run out. Although no accurate estimate of the damage can be assessed, it is assumed that 70-80 planes were destroyed on the ground. Only 10-15 fighters intercepted, and one of these was definitely destroyed. A bird to the 71st Squadron, which became confused and struck But instead of Dagua.

The only other ship in the air was Murphy on his lonely New Britain recco. The guy is becoming a fixture over there.

Wednesday, August 18

(Capts. Guerry and Rennels and F/O Rigsby went to Wewak, but) bad weather prevented our reconnaissance, and the three men returned empty-handed. The bombers, however, got their lick in driving through heavy rain and clouds. The heavies and B-25s made their attacks and left more wreckage and devastation behind. The bombers and their escorting fighters shot 32 enemy aircraft from the air and many more probables.

Southard had a bad tussle with the weather. After getting through a front at Gasmata, he couldn't find a hole through which to return. So he went back to Dobodura via Long Island, Fly River, and Moresby.

Thursday, August 19

They decided to let the Nips lick their wounds for awhile, so the only ships to Wewak were 8th Photo's. Churchill and Duke went up there and caught Wewak and Boram Dromes. Other photography was prevented by numerous Zekes who were rapidly gaining altitude. Guess they didn't get them all, but from the pictures we've seen they got most of them.

Murphy hauled the mail run, but nil excitement as he reccoed the western half of New Britain and then returned.

Friday, August 20

Just the heavies struck Wewak this morning, but they too took their toll with many direct hits; they destroyed six intercepting fighters...Loos and Langdon photographed after the strike, although with some cloud interference. We hate to say it, boys, but old Photo Joe Loos missed Boram Drome.

Sunday, August 22

Still on our one-mission-a-day schedule, Rigsby and Churchill took out for Kavieng this morning. A valiant effort was their contribution for, after fighting through one front, they ran into another and were forced to turn back....

Tuesday, August 24

Furgason, attempting to get off for the third time, had the old 2,000 RPM mag drop and once again retired to the Ready Room to wait for another crack at this flying game.

Rigsby, voted the man I'd like most to take pictures with, sallied forth to Wewak and picked up the four dromes there with the usual efficiency.

"Beaker" Ludtke went to Nubia, Alexishafen, and Madang, collecting pictures of all three enroute.

Wednesday, August 25

Captain Alexander Guerry, Jr., with F/O Furgason in tow, rode high and handsome over the Lae area yesterday. Pin points of Nadzab, Heath's Plantation, two strips in the Lae-Hopoi area, and a mapping strip places him well up in the week's ratings. However, if he doesn't quit asking the writer to look at the pictures, he will find himself at the bottom of the list where he so rightfully belongs.

Thursday, August 26

Guerry and Taylor took the Colonel on a bombing mission to the Markham. Bombs dropped in the kunai grass area west of Nadzab, and it was all a waste of time. Despite Guerry's comments, he would be in dire straits without Olson or Taylor to lead him around.

Sykes and Avery flew to Nubia but turned back at Atemble because of the damn weather.

Klages saw nothing unusual in the New Britain area, it being covered except for odd portions of the coastline. Don't waste the engine time boys.

Friday, August 27

...Taylor and Dobbs, off on their own, set out for Wewak but couldn't collect on account of weather. They did get the Hansa Bay area and a little A/A at 31,000. Come, come, boys, are you sure it wasn't just a little dark cumulus?

Saturday, August 28

Foster and Blum turned in a good day's work this morning. Rummy picked off the four dromes at Wewak and Blum the Hansa Bay area. The Zekes were really getting up there, 26,000 (feet), but couldn't reach our stratosphere boys...

Southard and Langdon did the New Britain job but could only cover the Western half of the Island. What are they trying to pull, Iron Man stuff? Two days in a row is too much.

Sunday, August 29

Rennels and Furgason traipsed over to Lae today and collected two K-18 strips in the Lae-Hopoi area. By their own admission, they weren't really on the money so we sent Murphy out to pick up the leftovers. Do we start calling him Scavenger?

Sykes is complaining again that the extra pair of eyes doesn't see everything it is supposed to see. He and Duke went to Wewak and collected photographs as well as five Zeros about 10,000 feet below them. Confidentially, boys, as I remember it, the old men didn't see too much when they first got here.

Klages is a veteran at this N. B. recco. He even collected pictures of Gloucester while running the circuit.

Monday, August 30

The circuit produced results today with Southard leading Farmer to Cape Gloucester. Plenty pix of Gloucester for the Sixth Army, but in the process, Southard lost Farmer. The new pilots should spend more time listening to the pilots. They have a lot to learn.

Foster and Taylor ran the Wewak job today, and the final straw has been laid across 8th Photo's back. The strike on Wewak was to occur at 1115. We were to photograph results one hour after the strike. At 1220, Foster and Taylor slipped across the dromes and returned to base. The pictures reveal the bombers just making the approach to the target. Guess they need Taylor and Olson as navigators on their easy mission.

Tuesday, August 31

(Except for one B-17, three F-5s and two F-4s, all other aircraft were shipped out of the squadron during the day —Auths)

Sykes and Duke landed at Marilinan and then took off for Hollandia. They couldn't make the grade on account of weather, but did collect three of the dromes at Wewak.

Murphy and his fighter friends were forced back from Rabaul by a front along New Britain's coast. Let's call it a day.

Wednesday, September 1

...Rennels, naively believing Taylor's weather forecast, set forth to Rabaul in high spirits, actually thinking he would return with pictures. Alack-a-day, the Gazelle Peninsula was just one big front and Rennels returned downcast and disillusioned. "Ole Hoss" had let him down.

Thursday, September 2

Our fighting leader, J. G. Foster, was forced to curb the indomitable spirit today and return to the fold pictureless. Hampered by two trailing fighters, he first turned back because the fighters had engine trouble and later because of an insurmountable front at Gasmata. That much for the newspapers. All true, of course, but he's just another of the boys. War weary, just like the rest of us.

Olson, ably assisted by Rennels and Davis, completed the mosaic of thirty mile. It was a noble piece of work, and unhindered by Guerry, who was sleeping, was completed in a minimum of time.

Friday, September 3

Old Fred Rennels had his troubles today. He set out for Wewak leading a fighter gently but firmly. He nicely stayed below the overcast at about 14,000' and throttled back to 20 inches, but instead of the fighter looking for Zeros, he spent time looking for Fred. For some reason even at 20 inches he couldn't get the fighter to fly formation in the direction of Wewak. It ended up with the fighter shouting, "I'm looking for you," as he headed back to Dobodura. Fred gave up in disgust and came down and photographed the Bogadjim Road. I don't know how the fighters explain it, but we have our own ideas.

Southard had better luck with his fighters to Rabaul. One of them was forced to turn back from Gasmata, but the other stayed right in there and the pictures were taken. Flight complete, nil excitement. Ten took off but never got close.

Sykes and Duke went off from Marilinan and up to Bogadjim Road. They got pictures of the road, and while doing so a Zero flew calmly between them. He either didn't see them or was just hoping they didn't, for no one made a move.

Saturday, September 4

Gentlemen, we have been encroached upon! Air Force yesterday afternoon ordered all of our remaining planes and one of our Marilinan ships to Dobodura. Foster and Rennels went over this morning, and Fairbanks and Dobbs, with an assortment of mechanics, camera repairmen, and communications men went over by transport at 0430/K. This motley crew will fly New Britain reccos for "D" Day and the "D" Plus days. God help them if they miss a Jap raiding party.

Flash! The Navy put ashore an amphibious party at the Buso River in the early hours of this morning. Lae is about to be enveloped by our forces. Place your bets, Gentlemen. My own estimate is September 24th.

The above-mentioned boys from over the Hump flew three missions to New Britain with six ships. Nothing happened, and they left the area at 11:30 as ordered, and at 1230 the Japs came down in force. Our fighters still messed them up a bit. 23 definites.

No action from this side. Guerry, Olson, and friends rested for the day.

Sunday, September 5

The B-17 (crew) produced wonderous results and individually had the time of their lives covering the Nadzab activity. Photos were taken of the entire landing operation. At 1018 the B-25s bombed and strafed Gabsonkek and Nadzab. At 1020 the A-20s went hurtling by with great trails of white smoke issuing therefrom. These quickly settled into thick walls of white which surrounded Nadzab on the east, west, and north. At 1025, in swept approximately 85 transports, and a moment later the air was filled with a thousand mushrooms. The white chutes of the men, the greens, reds, blues, and orange of the various supplies, all fell out with machinelike precision, and the whole spectacle provided a Kaleidiascope of color. They fell behind the great walls of smoke, and after landing and rushing to the supplies they began moving through the kunai grass....

The "17" also investigated the landing of the previous night at Hopoi, but it looked more like a summer resort than an advance on the enemy. The landing barges were riding serenely at anchor, the troops were swimming in the Buso River, and nary a Jap was in evidence. Passengers aboard on this trip were Major General Vassey of N. G. F. and Vern Haugland and Van Atta of the UP and INS. Also, Combat Camera Unit #5 provided Lt. Blake and an assistant, who photographed the whole action with 35mm movies. Colonel Jennings of the paratroops watched with tremendous interest the entire landing from the radio compartment. Everyone had a big time.

Lt. Duke from Marilinan Detachment delivered the goods with pictures of But and Dagur and 9,000' pix of the Bogadjim Road.

Monday, September 6

Blum made the long, tiresome (first) trip to Hollandia today and found it clear as a bell. The Nippos have done a good job, and the strip is close to 6,000 feet long with a revetment area. There are at the moment 42 planes on deck and will handle a good many more. Looks like another place we have to drive them out of.

The really good news tonight is the arrival of Lt. Col. "Pop" Polifka, with innumerable stories of the war in the other theaters that he has seen. He is imparting some good info on what we can look forward to on return to the States. "Pop" will be with us for three days, then off again for a tour of the other theaters. Incidentally, despite what they say about rationing, "Pop" has added about fifty pounds to his frame, so things can't be too bad.

Foster and Rennels, returning from Dobo, brought 8 rolls of film and an asortment of poop sheets. We spent an hour fitting the right poop sheet to the right film. Sixth Army shouts with glee as these cover those areas they've been hollering for. The big news on these reccos we're shooting out from Dobo is the annoying fact that after patrolling for six hours a day, we finally desert for good full reasons and then the Nips send a raiding party down half an hour later. We know the answer, but will the Generals figure it out?

Wednesday, September 8

The B-17 gave the Madang area the old one-two-three today. Nulty and Co. photographed the shore from Cape Croiselles to Kepler Point. A little film trouble marred the day's effort, but the stuff still looks good to everybody but ourselves. The hypercritical eye to the experts, of course. Nothing but perfection will fill the bill. In addition, the boys collected those low obliques of Rooke Island everyone is screaming for.

Lt. Lamdin, Doc Robertson, Horatio Holton, Tom Farmer, Dick Shipway, Bill Gailfus, Byron Dobbs, and Thadeus Jones at Nadzab around the end of 1943. (Gailfus)

All in all, a good day's work.

Duke seems to have caught the war spirit up there at Marilinan. He photographed Nubia from 12,000 and Alexishafen and Madang from 10,000. That's not recommended procedure, but it's hard to chastise a man for a job well done.

Avery couldn't get into Wewak because of weather conditions, but he did collect Alexishafen on his way home.

Thursday, September 9

...Southard did the Wewak job in fine style this morning, catching all four dromes. Dagua looks like it is loading up again. About time for the 25s to work it over again.

Blum did a tri-met job for the Colonel of the Nadzab to Cape Gerhard and then flew in with the film. The boys seem to like the outposts.

Friday, September 10

We flew no missions today, for all of the F-4s and the F-5s were either on the other side or not in commission. However, the boys started coming back from Dobodura. This bit of good news was changed to bad by the disappearance of one of the new pilots. Lt. C. O. Taylor was returning from Dobodura with Captains Foster and Rennels and Lt. Sykes. As they started to cross the ranges, the signal to break formation was given, and each man was to get through the weather in his own way. Capt. Foster went through on instruments, Capt. Rennels came through a hole, Lt. Sykes went over the top of the whole thing, and Lt. Taylor has not been heard from. The search of the Allied Dromes yielded nothing. Taylor was an eager guy and would have made out fine. Sure hope he turns up.

Saturday, September 11

The other boys returned from Dobodura, leaving only Lts. Murphy, Langdon, Farmer, and F/O Furgason to carry on the New Britain recco. The recco will now be flown by 8th Photo pilots in fighter planes. This will relieve us of a duty that was wasting our precious few photo planes.

Old Ludbutt went over the top today escorted by two fighters and got to Wewak but couldn't photo. He came down the coast and picked up Uligan or Eitel Freidrich Harbor, they are both the same place.

Avery and Lankford did the circuit run, but Finschhafen and New Britain were loaded up with a front so they returned emptyhanded.

Monday, September 13

...Sykes journeyed all the way to Wewak but couldn't find anything open except the town area. Dobbs and Avery got some more of those "extra hurry—rush work" pictures in the Lae area. Radio security was completely maintained as one of the boys came forth with this news to the ground station: "I'm over Lae at 10,000 feet taking pictures. The weather doesn't look good for mapping." Try that one on the way to Rabaul some day and you'll probably get a welcoming committee to greet you.

Tuesday, September 14

Off went the B-17 today to get pictures of the south coast of New Britain and to look for Zeros. The route forecast was excellent, and so naturally there was a big front in the middle of the Solomon Sea that had to be widely skirted. Once over to New Britain, however, things cleared up nicely. Nulty had a field day with five rolls of K-18. Off Gasmata Taylor yelled, "Get the hell out of here before they shoot us down." Came the simultaneous and encouraging reply from Foster, Guerry, and Fairbank, "Shut up." Highlight of the trip home was Fairbank doing acrobatics on instruments.

Off went Ludtke to Hollandia today, but according to him we had to turn back at "Atiap." Our map specialists found he was talking about "Aitape." That's right, Ludbutt, you fly 'em and we'll pronounce them.

Duke and Klages tried themselves off on Ye Olde Circuit, but 'twas the usual question of bad weather. Klages did manage to aid the cause a bit with some Cape Gloucester K-18.

Wednesday, September 15

Part of the heart and soul of Eighth Photo left us today...Olson and Rennels climbed aboard a transport homeward bound this morning, and Sowers will follow tomorrow...And with these three officers went two of our enlisted men, Able and Pugh...

...Sykes spent the day going to Hollandia to grab some pictures as he buzzed the drome at 14,500'. The Japs were so amazed that they didn't fire a shot. Blum started out for Wewak but had oxygen mask trouble at Kerema and had to return.

Murph with Duke along picked up a little in the Kaiapit area on the General's special request. Klages, flying a matinee mission to Boana and Sio, managed to get a few shots of the latter despite generally bad weather.

Thursday, September 16

...Churchill and Blum went to Marilinan enroute to Hollandia and Wewak, but only one fighter was there to accompany. Hence, Church proceeded to Wewak, and Blum came home. As Church was beginning his run over Wewak at 27,000 feet, he spied six fighters coming up to intercept him and rapidly drawing into range. No doubt hoping for a grandstand seat at a good show, our photo pilot bravely said to the fighter: "Do you want to stick around and get into a scrap?" "Well, no!" came the reply, "There are six on their side and only one on ours." Accordingly, both pilots left the area with all possible speed.

Duke and Klages took the circuit today and piled up over four hours flying time. Some pictures resulted, but as usual, the weather was mostly bad.

Friday, September 17

...One of the new boys damaged a fighter over at Dobodura today, and loud yells from the 9th Fighter are expected any moment. First reports indicate he just plain taxied into a ditch. The new pilots have now destroyed two airplanes in only a month of flying, and, brother, that ain't good!

Saturday, September 18

Lots of effort, but not too much in the way of results today. Murphy tried Hollandia and Wewak but ended up with a strip in the Ramu. Blum and Duke took the circuit and brought back odds and ends of value here and there. Sykes went out to get Cape Hoskins but got nothing more than brake trouble at Marilinan. In the afternoon, the Officers finally got together enough players for a softball team and trounced Compilation 9-8 in a rough-and-tumble affair.

Sunday, September 19

...Blum was sent into the Dumpu area to get low obliques, which he did beautifully. Then Air Force decided they really wanted verticals. Duke and Klages went over to Dobodura and then took off for Finschhafen. They covered this and cleaned up the urgent strip in the Dampier Straits. All out of film, they returned to base.

The B-17 had an eventful trip to Townsville today to pick up alcoholic supplies. Ground fog cut down the visibility to half the length of the runway, but realizing the importance of the mission, Capt. Guerry pulled *R.F.D. Tojo* off the ground at 0600, and after a few hundred feet on instruments broke out and headed south. At Townsville, Capt. Foster took over for the landing and got it in after three passes at the field. The first time copilot Guerry failed to get the flaps, and the second time the horn indicated landing gear trouble.

At Townsville, the B-17ers found Capt. Loos waiting with 18 fighters under his direct command. Garbutt wouldn't clear him to Moresby without a B-25 or B-26 to guide him in. We wonder how Garbutt would feel about our little jaunts to Wewak, Rabaul, and Kavieng. The crew of the B-17 was in complete despair when it discovered that Gibson had not a single pint of beer to send back on the plane. Chaseling turned out to be the man of the hour as he lined up some Aussie Cobber of his and got us beer and gin in abundance. NFG's always high priority was raised even more, and Fairbank's slipped a little bit lower.

On the way home, Navigator Taylor missed Moresby by 120 miles, so far that at first Guerry and Foster couldn't determine their location. Fortunately, Foster soon saw a spot he recognized and the boys were able to head for Moresby and land there in the rain ten minutes before dark. We don't expect to hear much more from Taylor about navigation.

Leonhardt got his captaincy today, and Sowers broke through with a majority. The beer from the south came in very handy for a big celebration.

Monday, September 20

Klages took off for Marilinan and Hollandia but couldn't find his fighter cover. He called in for instructions and Taylor with his head way up sent back word that fighter cover was supposed to be picked up at Marilinan. In the meantime, the fighter cover from the 80th had tagged onto a 39th Fighter over our field by mistake. He didn't realize his error until he reached Marilinan and landed; but all worked out well, as Klages came in only a minute or two later.

Murph did a swell job over Rabaul, but strange things happened to him, too. He took four shots of Rapopo, and the third picture with the drome apparently right in the middle was a complete blank.

Guerry brought back lots of pictures in the Madang and Dumpu areas. His right engine cut out completely on the way home, and so he feathered it and landed on one. That puts him well out in front of the "Engine-out Landing Club," with two such landings in a P-38 and one in a B-17.

Sykes dropped over to New Britain and then came back by way of Kiaipit, getting K-18 both places.

Tuesday, September 21

Remnants of the fighter pilots from school arrived today by transport after five days in Brisbane to ferry planes back. Such awful luck! Captain Loos arrived on the field day before yesterday with six brand new fighters (P-38H). 8th Photo now has a complement of photo ships, fighters, and one B-17. My, my, what a squadron! Now we fly our own fighter cover, and good luck to the boys. We have two new members in the squadron with the arrival of 1st Lt. Charles K. Taylor, Jr., and Charles E. Bateson from the 80th Fighter Squadron. Two of our men, Furgason and Langford, went to the 80th. Not a bad swap, because we got two men who have lots of hours. We shall get plenty of what we're looking for, and that's fighter cover.

The missions today were Klages to Kavieng. He turned in a very good job. Major Foster landed at a field today that used to be a hot spot for the old 8th, namely Lae. He reports the field suitable for light planes. He was a little sore when they wanted to charge him 30 pounds for a Jap rifle. He did some trading with the Aussies though—a rusty Jap rifle for two cartons of Camels (brown with mildew).

Blum and Dobbs flew the recco of the North and South coasts of New Britain.

Wednesday, September 22

...Churchill and Ludtke up to the Markham for that area so hard to find, Dumpu. Three nice mapping strips along the top of the ranges and around Bena Bena were also obtained.

We are glad to announce that this cleans up the Markham and Ramu Valleys of all mapping. Much of the credit goes to these two men. Fairbank has been struggling with this area since last September. We'll admit that if he hadn't driven us so hard we'd still have half of it yet to fly.

Friday, September 24

...The weather man was tough on the missions today. Foster to Kavieng was stopped by a Solomon Sea front. Rigsby and Holton, who flew his first mission, were stopped by a New Guinea front. Sykes turned back one hour out. We have a new system on the weather reports. Take the report and translate it exactly opposite, thus giving you the actual weather.

Saturday, September 25

For the first time, and this goes for the other theaters as well, a photo squadron flew its own fighter cover with its own airplanes and pilots. Capt. Loos escorted Lt. Southard to Wewak. Camera trouble, but Dagua and But Dromes came out satisfactorily. Lt. C. E. Taylor escorted Major Foster to Hollandia. The pictures were very good, with a nice mapping strip from Piore River to Suain. The fighter boys report nil enemy planes sighted, thus nil victories scored.

The other photo missions were Churchill and Ludtke to Lepsius Pt. and Saidor. Good picture which shows the boys are still in the groove. Churchill picked up two mapping strips on Lang Island. Murphy and Klages to New Britain. Trimet photos Unea Island to Garove Island and operational photos Hoskins and Gloucester Dromes. Recco 100% completed. Eight planes in the air sets a record.

Sunday, September 26

...Lt. Duke, with Moffat and Clark as escort, took off for New Britain. Clark lost a canopy and Duke had engine trouble, so the mission was canceled.

8PRS F-4 #17 undergoing repairs at 14-Mile (Reindl)

Farmer and Blum took the circuit and photographed the coastline from Sio to Saidor. Good work.

Tuesday, September 28

...Sykes to Hollandia with Bateson as escort took the best pictures obtained thus far of that area.

Churchill turned in some excellent flying by covering the Bogadjim Road from 9,000 ft. It was so good that a mosaic was laid and reprinted for the heavies. Klages accompanied him and took another coastline strip around Saidor, which cleans up the original request.

Taylor and Jones escorted Southard in two vain attempts to reach Rabaul, each time turning back with engine trouble. Here's hoping for better luck next time.

Langdon, escorted by Rigsby to Wewak, looked over the areas the B-24s hit earlier with small eggs ranging up to king size. They report a good job by the bombers, but the photos only cover Boram and part of the town area at Wewak.

Wednesday, September 29

(Three missions—Ludtke with escort to Rabaul, Major Foster to Kavieng, and Blum and Farmer to Markham Valley and Cape Gloucester—were all aborted due to weather. -Auths.)

Thursday, September 30

...The day's orders called for Hollandia, Wewak, Markham, Kavieng, and Rabaul. All scored standing up save for Langdon-Loos duo, slated for Hollandia. They took off from Lae with belly tanks bulging, but returned when Langdon discovered his oxygen equipment wasn't complete. DeLasso put his fighter down with a bang, the nose wheel collapsing. Inasmuch as a woman is the only thing that can harm a Texan, the good Captain emerged unscathed. Major Foster and Johnny Nielsen flew to Lae in 2130 to check the damage and to see if a Lae junk dealer wouldn't give two bob for the wreck if Loos were thrown into the bargain. No deal.

After shooting Wewak assignment, Lt. Duke and his bodyguard, Lt. Moffat, set out for Moresby and the fireside. Then Lt. Duke spotted four Tonys 2,000 ft. above him. Of course, Moffat insisted on taking them all on. Duke finally talked him into leaving the area—just as the Anthony's started to peel down.

Saturday, October 2

And so it came about. The weather gent said to give a go. Result: Murphy turned back at Marilinan when he smelled a front, and he returned to base with Loos and Jones. To hell with Wewak, Alexishafen, and Madang.

At mid-morning Lt. Klages and Farmer took off for New Britain. Weather, engine trouble, separation, gremlins, and weather, weather, weather, sent the two back home.

Sunday, October 3

The Sabbath was properly observed today. No missions. The day was spent lugging lumber at the new Officers' Club, sleeping, and second guessing. Rigsby and Sykes couldn't keep their minds on their work, thinking of their leaves which start tomorrow.

Monday, October 4

Back to normal standards today, with eight planes in the air. Weather was good in the New Guinea area, and Lt. Langdon, with fighters Moffat and Clark, got thru to Wewak and covered the dromes completely. Blum, Jones, and Bateson weren't as fortunate with Rabaul, and they returned fresh out of pictures.

Klages and Farmer took the milk run and milked out photos of New Britain.

No excitement on any of the mission pictures, but still no Zeros. Sykes, Rigsby, and Murphy got off early this morning for Sydney. Murphy, with hopes for a better trip than last time—Rigsby with a peculiar gleam in his eye—and Sykes cussing like hell because it would be another night before he could begin his week's sack time!

Tuesday, October 5

Rabaul attempted by "Photo" Duke and fighters Loos and Taylor today, but the weather was still bad and the flight returned pictureless. Churchill and Ludtke took the circuit and couldn't find a damn thing open for pictures due to excessive frontal activity. Major Foster and Capt. Guerry even set out for their ass buster to Wakde today, but a poor weather report at the last minute kept them on the ground.

Foster and Guerry then busted old 27 loose from her ropes and drove up to the Madang area to catch some ground support photography. Our cool and steady navigator, "Hoss Taylor," was again up to his tricks. On being jumped by four P-39s in the Ramu Valley, Hoss lost his usual composure and began tangling himself with parachutes and guns. He didn't get to his guns, thank God, or we probably would have been casualties, but he did get to his parachute. Swore the 39s were 47s, too, just to add a little confusion to the crew. A while later he had the 17 going down in flames over Bogadjim from accurate ack-ack, but that turned out to be prop wash from a steep 360 degree turn. He did get us back home, however, after losing two bob to Guerry betting that a piece of land sure as hell wasn't Yule Island...it was, and he missed his ETA by a full twenty minutes. It wasn't all horseplay, however, because six rolls of K-18 were expended, getting strips around Dumpu and the Bogadjim Road, Fairbank again directing photography, and got by without any serious error.

Wednesday, October 6

"Joe" Klages with Moffat and Holton got through to Rabaul today and brought back nice pictures of dromes, town, and harbor. Klages' first trip to our beloved spot, and damned if he didn't think they had brought in the whole Jap fleet for him to photograph. No excitement, however, except controlling the pilot's enthusiasm in the briefing room after his return. Intelligence is going to install wall chains for use on these eager war pilots. Southard and Dobbs photographed the required areas on the north coast of New Britain, and also a few shots in the Sio area.

Officers lost the afternoon ball game to the Squadron, 6 to 1, but intend on doing better later in the week. "Iron Ass" Loos still driving on the Officers' Club, which is coming along nicely. Should be done by the first of the month.

Thursday, October 7

Air Force is still mightily interested in Rabaul pictures because of the intended strike there in the near future. Blum, (Photo) Bateson, and Jones give it a go today, but again the weather was too poor to flub around in, and the boys came home unhappy. Farmer and Avery picked up good K-18 recco material in the Gloucester, Sio, and Madang areas to keep up the average of the day. No excitement, and still no Zeros.

Friday, October 8

Pilots Langdon, Taylor, and Clark to Rabaul today, but the usual weather trouble was encountered and the trio returned without pictures. Churchill and Duke to the Ramu, Madang, and New Britain, but it seemed they conspired against Fairbank and only obtained pictures for our dinkum Aussie, "W. T. (Whiskey Tenor)" Chaseling. (The Intelligence Dept has been investigating Captain Chaseling's voice for some time, and it still can't determine what makes it that way.) Late in the afternoon our good friends in Air Force decided they needed a look at Alexishafen Drome to see if the 30 planes that had been present on the drome for two days were still there. Lt. Ludtke with fighters Bateson and Holton skipped off at 1313 to see if they could please them.

Ludtke and Holton lost sight of Bateson somewhere in the Madang area, and the last message received over the interphone from Bateson was, "Bandits at five o'clock. Let's get 'em." Evidently Bateson had seen the Japs and was maneuvering for an attack when the other pilots lost contact with him. We have no word from Lt. Bateson, but we have every hope that he got himself a couple of little bastards and will come walking in one of these days. Although relatively new and unknown to the Squadron, Charlie was a veteran fighter pilot of this theatre with over 90 combat missions in 39s and 38s. Our association with him in the few weeks he was with the Squadron proved him to be an excellent pilot and a hell of a good felow. Our thoughts and hopes are for him and safe return.

Saturday, October 9

Dobbs, with protection by Moffat and Loos, came thru today with pictures of the installations in the Rabaul area. When we get one, we always have trouble with the other. No pictures from Avery, Jones, and taylor of Wewak and vicinity due to old man weather. The milk run ships, piloted by Southard and Klages, did get operational pictures of the Madang area, so we are still batting .666. Nothing of interest to bull about...

Sunday, October 10

Another record flight made today by members of the Squadron. C. O. Foster and Ops Guerry took off bright and early for their pre-planned trip to Wakde Island. They made it all right, mapping all the way up and back and stopping at Hollandia on the way back for excellent photos of the drome there. 690 miles from Lae to Wakde makes it by far the longest trip ever made by pursuit type aircraft in this theater...

Moffat turned photo today and accompanied by Jones and Taylor photoed hell out of Rabaul. Langdon and Blum experienced results by shooting Madang and Alexishafen and a bit of the Bogadjim Road.

Monday, October 11

Air Force and Rabaul—Churchill got it for them today with Loos and Holton providing that good top cover. Duke and Farmer K- 18'd operational points on the north coast of New Britain and over in the Madang-Sio area. This milk run is boring to write about, but it really picks up the pictures. Imagine it's boring as hell to fly too, but that's war...

Tuesday, October 12

The big day arrived and 8th Photo was there with almost everthing it had. 100 odd B-25s strafed the Rabaul area at about 1000 this morning, concentrating on the fighter dromes. At 1200 approximately 80 B-24s went for shipping and sundry targets in the harbor and town areas. Really had the big hopes for a complete surprise and plenty of destruction, but leave it up to the 8th to mess up the works. Pictures were taken by Foster, with plenty of good support from Charlie Taylor on the fighter end, the pair remaining in the area for about 90 minutes so as to make the job complete. Southard, with Loos and Jones as support, took color pictures about 15 minutes later, and finally at 2:30 Ludtke and Moffat, with "Killer" Clark protecting, finished off with more K-18 runs over the supposedly washed-out Rabaul. When all the pictures were developed, the observed damage wasn't nearly what was expected, and all afternoon Generals and Colonels were calling the pilots, pleading with them to say that they personally observed 5 warships roll over and sink, etc.—they had to, damn it—didn't 80 B-24s bomb the harbor? Next morning's A-2 report from the bomber crews substantiated the fact that they can't even see to work a bombsight, let alone observe direct hits from 23,000'. According to the heavies, they sank everything in the harbor; according to 8th Photo's pictures, they're damn lucky if they sank a total of five good-sized ships. Oh, well, maybe they'll be better next time.

Not being satisfied with 8 planes over Rabaul in one day, Klages, Dobbs, and Avery took the F-4s on the milk run and brought back photos of Gloucester, Dampier Striats, Rooke Island, Long Island, and operational photos of Madang and Alexishafen area. So ended the most active day in the Squadron flying for some time.

Wednesday, October 13

Langdon and Taylor took the Wewak mission today and came home with the bacon. Saw a few Zeros, but even C. Taylor wasn't about to go down after 11 of them at 5,000'. Farmer and Duke were NG Force boys today and were content to run out their K-18 cameras in the Ramu Valley areas. Rabaul attempted by Blum, Loos, and Holton, but weather has set in again and no pictures taken. Old 27 spread her wings again, much to the lab's disgust, and flew around the north coast of New Britain, taking 1000' off-shore obliques of most everything they could find. Wound up with ten K-18 rolls, and immediately the Lab began undoing the labors. I think they salvaged four out of ten rolls, but the other six look as if the jungle crud got to them. Believe all the pictures can be used, but God help the photo interpreters.

Note a few statistics on last week's flying by certain of 8th Photo's boys. Wish someone would ask Polifka about the hottest photo pilot in the theater after getting a look at this: Moffat has been to Rabaul in either photo or fighter ships four days out of the last eight, plus a B-17 mission of seven hours. Loos to Rabaul five times in the last eight days in fighters, while Charlie Taylor has hit Rabaul or Wewak six times out of the last eight. Brother, that's flying!

Thursday, October 14

Lts. Ludtke and Churchill handled the N. B circuit admirably, shooting everything from K-18s of Gloucester and Borgen Bay, Cape Raoult and Rein Bay to excellent mapping of the "water" in the Dampier Straits. Southard and an 80th Fighter vigilante smacked into a front at Mt. Hagen, so Wewak went unreccoed. Lt. Taylor and Lt. Clark provided top cover for Brother Dobbs to Rabaul. Clouds prevented photos, so a visual recco was followed by shots of Hoskins Drome on the route back.

Sunday, October 17

Six pilots of the squadron took off from Schwimmer with high hopes of getting beautiful pictures. Soaring over the cloud-covered Markham Valley, Farmer and Langdon were stopped cold. Langdon, not to be outdone or come home with that "no pictures" feeling, took a K-18 run over Tolokiwa Island. Who knows, that might have been out next photo request.

Ludbutt, sometimes known as Lt. Ludtke, guided two of the 80th fighters toward Wewak. Around Bena Bena they ran into one of the highest, longest, blackest, wettest, and meanest-looking fronts in the area, so a quick 180 degrees was executed.

Southard had his hands full on the Rabaul mission and also ran into a little tough luck. With Capt. Loos and Lt Taylor keeping careful watch on his tail they started over Rapopo at 26,000', the weather forced them down to 20,000' over Lakunai. That's bringing the pictures back. On orders from Bomb Com(mand), Southard landed at Dobodura to have the film developed and printed for the medium units. The photo lab (in name only) messed up practically the whole roll trying to develop it. Southard lent a hand and managed to salvage enough to show them what the score was for tomorrow's raid. He landed back at Schwimmer at 1915. Good work.

Monday, October 18

(Unescorted raid of B-24s and B-25s hit Rabaul fields and destroyed a number of Japanese aircraft on the ground for the loss of about nine bombers destroyed or badly damaged—Auths.)

...Sykes, Rigsby, and Jones to Rabaul. Forced to turn back 10 miles off Buna due to weather.

Dobbs and Avery and stinko weather made the mission entirely nil.

Guerry flew co-pilot on a B-24 which was forced to turn back due to weather. From what I could gather they ended up over Kiriwina circling one direction and then another in a very small opening in the clouds. Dizzy guys, these bomber pilots.

Tuesday, October 19

At last the 8th Photo fighters tangle with the enemy. Lts. Taylor and Jones in fighters with Churchill in a photo ship were jumped by nine Japs over Wewak. Belly tanks were dropped, with photo ship climbing to 30,000 feet and returning to base.

Taylor was being followed by two Nips at a slightly lower altitude. Turning sharply into them and diving, an 80 round burst was fired. Instead of pulling up into a head-on pass, the Nips dived out of it. Taylor, not giving up, kept his head until he was practically on his back. It paid off, too, because Nip number one was claimed as a probable. Jones dived in on a 90 degree pass, but the Jap turned into and away from him, thus giving a chance for only a short burst. No damage observed. After the single pass and being slightly outnumbered plus 500 miles from home, They returned to Lae with plenty, so on to Schwimmer. Four fighters up there instead of two is all we wish for.

The Rabaul mission turned out to be quite a success. Murphy took the pictures with very little clouds present. On his left was Holton, and his right, Rigsby. Ack Ack was received at 33,000', first time at that altitude. On the way home Murph caused a little excitement by sighting two probable P-40s or P47s. He just could not point them out to the fighter boys. It seems there's never a dull moment.

Foster, Guerry, Tarkington, and Taylor prepare to leave for beautiful Sydney in our B-26.

Wednesday, October 20

At early dawn, the B-26 piloted by Major Foster and Capt. Guerry took off smooth as silk. Heading for Townsville, Brisbane, and Sydney, they will get there tonight, says Taylor. They are to bring back supplies ranging from photographic to Officers' Club furnishings, with emphasis on the latter. Capt. Loos has been driving the boys hard, and the club is progressing nicely. Lack of materials has caused a slight let-up for the present, but DeLasso, who is C. O. in Foster's absence, says, "You all will finish that club by the first or else." I guess we'll just have to humor him.

The flying weather proved to be a disappointment today. Loos, Clark, and Ludtke turned back unable to get into Lae. The circuit ships to Ramu, Finschhafen, and any other place that is free from clouds turned back due to weather. After bad weather the last few days we look forward to tomorrow and photo weather, we hope!

Thursday, October 21

The circuit ships cleaned up shooting two full rolls of K-18 and part of a tri-met roll. Photos of Satelburg, which spot is becoming more important each day, were obtained with a run north of that area around the Song River. Fortification Pt., Alexishafen, and Madang were covered with K-18. The tri-met run was from the Mindjim River to the Gusap area. We have Lts. Southard and Duke to thank for that mission.

Ludbutt, Taylor, and Holton attempted to reach Kavieng, but the weather proved to be rather difficult. The only results were several hours engine time on the planes.

Two fighters from the 80th Sq. were sent to Wewak with our photo ship piloted by Lt. Langdon. One turned back at 30-Mile and the other in the Madang area—some protection. Undaunted, Ole Photo Joe continued to Wewak; bad weather over the target, so Nubia (Hansa Bay) and a short coastal strip were taken. A new high for ack-ack—33,700' over Hansa Bay.

Congratulations to Murphy, C. K. Taylor, and Hamlin, who are now captains. It was a long, hard struggle, but the men made it and bought the beer. That's the part we Lts. look forward to—the party after the promotion.

Friday, October 22

...Churchill and C. K. Taylor are two tired boys tonight. They had quite an experience which called for plenty of topnotch flying ability. They flew to Buka Passage through frontal activity. After braving the ack-ack and obtaining beautiful pictures, lo and behold, the hole they had flown through on the way out had disappeared on the way home. They hunted high and low. No hole. Sucking in their guts, they entered the front at 18,000' and experienced some terrific instrument flying, and a P38 was never meant for that kind of stuff. It's all over now, but not forgotten by these two men.

Farmer to Rabaul with good photos. Job well done. The weather is still holding out on the circuit and as a result we get New Britain and Finschbafen. Avery and Dobbs do the good work...

Saturday, October 23

(Captain Charles K. Taylor was listed MIA in the Open Bay area of New Britain on a Rabaul mission.—Auths.)

...The Rabaul missions, fast and furious, came off as follows: Murphy, Taylor, and Holton were to go in after the bombers. Sykes, Jones, and Rigsby, 30 minutes after the strike. The first flight with Murphy had to circle and wait, so when the photo run was started, the Zekes were up pretty high and trailing them. Holton got separated over the target, and after being followed by two Zekes for awhile, he returned to base. Murphy and Taylor, followed by four Nips, ran into the Sykes flight over Keravat. Sykes turned the flight around and broke off to return to base after talking the situation over. Rigsby and Clark saw Taylor and Murphy pass beneath them heading back to base. It was decided to take one pass at the four Zekes. Clark could drop only one tank and was forced to climb and return to base. Rigsby dropped both tanks and made a rear quarter attack. The first one (Zero) attempted to turn into the P-38, and the third one was a little higher so he was singled out, but as the range was shortened he flipped over on his back and Split "S" out.

Rigsby broke off and was followed by the Zekes for a couple of minutes. Meantime, Sykes, who had started for home, ran into four Tonys, the first two opening fire on him. He ducked into a cloud and out again—still there, so back into the cloud. He finally lost them and was returning home when he got a call from Rigsby, whose left engine was out and was over Wide Bay at 9,000' on one engine. Sykes turned back and dropped down to that altitude searching the area in the photo ship until he picked up Rigsby five or ten minutes out to sea from Cape Orford. He flew with him to Kiriwina and Rigsby says (the) company was appreciated. Everyone returned safely, except Taylor, with Moiph getting Rabaul pictures and Sykes picking up Keravat.

Ludtke and Duke to Madang and Alexishafen for operational photos. This morning, Major Foster, Capt. Loos, and Fairbank took on leave to Sydney, leaving Guerry as C. O.

Sunday, October 24

The circuit was successfully run by Farmer, and Avery catching operational and mapping stuff in Talasea, Madang, and the Ramu. Langdon and two fighter pilots from the 80th set out for Kavieng, with Langdon and one of the escorters reaching the New Ireland base. Photos of the dromes were taken, and a run over Garove and Mundua Island were made on the way home by way of crossing the T. On the way up, Langdon spotted a couple of vessels—maybe DD and one M/V. He sent in the sighting to 8th Photo communications. The position was relayed to the operations. The wrong grid card, inadvertently dated October 24th by Bristowe, was picked up. Captain Guerry was given the position as being on the beach at Buna Bay, practically. He called Air Force, then went to communications only to learn that he had given AF the wrong position. He called AF with side remarks as to the background and ancestry of Bristowe, Duke, Chalupa, and others who had ____ed up. Langdon landed and reported that it was a DD and large M/V above Garove Island.

Dobbs with Jones and Clark scored standing up with operational photos, spotting a DD leaving Blanche Bay.

Monday, October 25

While Churchill and Ludtke hit the milk run, Guerry and Sykes in the B-17 answered requests at Nadzab and Gusap; Murphy couldn't get to Madang, and Duke, Rigsby, and Jones hit poor weather enroute to Rabaul. But who cares! For today Captain Post returned to 8th Photo with his immediate future undecided. Since June 20th the squadron has been without his services. He was on N. B. Island after having been jumped by Nips on the way home from Rabaul. His experiences are thrilling and interesting...after five months of harrowing experiences, he was picked up and taken to Hawaii on a submarine. He had no orders to follow there, so he came home to 8th Photo. The boys were all ears as he related his story. He had a warm look for Bowers. The Nips were on his tail at 10,000' when he bailed out of his burning plane, so he did not pull the cord until he could see the ground coming up to meet him, so to speak. The chute opened in due course, and all was well for the nonce, at least.

Captain Post brought back encouraging news about Lt. Fred Hargesheimer, missing three weeks before he was. He believes Hargie is alive but ill and in not too safe a spot. Word of a tall pilot, young looking, who might have been Lt. Ken Murphy, reached Capt. Post. It was believed this pilot is a Jap prisoner, possibly at Rabaul. Our prayers are with Hargie and Shapeless. May God bring them back to us soon.

Avery jumped from TSgt to F/O today with the good wishes of the Squadron.

Tuesday, October 26

Southard rolled out of his sack early to fly a F-5 to Dobo. He was to take off from there and shoot Rabaul before a B-25 strike. He followed instructions and concentrated on the shipping. Langdon was to have been protected on a post-strike photo run by two 8th Photo pilots in 80th Fighter ships. After Sykes threatened to have 80th Fighter court-martialed for failing to send the ships over, he got two planes and one pilot. Holton piloted one plane, and Lt. Adams of the 80th, the other. Holton's cut out at altitude just as it was supposed to do, and Adams' job wouldn't climb high enough to cover Langdon on the photo runs. So, with Rabaul in sight, Langdon and Adams did what Holton had done earlier—returned to base. Rigsby gave the Holton plane—one we were given—a test hop in the afternoon. His comments are not printable.

Farmer and Avery hit poor weather on the mail route and came home from Talasea.

The movie tonight was a bitch kitty—"Reap the Wild Wind."

Wednesday, October 27

(The morning missions were all frustrated by weather. - Auths.)

By 1100, Operations was as quiet as a hormone, so the lads took off for their own pleasures while Ross and Bristowe alternated on the cots in the pilots' room, sleeping off the effects of the straight shot (in the arm) administered by Demon Doc Stark last night. Capt. Post flew 2130, marking his first crack at the wheel since his bail-out in June. He said it was as natural as hell, then devoted the afternoon to making another Dan Beard out of Guerry. He taught him how to drink water from a vine, plus other helpful hints.

Me fellow belon 8th Photo. Pidgin-English speaking Major Art Post took off at early dawn for a well-deserved leave to Sydney. None of this seven days for Art, he's taking two weeks. Of course, it may take him a week to learn how to drink out of a glass instead of a vine, cross the street, and to walk on the sidewalk. We'll admit life in Sydney is still in a savage state, but a little advanced compared to that of New Britain. Have a good time, Art.

Southard to Kavieng, good weather but the fighters from the 80th turned back with engine trouble. The same thing has happened on the last three escorts from other squadrons.

Avery, wearing his shiny blue bars, and "Goldie" Farmer took areas on New Britain and around Finschhafen. Farmer must have looked cross-eyed at the coastline, because he was in the wrong area at the right time.

The reader may not believe this, but Guerry, according to a number of eye witnesses, was parading around in a pair of "pinks." And in New Guinea, too!

Friday, October 29

Duke, escorted by Moffat, who's back from leave as of yesterday, and Holton did up the Rabaul mission. The photos were clear and turned out very well. The lab impressed Fifth Bomb by their speed in developing and printing. Prints were out and on the way to the General one hour and forty minutes after the plane landed. Lt. Grigg has handled the lab efficiently during Hamlin's absence.

Capt. Murphy's mission Snafu to Kavieng. Another day of bad weather with apologies from the weather man.

Ludtke had everyone in the squadron looking skyward for a lone F-4 on one engine. The radio operator heard Ludtke say something about a bad engine, and in 20 minutes the word was all around camp that Ludtke was coming in on a single engine. It was only prop trouble, so no single engine landing to sweat out. Churchill and Ludtke secured pictures in Finschhafen and Aisega areas.

News comes from the mainland that six new photo pilots have arrived. Their destination: 8th Photo. The older pilots look eagerly at the replacement list as their thoughts drift back to the good ole U. S. A.

Saturday, October 30

Frontal activity, nil photo weather. Again the weather stops us and no pictures obtainable at Kavieng and Rabaul. Blum and Klages respectively to the above targets.

Sykes and Rigsby manage to shoot Madang and Alexishafen with two strips of coastline. They couldn't figure out which one had more land and least water in the coastline strips. Both strips ran too far out into the water with the coastline on one side of the picture. Anyway, their overlap was good.

Flash! News reached the squadron that Capt. Guerry is to be in Air Force. A look into the future tells us that jump in grade

8PRS Mechanic Andy Moore at Port Moresby. (Earl Lee)

P-38 and F-5 crew chief Arthur Steiner at Port Moresby. (Earl Lee)

and a trip home is about all that is in store for him. Who could ask for more except the Legion of Merit and, according to Sgt. Yourman, that is through and the orders will be out soon. Capt. Guerry has been part of the very foundation of the Squadron (according to Guerry) since its arrival in New Guinea in September 1942. With his well over 400 combat hours he has probably contributed more to the success of the squadron than any other man, including Polifka. His low obliques of New Britain and New Guinea are still the rage of 7th Fleet and 6th Army. No doubt his services with the squadron were outstanding, and we wish him every success in Air Force. He's still with the Squadron and will be C. O. until Foster's return from Sydney....

Sunday, October 31
(All operations for the day were canceled due to weather.—Auths.)

Tuesday, November 2
As of today, the Squadron has six new pilots. They look like pretty good men, eager, etc. Capt Sykes in an effort to get them off on the right foot gave 'em a little pep talk about the area, Nips, weather, and flying in general. It seems we either have too many planes and not enough pilots, or vice versa; someday maybe we'll hit a happy medium. Sgt Bowers did the honors with the jungle kit, explaining its composition and its many uses, while "Doc" Stark went deeper into it from a medical point of view. They were followed by Lt. Aucoin, who went thru the radio procedure.

At last the weather has cleared up with every photo ship bringing home the bacon. F/O Avery off early to Rabaul and got most of the town and harbor, his primary target, plus Tobera, Rapopo, and Vunakanau. Good job with clear photographs.

Capt. Murphy and Lt. Blum to North coast and New Guinea, picking up Madang, Alexishafen, and the two dromes at Hansa Bay. "Murph," remembering Fairbanks, flew tri-met from Madang to the Ramu River, cleaning up that area for good.

Southard, fifteen minutes after the bombers at Rabaul, photographed their results, and the prints were rushed over to Bomb Com. From his account the raid was quite a success. Who would complain on a day like this?

Wednesday, November 3
Klages to Rabaul, picking up all dromes and most of harbor and town area. If we were called once from Colonel Cooper's office we were called a dozen times. Fifth Bomb was really eager to see if anything was left at Rabaul. Needless to say, the Harbor still had ships and the dromes airplanes, but the B-25s on yesterday's strike did a good job, getting numerous direct hits on the shipping and shooting down 40 enemy aircraft with a little help from the peashooters.

Langdon and Jones got two rolls of much needed photography in the Finschhafen area.

Rigsby to Wewak with a Lt. Colonel, a Major, a Captain, and 1st Looey flying P-47s for top cover. Reports they did a good job and seemed very effective.

Two new pilots, Lts. Erb and Bayard, flew the circuit of friendly dromes. After two hot-pilot approaches they carried their base leg out a few miles and hit the strip. Don't worry, boys, a few more flights and you'll be old timers on the approaches. Bayard's plane is in the service squadron, having a new nose strut and wheel installed. No show tonight, but plenty of loud noise coming from Duke's tent. This liquor seems to affect a few people.

Friday, November 5
Capt. Murphy, Moffat, and Lt. Ludtke find themselves cruising over Wide Bay at 17,000'. The overcast at that altitude covered the entire area, so nil photos of Rabaul, but Hoskins area was completely covered.

Southard with escorts sighted six U/I SSF around Rooke Island. Full throttle and a quick 180 degree turn bring them back to base. Fairbank frowns as New Ireland goes unmapped.

Lt. Bayard flew his first mission and secured pictures under the wing of Captain Clark M. Sykes. Good stuff from both pilots and 6th Army just loves it.

The show tonight was "My Heart Belongs to Daddy" and an Ina Rae (Sex-Box) Hutton short. Compliments of Motion Picture Industry.

Saturday, November 6
Churchill received quite a surprise today. Landing at Nadzab to refuel for the Kavieng mission, he ran into four enemy planes, apparently strafing the area. He evaded them and came back to base.

Blum, Loos, and Rigsby attempt the Rabaul mission, but the flight was turned back due to weather over the Owen Stanleys. F/O Avery scores on the Wewak mission, staging out of Nadzab with P47s he covered all the dromes and returned to Schwimmer.

The work on the club continues and is shaping up nicely. Saturday, November 13th has been set as the gala opening. News is in the air of a B-26 trip to Sydney for much needed club furninshings.

Red alert today at 0855, caused by Tojo's Kids raiding Gusap and Nadzab. Some damage and casualties.

Sunday, November 7
Rough and tough, cigarette-smoking DeLasso with Rigsby attempted Kavieng. Bad weather still dominates the area, so a full roll was shot on north coast New Britain and Unea Island.

Ludtke to Rabaul with 39th Fighter escort finds himself headed toward Buka instead of Rabaul, so target not reached due to weather. These fronts are perfect barriers. Langdon and Klages get operational coverage of Alexishafen and Cape Gloucester dromes. A couple of tri-met runs for the Army and Navy were secured. Plenty of pictures of New Britain today. Maybe Sixth Army will be satisfied for a change.

Our silver piggy-back plane slipped off the jacks, falling on its left wing. It looks like a deport job, so should be out for a couple of weeks.

Tuesday, November 9
The weather can't keep us down forever, and given half a chance we 100% with photos. Blum covers all the important places at

Rabaul, sending in a sighting of five ships, heading north out of Blanche Bay.

Major Foster has the wires buzzing to 5th Bomb about a convoy south of New Hanover consisting of four M/V and three warships. Photos were taken of the convoy, a new strip southeast of Panapai, Kavieng, a run across the harbor and a couple of trimet strips across New Hanover. All the photos turned out well, except the overlap on the tri-met runs on New Hanover was about 50%. DeLasso escorted the mission, but aborted over New Hanover.

Churchill and Avery take off for Alexishafen and Madang, return to base as soon as possible. On the trip home Church gets photos in the Gusap area for 5th Fighter. The mission went off 100%.

Orders have come through on Major Guerry's Silver Star for the flight over Rabaul last month. The entire crew received the same award—Capt. Barnes, Guerry, Thomas, and to Capt. H. H. Olson the Oak Leaf Cluster to the Silver Star. The Fruit Salad on Guerry's chest is beginning to shape up.

Wednesday, November 10

Two ships off today, Sykes to Rabaul, Klages to Wewak. Sykes secured excellent photos of Lakunai to Vunakanau. The other dromes were overcast.

Klages, at 28,000', was intercepted after his run over Wewak and Boram. His fighters took on the Nips and Klages turned around, climbed, and returned to base wia Nubia.

On orders from Col. Cooper and direct orders of the C. O. the 8th Photo will take photos of Rabaul, Wewak, Madang, Kavieng, or any of those places under 33,000' true. The policy seems to have changed, because several months ago they kept asking for lower altitude.

Oh, for the days when only one flight went out and five days of the diary could be written on one typewritten page.

Thursday, November 11

(Eight planes set out—for Rabaul, in general—and were turned back by rough weather.—Auths.)

Friday, November 12

Rigsby to Rabaul, securing photos of all dromes except Keravat and the harbor at 33,000'. Eight SSF attempted interception over the harbor at 30,000'. The two fighters from the 39th Fighter and the photo ship outdistanced the Nips and returned to Schwimmer.

Lt. Blum, with P-47 escort, attempted Wewak, but nil photos due to weather.

Capt. Vince Murphy left this morning for the good ole U.S.A. He flew 85 missions. Most of the officers were overjoyed to hear of his leaving. Of course, they wished him all the success, etc. We present Colorado Springs with a Christmas gift.

Saturday, November 13

Major Foster took off with two fighters from the 39th Sq. this morning for the all-important Rabaul mission. Flying light instruments off the coast of Dobodura they ran into a cumulonimbus cloud. The up and down drafts and the icing conditions were terrific. Major Foster's plane was flipped over on its back and the (pilot) tube iced up, indicating only 100 mph. He flipped on the heat, and the speed jumped to 600 indicated. On breaking out of the instrument weather he had lost 10,000 feet. One of the fighters from the 39th failed to return.

A low ceiling of 27,500 feet stopped Ludbutt from taking Alexishafen after the strike. Similar weather was encountered by Lt. Klages. Needless to say, the men are a little pissed-off, but orders are orders.

Avery went to Wewak, but heavy stratus prevented photography.

At last the long-awaited day is here. Officially at 0900 the new Officers' Club was opened. Rush construction on the bar doors and interior decorating made the opening possible. Capt. Leonhardt and Capt. Loos take the honors for the very good job of construction and design. Other officers of the squadron worked daily from start to finish. We now claim the finest club in the Moresby area....

Monday, November 15

Lt. Langdon was given a mission from Dobodura this morning. He took photographs of all dromes in the Rabaul area, bringing them back to Schwimmer. There was a heavy haze over the harbor, but the shipping was clear enough for interpretation.

Capt. Loos goes artistic on the Squadron and shoots a roll of color film in the Aisega area at 15,000'. He and Lt. Blum, also in an F-4, were heading toward the village of Kulungtufu, when two U/I SSF were seen above them. Thinking of something to do at camp in a hurry, they came back to Schwimmer. After ComBomCom Victor gave us the old stuff about the mission must go through, etc., Churchill and Walzak take off to complete the said mission, but find the weather closed in over the ranges.

Rigsby to Wewak escorted by P-47s gets photos of all dromes and a ten-mile strip along the Ramu River.

From the number of visitors Operations is receiving, it would be wise to build a waiting room. Several officers from Sixth Army and Naval officers from Seventh Fleet came down to "see the set-up" of the Squadron and look at all available photographs.

Tuesday, November 16

Sykes and Loos take operational photos of Kulungtufu to Masawent R; Wald Bay to Kalasa; Karako to Headwaters of Song River. Capt. Chaseling picked up the copies for N.G.F.

Lt. Ludtke got as far as the Sepik River on his mission to Wewak. What appeared to be a thin layer of stratus turned out to be several thousand feet thick. When he broke through he was alone and his fighters had returned to Nadzab. The target was covered anyway, so nil photos.

Klages in F-4 2209 took operational photos of Hansa Bay; Alexishafen and Madang were cloud-covered. He returned to base while fighters returned to Dobodura.

There are rumors in the air of another B-26 trip to Sydney and Melbourne, possibly tomorrow.

Thursday, November 18

Out of the five missions planned for this morning all were canceled except Wewak. Lt. Duke went to Nadzab in 3105 to pick up fighters and then got as far as the turn in the Ramu before turning back because of bad weather. The lab gets another day off with no photos today.

The show tonight was "Two Tickets to London." It didn't turn out to be as bad as expected. If the shows are no good, we just walk out and go up the hill to the club where there's peace, quiet, and plenty of good music. Well—there's good music anyway.

Friday, November 19

As soon as Major Foster left for the south an urgent request came in for obliques in the Gasmata area. Capt. Loos has been over to Fifth Air Force about ten times today, explaining, etc., and getting the mission set up. The B-17 has been on the ground so long a few more days won't make any difference.

After much quibbling from Air Force and Bomb Com, two missions were sent to Hollandia. They took off from the Nadzab strip with fighter escort from the 80th Squadron an hour apart. Ludtke took the first flight and covered all the dromes in the Wewak area—al least he thought so, on his way via the sea route to Hollandia. He must have gotten up on the wrong side of his bunk, because only half the dromes he attempted were covered. Thanks to Klages, who took off an hour later and flew the same mission, the dromes at Wewak and Hollandia were all covered. A tri-met strip was taken from But to vicinity of Humboldt Bay. What looked like a new drome to Klages was photographed east of Hansa Bay. It is an old site first constructed in 1930. The photos showed a new strip under construction at Hollandia. Both of the men did a good job, but did not see the convoy supposedly in that area.

Saturday, November 20

Major Post ferried a brand new P-38H up from Brisbane and arrived here at 1600. He learned that his orders are out and, after a week up here to finish up business, he returns to Brisbane to await transportation to the U.S.A.

Sykes, Rigsby, and Jones covered the strike on Hansa Bay. Reported two large fires. Clark was giving the Nips hell for throwing ack-ack up to 33,000'.

R. D. Erb, KIA December 30, 1943. (Dobbs)

Lt. Daniels, with fighters from the 80th Squadron, did a good job on the "before and after" mission deal on the Ring Ring strike. Good average.

Farmer to Rabaul staging out of Dobodura. He brought back pictures, but weather over the ranges forced him to land at Dobo. After another try at getting back to Moresby, he stayed the night at Dobodura. He will fly back at first light tomorrow.

Sunday, November 21

...Major Darnell, C. O. of the new 6th Photo Group, with a few of his staff officers, arrived on the plane with Fairbank. They will be with the squadron a few days to study our procedure, etc.

Gailfus to Gasmata to photograph before and after the strike. Because the escorting fighters were delayed in taking off, the mission reached the target late, and Gailfus, no doubt being amazed at the number of switches, turned on the 6" cameras instead of the 24". Outside of the scale, the pictures were good.

Davis did a good job at Wewak, securing all dromes and a short tri-met strip in that area. He was escorted by Moffat and Loos in 43 and 48.

Major Darnell put on a little exhibition in 30 this evening while Truman sweat blood.

Monday, November 22

Weather turned the Gasmata missions back, but Duke slipped through the weather and got Rabaul, although quite a few cumulus clouds were present. Walzak ran into bad weather going to Gasmata, as did Churchill, Jones, and Rigsby. Church went through a little hole in the front and found the flight in one large hole. They had to climb to altitude to get out through the breaks. Langdon, with P-47s from Nadzab, ran into a 29,000-foot broken layer of clouds off land at Wewak. Staying at 33,000 feet, it was open enough to get part of Wewak and Boram.

We announce at long last that "Gabby" Garcelon and "Stinky" Davis have finally arrived from their seven-days leave. We were beginning to wonder if they were on (detached service) or had joined the first line of defense for the "Battle of Sydney."

The G. I. move tonight wasn't quite up to scratch without the usual Private SNAFU.

Tuesday, November 23

...at noon Bomber Command called and ordered us to send a ship to Cape Arawe on New Britain. Ludtke flew the photo ship after outranking Sykes. Moffat took the fighter. The weather wasn't too good, but Lud shot nearly all of his film. A mission is a mission, and that was about eighty for Ludbut.

Everyone got quite a laugh out of the show last night—a musical comedy "Class B" entitled " Mr. Big."

Wednesday, November 24

At 0622 the B-17, piloted by DeLasso and Darnell, took off for Townsville. The take-off must have been on instruments because the visibility was very limited. They went down after the goodies for tomorrow's Thanksgiving dinner. From last reports they won't be back until tomorrow morning, and not this afternoon as planned.

L-R: Vic Heldenbrand, Bill Kumic, Hank Meade, John Nielson by F-4, serial 41-2209. Lt Charles Erb was lost in this F-4 on December 30, 1943. (Woods)

Plenty of pictures were taken today, but the Gremlins were busy on each mission. I guess this all started the other day with Ludtke. Farmer to Wewak covered Boram, Wewak, Dagua, Anwar, Madang, and half of But and Nubia dromes. He was escorted by Rigsby and up to the Rabaul mission but missed Vunakanau and Keravat dromes. He was escorted by the 80th Fighter Sq. Sykes and Daniels went in at Gasmata after the strike. Clark with color film and Daniels with black and white. Daniels being confused over the intervalometer set it at 18 seconds instead of the usual 9. The 24" had no overlap, but the tri-met was satisfactory. We'll mark this up as one of those days, and profit by experience.

Thursday, November 25

Thanksgiving was observed at the line today in the classical tradition....

After corned beef for the last ten days, the officers and men put on the feed bag and slowly diminished the pangs of hunger. It was cooked and served in the Thanksgiving style becoming a G. I. in the States. Turkey and dressing, cranberry sauce, fresh mashed potatoes, fresh peas, fresh celery (didn't see any of that), olives, pickles, biscuits, fresh butter, pumpkin pie, iced tea, and coffee, and last but not least—ice cream and watermelon...

...Armstrong flew his first mission with Moffat and Davis. All the Wewak dromes were covered by Davis who also sighted 12 to 15 barges in the harbor. This was the only mission today.

Friday, November 26

The war must go on. So, despite the desire to stay in the sack this morning, the pilots and men got five aircraft off on missions.

Lt. Duke got off early and brought home the bacon with excellent photos and coverage of Rabaul. On the trip home, Gasmata was also taken. Major Darnell and Capt. Loos attempted Gasmata after the strike, but electrical trouble on DeLasso's plane forced them to return to base.

Lt. Farmer took the ass-buster to Hollandia. After flying all the way up there, the dromes were covered with clouds. A strip around Humboldt Bay was taken, a short tri-met strip around Humboldt Bay was taken, a short tri-met strip around Aitape, and But and Dagua were covered.

Lt. Rigsby to Wewak secured photos of all the dromes in that area, also Hansa Bay and Alexishafen.

Southard and Garcelon, along with Stark, drew up a few rules for the club. Gabby spent about a half hour explaining about the 10 pounds the officers shelled out for the coke machine. It seems it will be returned eventually. Ludtke and Churchill pulled out for Sydney at last.

Saturday, November 27

Two missions went out today. Klages to Wewak after the strike by the B-25s escorted by Capt. Loos and Lt. Jones. A few fires were observed around Boram and all dromes were covered.

Southard and Gailfus, escorted by P-47s, landed at Nadzab before going on to Arawe, Southard took very good runs and the desired tri-met and K-18 requests. Gailfus became separated and proceeded to Cape Bushing. Thinking that area to be cloudy, he returned to base.

The show tonight was a murder mystery entitled "Murder" with George Sanders. What we need is another show with a little sex in it.

Sunday, November 28

Major Foster took the "After the strike" mission to Wewak this morning. He was escorted by Walzak and Counselman in our fighters. Several strips were taken over the target. Other than some ack-ack over Dagua, the flight was uneventful.

This was the only mission that went out today, but Capt. Moffat got in a little flying with three test hops. Lt. Thompson, another addition to the Squadron as of several days ago, flew in the local area. Committing a few of the newcomer's mistakes, he taxied out to take off along the side of the runway instead of on it. Luckily, no

8PRS F-4, serial 41-2139, POUTING PEGGY at 14-Mile. (John Nielson)

damage resulted, so he looked the area over and came in and landed on the right strip.

Rigsby and Bristowe neglected their duties today and put out a double-header washing. We looked forward to the Squadron laundry getting back into business.

Monday, November 29

...The only mission that went out was Daniels. Sykes and Darnell to Wewak and Aitape. Wewak was cloud-covered and Aitape was not reached because an engine cut out on the photo ship. The results of today's efforts were nil.

Tuesday, November 30

The camp got a thorough drenching last night. The downpour only lasted a few minutes, but was accompanied by a stiff breeze which made everything unpleasant. Must have been a number of wet beds last night.

Bayard and Loos along with Duke attempted the Wewak milk run but got no further than Kerema. They returned after an hour and a half of flying. Ole George, the weather man, is off the ball again. Blum got as far as Rooke Island on his way to Kavieng before turning back because of bad weather.

The only mission that got pictures was the B-17 piloted by Col. Hutchison. They took five rolls of K-18 photos from 1,500 feet. All the film turned out good except (there is always that "except") the first two rolls. Lens condensation ruined them. As said previously, that is pretty expensive condensation.

Major Foster and Capt. Sykes took off early this morning in the B-26 for Brisbane to ferry eleven pilots of the new group back to Moresby. We see why the squadron is called heavy, medium, light, *transport,* school and service.

Wednesday, December 1

Lt. Erb, after checking the weather, which he always does after being stopped by Hutchison, took off for the Finschhafen and Madang areas. The Madang area was cloud-covered, so a full roll of K-18 and two tri-met strips were taken from the Song River north to Wald Bay. These were areas heretofore unphotographed and just what the Army wants.

Lt. Farmer, with two fighters from the 80th, to Wewak and Aitape. Excellent weather was encountered so Farmer made the most of it. He photographed all Wewak dromes and the strip about 665 miles north, Tadji. The Aitape strip about two miles north of that could not be found by "eagle eye" from 33,000'. A very good tri-met strip was taken along the coast and another in the Sepic River. Not a bad day's work.

...Major Foster returned with the B-26 at 1600 hours. His flesh and blood cargo took a look at their new home for the next year. No flat tires, no bent nose struts, no bad weather, so for a change the trip turned out successfully.

Thursday, December 2

The fighter planes got a rest today as Duke took off for Kavieng without benefit of escort, and F/O Davis headed for Arawe under similar conditions. Duke landed at Nadzab, refueled and got as far as Sio on the second leg of the trip when weather fouled him. Davis reached the Solomon Sea near Arawe, but clouds over the target served to turn him back.

While Lt. Klages was moaning about the slow-changing status board with unescorted missions, the B-17 took off for the Madang area. Major Foster was in the slot aided by Capt. Loos. Homer Taylor took it easy in the navigator's cushioned seat, and Fairbank acted as technical advisor to Photographer Reindl. Madang targets were (no good) due weather so K-18s of Arndt Pt. and the Finschhafen fighter strip were taken to save face and to keep the mission from going to waste.

The Red Cross girl's visits are less pleasant now because she very wisely brings a No. G. I. boy with her to keep Daniel at his proper distance. Even the drink she brings stinks to high heaven. Some action against the "odd" Elaine brings with her will have to be taken.

Saturday, December 4

The lone mission that went out today was flown by Capt. Armstrong, (Operations Officer) of the 6th Group., in 2139 to photograph Cape Gloucester after the bombing strike. Crossing the ranges, he encountered a front and stuck his nose in and pulled it out again promptly because of severe turbulence. He broke out going about 450. After another try at going under the weather, he looked around and found a hole back to good old Schwimmer. Instrument flying in a P-38 type aricraft in this Squadron is discouraged unless absolutely necessary. The importance of aerial photographs using the policy "at any cost" is negligible in this theater compared with others. Photographs the next day or a few days hence seem to serve the purpose. So take heed, all ye eager beavers, and do your photographing on clear days.

Sunday, December 5

Another unexpected tragedy hit the Squadron today. One of the new pilots, F/O (Fred) Cross of the 25th Sq (L), 6th Gp., crashed in F-4 #2122 near the Hood Point strip about 1000 hours during a local hop designed to acquaint him with New Guinea. He was burned severely and was flown in a transport to the 171st Station Hospital in critical condition. He and Lt. Danvers (2130) were flying together. Cross was apparently flying low over the water when he

Pilots Erb and Bayard somewhere in what appears to be Australia. (Gailfus)

lost control of the plane. Bomber Command phoned Operations, and Capt. Sykes flew to Hood Point in Bom Com's L-5 to pick up the doctor and investigate the accident. Lt Danvers left 2130 at Hood Point and flew to the hospital with Cross.

The ship was demolished. Part of a native village was struck before the plane hit a tree and burned.

No missions were flown today, although Colonel Hutchison took the B-17 loaded with new pilots of the 6th Gp Squadrons over to Nadzab.

Churchill and Ludtke returned from their "rest" in Sydnew looking as if they had just taken Satelburg on a horse.

The Officer's Club is still jammed with new and transient faces as the Mess Officer worries about a food shortage, and Doc frets about a fire water shortage.

Monday, December 6

F/O Cross died early today as a result of burns sustained in his plane crash yesterday at Hood point. The tragedy is made more severe when one realizes that Cross's father died a week ago. While none of the 8th Photo knew Cross well, his loss is felt deeply among the officers and men of the 25th Sq.

Capt. Loos and Lt. Bayard flew the top cover for Lt. Klages this morning on the Karavia Bay mission. Just this side of New Britain, the F-5 developed engine trouble and the flight returned. Loos, the eager Ops Officer, radioed to his base for three more pilots and a fresh photo plane so that the mission could go out again.

Jones, with Walzak and Holton in the Hs, set out in 02 at 1045 and managed to get to Rabaul for photos of Karavia Bay and most of the dromes.

Oddly enough, Rabaul was covered twice today. Rigsby set out for Borpop on New Ireland and hit Namantanai on the way to Borpop. The mapping weather was pee poor but Rigsby was not to be outdone. He saw Rabaul clear as a bell so he hit the Jap base full force on the way home. He was griped because nobody received his message about the cruiser in the Bismarck Sea.

A G. I. movie helped to pass the evening.

8th Photo Recon Squadron campsite at 14-Mile. (Woods)

Charlie Bateson came from the 80th FS to provide the 8PRS with an experienced fighter pilot for escort. He was KIA in 1943. (Norbert Ruff)

New ruling today from Gen. Whitehead that all bars would close at 2100 unless there was a "special occasion." Ludtke immediately looks for his book "365 Days of Special Occasions," or some such title. All he could find to observe for tonight was "Anniversary of the Acquisition of Puerto Rico."

Flash—Rumors are that Rummy Foster is just about on his way to the good ole U.S.A.

Tuesday, December 7

While Homer Taylor recalled the Pearl Harbor attack and the part he played in it, Sykes tried for New Ireland unescorted in a pair of fatigue overalls reminiscent of the days when we had a "new pappy on the Santa Fe." Counselman went to Bushing, and the B-26 started earning its keep by flying to Cape Gloucester for low obliques.

The weather in the Bismark Sea was too much for the San Antonio Rose, so he and his coveralls came back. Counselman got to Bushing just after some clouds, so he hit for Finschhafen and gladdened Chaseling's heart with a strip around the Song River. The B-26, Moffat Boss Boy and Ludtke No. 2, dropped to 1,200 feet for good coastline obliques.

The movie tonight was "Young Ideas" with (Herbert) Marshall, Mary Astor, and a cute dish with an inviting mouth by the name of Susan Peters. We all had young ideas after watching the quiff cavort on the screen.

Just after chow, Major Foster said au revoir to the members of the Squadron. He is slated to leave tomorrow after having commanded the Squadron since June 26th. He has an enviable record with 8th Photo and his departure marks another great loss from that stellar group who used to swim with Weidner on the bank of the river to shoot crocs.

F-4 #30, MALARIA MABEL, at 14-Mile. Alex Guerry at extreme left and Fred Rennels at extreme right. (Nielson)

Clark Sykes banks away from B-17 in his 8PRS F-4. (Sykes)

Thursday, December 9
Another day with no missions.
All pilots hit the sack, the bottle, or both.

John Nielson posing before one of the 8th PRS F-4s, MAP HAPPY PAPPY at 14 Mile. (Nielson)

Capt. Loos became our new C. O. today, stepping into Major Foster's boots. We wish him success, and knowing Loos, we know he will enjoy it.

Friday, December 10
Our new 1st Lt., Allen H. Blum, took off for Kavieng, silver bar and all. He couldn't get photos due to weather so decided to practice up on his instrument flying. After flubbing around in the fog and running into a few thunderheads, our boy Blum returned to base.

Lt. Erb took one strip over Finschhafen, had trouble with an engine, and had to come home. Flying through thundershowers and over mountains on one engine is routine for "H. P." Erb. He made home base o.k.

Lt. Daniels had bad weather again today standing in the way. He had to return to base when he found his New Britain target covered. He tries hard.

Sunday, December 12
No missions for the day.

Capt. "Doc" Stark had his clothes ripped from his body during the party given in our new club as a farewell salute. Major Foster was honored the same way a few days before. We wish them both all the luck in the world and hope they have a pleasant trip back to the States. They have both well earned it.

Wednesday, December 15
Lts. Jones and Gailfus took off to get photos of Hansa Bay and the Bogadjim areas. They became separated somewhere in the clouds over Hansa Bay. Each took his pictures and came home, Gailfus returning one half hour after Jones.

When Darnell, Armstrong, and Fairbank took off for Gloucester in the B-26 this morning, little did they realize what was in store for them. Over the ranges, the No. 8 cylinder of the left engine blew up, belching oil in its dying moments. The colonel feathered the

F-4s numbers 41-2139 and 41-2177 at 14-Mile Strip. (Fairbank)

Pilot LeGrand Kneeskern on F-4 #41-2156 LIMPING LIZZIE. (Fairbank)

engine and headed for Dobodura, losing altitude steadily. The old gal just "ain't what she used to be" when it comes to holding altitude on one engine. The nine men aboard threw out everything they could get their hands on, and the Colonel finally set her down at Dobo as gently as a kitten. If only Homer Taylor had been along—well, maybe it's better for his heart that he wasn't. The crew returned home on a transport.

Thursday, December 16

Lt. H. L. Holton, "Tojo," or "Horrible Little Holton" (he answers to the latter with a —— you) took off for Hansa Bay, ran into weather over the Finsterre(sic) Ranges and returned. Keep this boy in mind. He's going to get Hansa Bay yet.

Lt. Walzak flew to Rooke Island and got the requested photos. On the way back he was to shoot some tri-met in the Finschhafen area, "snafued" on the intervalometer, and got only two exposures. Sad case this.

Ludtke and Moffat took off for Cape Hoskins but had to turn back because of weather over the ranges.

Friday, December 17

Lt. Counselman and Lt. Thompson flew to Hansa Bay but found nil photo weather, then continued on towards Wewak but found nil flying weather. They returned to base.

Col. "Hutch" and Moff flew the B-17 on a low oblique mission in the Saidor area. Loos, Armstrong, and "Ludbutt" escorted the '17 with our fighters. Upon landing, it was found that no one on the B-17 knew they had an escort. The navigator, Colonel Smith, saw one of our boys once, but the plane was so far away he could just about identify it as a P-38.

Lt. Klages tok off for Madang and Saidor areas loaded with color film, but the wrong filter. Lucky enough for Camera Repair that the weather was bad, and the film wasn't wasted because of the filter. On the way back, Klages flew low over the wrecked P47 he and others had spent two days and nights getting to. A few hundred yards from the '47, he noticed the tail of a L-5 sticking up out of the swamp. A special flight was made over the wreck, and the ship was identified as the one Capt. Henry Leonhardt and Lt. Wayne Mueller had been flying a few hours earlier. A party was launched from here in two rubber boats on the Laloki; another party, Australians, took a power boat up the Laloki from Red Scar Bay.

The Aussies reached the wreck first, after tedious hours of work plowing through swamps and kunai grass. The bodies were found and identified as those of Lt. Mueller and Capt. Leonhardt.

Lt Mueller was one of the best glider pilots in this theater and had an enviable record in assisting A-3 in planning airborne operations. For some time he had been attached to the 2nd Air Task Force at Marilinan and had made countless rescue flights up into the Ramu and Markham Valleys, often far over Japanese lines. While Lt. Mueller has not been with the Squadron for some time, his loss hits

Port Moresby 7-Mile Strip (Jackson Dome) view looking southeast. (Fairbank)

14-Mile Strip center and 12-Mile Strip at right. (Fairbank)

Looking across Dobodura's main 10,000 ft. runway to runway 4Y. (Fairbank)

us just as hard as if he were now one of our own men, and the theater and Fifth Air Force suffer a distinct loss.

Capt. Leonhardt came over with "B" Flight in June 1942 and has been a mainstay in the ground echelon ever since. He has been responsible for all the extensive construction carried out by the outfit since its transfer to New Guinea, and, by actually rolling up his sleeves and helping ours, has endeared himself to all the officers and enlisted men of the organizations. Henry is the sort of fellow who is almost impossible to replace.

Saturday, December 18

Lt. Ludtke flew to Rabaul but couldn't take pictures because of an overcast. On the way back, he took pictures of Hoskins. Lud has to bring some bacon if not the bacon. He claims he saw an explosion in the water 20 miles SW of Gasmata, but we know he has been over here long enough to mistake it for a spouting whale.

Sunday, December 19

Lt. Colonel Darnell, 6th Group C.O., flew his DSC mission today. Unescorted, alone, all by himself, he flew one F-5A (P-38 type) aircraft at 7,500 feet over the Jap stronghold at Kavieng. The Japs were so surprised they didn't know if they should __ or go blind. This element of surprise played a big part in the success of the mission. Darnell forgot that the intervalometer doesn't count on runaway, so he proceeded to turn around and fly through the storm of A/A and fighters to take another strip manually. He didn't get a scratch and came home with beautiful K-18 shots of the dromes, harbor, and installations.

Capt. Loos today took the first photos of Manus Island to be taken in a light ship. He covered the dromes at Momote and Lorengau with good K-18 photos. He also shot a mapping run from Lorengau to the Mouke Reefs.

Erb brought back good pictures of the Madang area.

Blum, our new Asst. O. O., did his usual workmanlike job on DeKays Bay inland and got mapping photos of the Bogadjim Road.

Wednesday, December 22

Klages and Erb took off to photograph the effects of the strike at Wewak. They were to arrive shortly after the strike, but neither of them got there. Erb came back when he got lost in a cloud and found his gas supply low. Klages tried hard, but the weather won and he had to come back with no photos.

Loos did his usual quiet and successful job on Cape Gloucester and Borgen Bay today. The pictures were good, and the invasion forces can use them soon to good advantage, we hope.

Lt. Thompson tried to get to Hansa Bay, but weather intervened so he settled for photos of Saidor. They were supposed to be K-18 and he shot K-17. He'll get a chance to redeem himself—we all make mistakes.

Thursday, December 23

The prize mission of the day was taken by "Tojo" Holton. He took beautiful pictures of what he thought was Hansa Bay, only to find when they were developed that he had taken Madang. We still can't figure out how the little man made this mistake. Stick around—he's going to get a complete mission yet.

Rigsby, Clark, and Langdon got to Wewak (At last somebody got through). Rigsby took excellent photos of all the dromes under the watchful eye of Langdon and Clark, his escort. The boys picked up pictures of Hansa Bay, Alexishafen, and Madang. Langdon couldn't resist firing the guns, so he strafed Madang from 20,000'.

Lt. Bayard and F/O Dobbs got photos of the dromes in the Markham-Ramu-Finschhafen areas. Their altitudes varied from 8,000 to 28,000' on different runs due to overcasts in the wrong places. Blum was stopped from taking photos of Saidor by ole man weather. He reported seeing barges, probably our own.

Friday, December 24

Lt. Klages flew up in the Ramu Valley and Madang area. The weather was good and he got his pictures. Lt. Counselman pretty well covered Manum Island today, getting all the coverage required.

Ludtke just about finished up the Hansa Bay Mission. It has been a pain in the neck all the way along, and we still have to get a short strip to complete the coverage.

Loos and Erb did an excellent job on Saidor today. Erb covered DeLasso's tail while he took pictures. When he finished, Erb turned right and DeLasso left, and that's the last they saw of each other until they landed...

Saturday, December 25

MERRY CHRISTMAS!

The only mission flown today was one by Col. Hutchison in the B-25 with Lt. Counselman as co-pilot. They lost their fighter escort around Dumpu, but went ahead and got the off-shore obliques of Gloucester and Saidor.

Christmas dinner was the best meal we have ever had. Roast turkey, cranberry sauce, dressing, mince pie, and all the rest. Wine was served with the meal which enabled everyone to eat more. Christmas night was a very quiet one, the piano, radio, and poker game in full swing.

Sunday, December 26

Lt. Clark today took his first photos in seven months. He has been a so-called escort "fighter pilot," one of the six trained at Charters Towers. They were of two strips of a mosaic of Nadzab and turned out pretty well.

Lt. Rigsby flew his assigned mission to Saidor, and then flew over to Gloucester to see how the invasion was progressing. He saw plenty of activity both in the air and on the water. Twenty thousand troops were landed on Gloucester, this time for keeps.

John Miller, crewchief on F-4 #41-2220. (Virgil Brown)

RFD Tojo has its photo taken from another aircraft. The day is typically clear with clouds and mist in the distance. (Andreanna Pappas)

Lt. Blum flew to Hansa Bay but couldn't take pictures due to weather. Langdon flew a red-hot mission to Gasmata and Hoskins this afternoon. This probably means the landing of more troops.

Col. Hutchison, Lt. Col. Darnell, Lt. Fairbank, T/Sgt. Laboda, T/Sgt. Manley, S/Sgt. Lane, Cpl. Rodgers, Cpl. Lynch, PFC McGee, Pvt. Young, Pvt Black, Combat Cameramen Capt. Carter, and S/Sgt. Hartman, War Correspondents Rayner, Morrison, Lennard, Taves—all took off in the B-17 at 0549 hours. There was an intense fog with ceiling zero. Guided by the headlights of two jeeps, the plane raced down the runway, leaving the ground after its normal run. At 0550, the plane crashed in the swamp just off the NW end of the runway. All but two, Cpl. Lynch and PFC McGee, managed to escape from the burning plane. Rescue squads ploughed a path through the swamp and jungle, evacuating the broken and blood-soaked bodies, under a hail of exploding ammunition. We hope the best for the 15 survivors.

Monday, December 27

Lt. Bayard took off for the Nadzab area to complete a mosaic. This he did, and then shot up the rest of his K-18 on the dromes at Lae and Finschhafen. The boy doesn't realize that these dromes were hot spots when we first got here. Lt. Dobbs (promoted from F/O to 2nd Lt. recently) flew to Hansa Bay, found (no good) weather and returned to base.

"Hog About Missions" Langdon stayed all night at Dobo so he could fly Saidor for the "General" next day. We know the weather was bad when he returned from his previous mission to Gasmata, and he had to stay all night, but to fly stuff recently covered is the pay off. Rigsby told him, quote: "Refer all these godamn generals to me after this." Unquote. What he meant was refer them to the Wing.

Tuesday, December 28

Churchill, Loos, and Armstrong took of for Cape Arawe—Loos and Armstrong as escort. Churchill got his photos, but not without some difficulty with the umbrella of fighters that we have had covering our little beachhead on Arawe. Everyone returned without mishap, and the pictures were good.

Lts. Holton and Klages took off for Hansa Bay again. They were looking for some uncharted lakes in that vicinity, but you should see what they brought back. They weren't lakes, they were mud puddles. Major Small can't say much because he just thinks there are lakes up there.

Wednesday, December 29

Last night's movie—Hi Diddle Diddle—was the cat's undies and all enjoyed it, mainly because it was unusual and because there was some toe curling kissing in it. After the regular movie a short reel of color photos showing the sexy pictures on the noses of bombers was shown, with the last few shots of the late B-17 RFD Tojo and the 8th Photo Camp.

Three missions werre assigned by the Wing for today's blow at the Axis. Rigsby to Hansa Bay; Ludtke, with Blum and Counselman as escort, to Cape Bushing; and Erb on a local job for some artillery outfit.

Of course Rigsby couldn't content himself with little old Hansa Bay. he took the four Wewak Dromes in addition to his K18s around Hansa Bay and his mapping in the (Sepik) area. There were several shipping sightings to report. The Bushing mission reached the target, but the weather was for the birds so the boys came back empty-handed. Erb spent an hour and a half in the Moresby area.

It became fairly definite that Lt. Shipway, 25th Sq., is lost as a result of a P-39 flight from Horn Island to Moresby. Simmons and Martin, new pilots in the 25th Sq., started for Milne Bay on December 23rd. Several days later, we learned from Angua that they had crash-landed and were uninjured. They are on their way back, we guess.

Thursday, December 30

December has been the worst month the Squadron has ever had from the standpoint of missing men, injured and killed. Lt. Erb is missing today after turning back on the way to Bushing. Dobbs and he were in photo planes—Bayard and Langdon in fighters. Off Cape Ward Hunt about 100 miles, Erb had engine trouble and turned back. The others went on. No word from Erb today. Langdon and Bayard went out again to search.

Loos tried Finschhafen, but weather forced him to settle for 30-Mile where a bombing experiment was being conducted...

Friday, December 31

Tonight every member of the 8th Photo will celebrate the ending of 1943 and the beginning of '44. We wish everyone a Happy New Year!

Klages with Armstrong and Blum as escort took off after photos of Cape Bushing, Arawe, and Moewe Harbor on New Britain. Weather was bad for photos at Cape Bushing. On their way to Arawe, Blum spots two Zekes at 11 o'clock. He contacts the other two ships and throws his combat switch. With his fingers on the trigger and the "relief" tube ready, he prepared to do or die for the photo ship. His chances for glory are shattered when the Zekes turn out to be our own P-47s on patrol over Arawe. The weather was bad all the way around, and the result: Nil Photos. On their way back from N. B., the search for Lt. Erb was carried out to the best of their ability. He is still missing, but we hold out the best of hope for him.

Churchill too had bad weather and nil photos at Dumpu. Everyone saw the old year out and the new year in through bleary eyes and the smoke from Southard's cigars...

So ends the 8th Photo Diary as kept by the Intelligence Section. It has had a number of authors, all of whom forsook accuracy to make a better story.

(Note: this entry ended the period when the 8th Photo Squadron operated virtually alone as the eyes of Fifth Air force and General MacArthur in New Guinea. After joining the 6th Photo Group the 8th PhS carried on as part of a larger whole.)

8PRS F-4 #41-2130 stripped down to bare metal on October 22, 1943 at 14-Mile, Port Moresby.

3

Operational Summary 1944-1945

1944 opened for the 8th Photo Squadron on a more optimistic note. When the squadron began operations early in 1942 there were only sixteen pilots in the unit and only one of them had any experience over enemy territory. Time for training was virtually nonexistent in view of the urgent need for photo intelligence. By 1944, however, there were more than thirty officers and flight officers in the 8th Photo Squadron, and there was sufficient time to train personnel in the proper method of obtaining and processing aerial photos. The casualty rate went down when pilots were schooled in the proper techniques of navigating over the jungle and water of the Southwest Pacific, and also of avoiding the flak and fighters which had claimed some of the best reconnaissance pilots of the squadron.

Laboratory facilities were improved with the third installation at Laloki at the end of 1943. A native style building with a concrete floor and three A2 trailers to form an additional space on one side of the main building comprised this third version of an effective lab. A refrigerator was allocated to the lab to finally keep photo supplies fresh in the pernicious New Guinea heat and moisture.

At the beginning of 1944 the targets covered by the F-4s and F- 5s of the 8th PhS included bypassed sections of New Britain and Wewak, as well as distant targets on New Ireland and the northern Solomons. Reconnaissance flights over the Admiralties during and after the invasion played a part in the sealing off of Rabaul by March 1944. Major DeLasso Loos was awarded a Distinguished Flying Cross for flying the first mission over Manus Island in the Admiralties on December 19, 1943.

After the successful invasion of Hollandia at the end of April there was little that the 8th PhS could do from the eastern end of New Guinea, although missions to isolated Japanese bases on the Vogelkop peninsula are recorded beginning in May. A station move to Nadzab was made in March by the squadron, but the need was becoming more pressing to secure a base from which the southern Philippines could be reached.

An air contingent was moved to Biak Island around August 11, 1944, and the entire squadron operated from the island from September 10 until October 20 when the invasion of the Philippines occurred. Most operations were flown to the Philippine area, while others were made to Western New Guinea, Ambon, Ceram, and Dutch East Indies airdromes. Eighteen missions were flown from Biak by October 12, and three days later the squadron began to pack for the move to the Philippines.

One sad event happened on Biak which involved an old hand and former commander of the 8th Photo Squadron. Major Art Post had decided to take crew chief Delbert Mendenhall on a hop in a F5A during the morning of August 25, 1944 (other sources list the date as October, but the squadron history is precise about the time). Something happened during one of the maneuvers, and the Lightning crashed about 1 1/2 miles from Sorido Village, out into the water around 800 feet from shore. Both men were killed, but the loss of Post must have been especially bitter since he was one of the oldest members of the squadron and had already returned after being downed in June 1943.

The Squadron loaded aboard the Liberty Ship SS Juan Cabrillo on October 15 and began to sail for the Philippines on the day of the Leyte invasion, October 20, 1944. The pilots and some mechanics remained on Biak to fly the planes up to the strips on Leyte as soon as they were serviceable. The Juan Cabrillo arrived in San Pedro Bay on October 29 and endured several savage air raids before the 8th PhS personnel could disembark at Leyte on November 3. The men could watch at least five Japanese raiders shot down, including one that was shot down by a P-38. The gunners on the Juan Cabrillo claimed one of the victories and painted a victory flag on the funnel of the ship.

On November 4 the squadron assumed its new location at Julita, Leyte. The operational buildings were erected by the advance party, and the squadron was ready to fly by November 26.

Two F-5s were reported lost on November 24, one due to Japanese bombing and the other during a preliminary mission flown from Tacloban.

Lt. Richard E. Erickson was reported lost in F-5E, serial 43-28953, but may have been recovered safely since the same F-5 was reported in service during December. Erickson was not listed on the final roster of dead and missing, so he may have been recovered safely with his aircraft after his mission to Ormoc.

Eight successful missions were flown during five days of flying in November. Reconnaissance and mapping photos were made of the Lingayen and Manila areas on Luzon, as well as airdromes and installations on Bohol, Cebu, Negros, and Panay Islands. The squadron history notes that older veterans in the unit were reminded of the original Port Moresby days when the 8th Photo Rcn Squadron was the only unit of its kind to give service to the Fifth Air Force.

On December 13 Captain K. W. Klages and F/O Clyde F. McConnell took off from Leyte at 8 o'clock in the morning for a photo reconnaissance mission over Luzon when McConnell developed trouble with his oxygen system and was forced to turn back, while Klages completed the mission.

McConnell was last sighted over Balayan Bay, Luzon, and was not heard from again until December 30 when it was reported that he had bailed out of his Lightning and was picked up safely by Philippine guerillas. Curiously enough, McConnel was flying F5E serial 43-28953. Thus, it seems that either Erickson landed safely with 43-28953 or that a rare error appeared in the records of the unit.

January 1945 began with a continuation of the coverage over Luzon. On January 2 a reconnaissance was made of Lingayen Gulf which made use of color verticals. The next day more color vertical photography was made of the same area and coverage was made of the previous strikes on Clark Field. After January 9 when U.S. forces landed in the Lingayen Gulf the 8th PhS missions moved up into Central and Northern Luzon. On January 11 there was a reconnaissance mission to photograph the road net on the infamous Bataan peninsula. While their missions ranged as far north as the coast around Aparri, the 8th also provided tactical coverage for the Lingayen landings. On January 14 a mission to Formosa (Taiwan) staged through Mindoro on the return flight. The last mission in January was a photo reconnaissance of the Visayan Islands airdromes by two F-5s.

Typical missions for the month included a mapping mission to the Balete Pass area of west central Luzon flown by Lts. Wald and Blank on January 5. The Balete Pass was weathered in, so the two F-5s concentrated on such targets as the town of Baguto and the Harbor at San Fernando. Altitude for the reconaissance ranged from 27,000 to 30,000 feet. The next day Lts. Monroe and Shuman were escorted by four Corsairs to photo recce the Lingayen Gulf shoreline at altitudes generally below 10,000 feet. On January 14 the squadron established a detachment on Mindoro Island to extend its range to China, Indo-China (Viet Nam), and Formosa.

Two typical missions for February included a mapping mission to the Visayans by Capt. Lamdin and Lt. Gray on the 11th and a reconnaissance to Formosa by Major Shipway and Lt. Thompson on the 19th. Lamdin and Gray photographed Bohol, Samar, and Cebu during the morning and covered several airdromes with their K-18 cameras. (Mapping missions usually were covered with K-17 cameras, but this mission prehaps had a dual purpose.) Major Shipway and Lt. Thompson successfully photographed the Jitsucetsu-Tan power installations on Formosa (Taiwan) and got some good coverage of the Koshun and Taito airdromes.

In May the squadron also set up an air echelon at Clark Field that lasted from May 19 through August 12. The range of the Squadron's F-5s was now extended from Borneo in the south to the southernmost areas of Japan itself.

Major Richard C. Bailey replaced Major Shipway at the end of March to become the last wartime commander of the squadron. Major Bailey saw the 8th PhS make its last wartime move on July 15, 1945, when the squadron boarded ship on Leyte and left for Okinawa.

Within a few days the 8th PhS had arrived on Okinawa and was set up on Motoby peninsula by July 21. Until the end of the war the squadron flew missions over Honshu, Kyushu, and Shikuku. On 28 September 1945 the 8th was based on Japan proper when it moved to Chofu. It moved to Irumagawa on January 26, 1946, and to Yakota in 1949. During the Korean War the squadron operated from bases both in Japan and Korea, extending its record of service into an entirely new era.

ESCAPE AND EVASION
THE EIGHT MONTH ORDEAL OF FRED HARGESHEIMER

During 1943 at least fourteen 8th Photo Squadron personnel were lost on operational or other types of flight. Three of those reported missing were lucky enough to be recovered either through rescue efforts or by their own determination.

Major Art Post was hit by a number of Japanese fighters over New Britain on June 20, and bailed out of his burning plane to land somewhere near Wide Bay. He was picked up by submarine on September 28 and transported to Hawaii. Since he had no orders, he simply came back to New Guinea and was flying again with the 8th Squadron by the end of October.

Lieutenant LeGrand Kneeskren had an equally harrowing return home when he bailed out of his Lightning on July 31 in the Markham Valley northwest of Nadzab. He was rescued by friendly natives on August 10, but didn't return to the squadron until August 17 in a ragged condition, including a missing boot.

The most impressive story of evasion and escape, however, was that of 1st Lt. Fred Hargesheimer, who was shot down over northern New Britain on June 5, 1943. Hargesheimer got up on the morning of June 5 and found that he was assigned to the coastline reconnaissance of New Britain. After a breakfast that usually consisted of powdered eggs, coffee with condensed milk, and toast covered with an unmeltable butter substitute, Hargesheimer went out to his F-4 and made the final preflight check with his crewchief.

Hargesheimer took off a little later in the morning and headed for the New Britain coast. He made the periodic radio checks along the route until his last communication over Open Bay just southeast of Rabaul. When he failed to return or check in by five o'clock in the afternoon, his comrades reluctantly added his name to the missing in action list, but silently hoped that he would somehow make it back.

What had happened when Hargesheimer made his last call was that word had reached the Ki-45 Toryu (dragon killer) twin-engine interceptor-equipped Japanese Army Air Force 13th Sentai that enemy aircraft were sighted in its sector. Warrant Officer Mitsugi Momotomi was off duty at the time, but was so excited by the prospect of meeting the Americans in combat that he implored one of the alert pilots to switch places for the scramble.

Momotomi got his fellow pilot to agree and was off with the flight to meet the Americans for the first time. When he reached about 12,000 feet Momotomi began to search the sky with his reputedly keen vision and eventually sighted an object that looked at first like a small bean in the distance. At first he thought it was a Mitsubishi Ki-46 twin-engine reconnaissance plane returning from a mission, but soon recognized the unmistakable twin-booms of the Lockheed Lightning. Taking care not to be discovered, Momotomi let his Nick, as the Ki-45 was codenamed by the Allies, settle in behind and slightly to the left of the American. Excitement for the Japanese pilot was high, but he forced himself to calm down and gradually closed the distance to about 200 yards before he opened up with his 37 mm cannon and 12.7 machine gun. Hits were scored on an engine, and the American pilot belatedly reacted to the threat by opening up both throttles and leaping out of range by several hundred yards before Momotomi could deliver the final blow.

Nevertheless, Momotomi and his gunner, Sgt. Kurihara, watched as the Lockheed fell with smoke trailing behind. Finally, at an altiude of about three to four thousand feet, a parachute appeared, and Momotomi restrained Kurihara from firing at the dangling figure beneath the canopy during a close pass because the enemy pilot was certain to be quickly picked up and captured. The Japanese crew exulted in the first certain victory over a Lockheed Lightning by the 13th Sentai.

Momotomi's victim was almost certainly Fred Hargesheimer. It was the first P-38 type aircraft claimed by the 13th Sentai and was listed in accounts of the Japanese units as being downed around the end of May, or perhaps beginning of June 1943. Hargesheimer was the first reported MIA flying a P-38 type aircraft in the New Britain area.

Hargesheimer was completely surprised by the twin-engine Japanese fighter that jumped him from the rear and set fire to both engines. The American avoided the killing burst of fire, but felt the blood running down his face that gave notice the enemy had nearly finished his purpose anyway. With a pull of the emergency release handle just above his head the battered reconnaissance pilot stood up into the rushing wind and was swept into space.

Relieved when the flapping material of the parachute opened into a bright canopy, Hargesheimer concentrated on his descent into the hostile country below. He did not know for certain at the time, but he was headed for the jungle near Wide Bay on the northwest side of New Britain. The ground came up with a rush, but he landed safely into the mud of the jungle. Taking stock, he was happy to learn that his only injury was a gash on the head, which he was able to bind with strips of the parachute.

The emergency kit that he carried contained a compass, knife, matches, three bars of chocolate, medicine, fishing equipment, and a canvas bag for water. This meager fare would be sufficient for perhaps a few days, and he would be required to trek through the thick rain forest for a full month. Within two weeks his provisions were gone and his uniform was in tatters from the inhospitable environment.

New Britain was about the worst place to try and survive during the war. The jungle itself was formidable, with many virulent diseases waiting for an unadapted American or European. In addition, there were a number of native tribes that still practiced headhunting, or were sympathetic to the Japanese. The Japanese troops themselves were the most ferocious in the Pacific, hating the enemy without reservation or thought of mercy. Some Americans who fell into Japanese hands were brutally killed on the spot at the pleasure of unreasoning fury.

This state of affairs weighed on Hargesheimer's mind as he made his way through the muddy slime and vines that barred his way and ripped at his clothes. He had decided to risk contacting one of the villages in the area even though he knew the penalty was either death or the almost equally painful prospect of capture by the Japanese. On the 31st day of his lonely trek Hargesheimer encountered some natives in a canoe who were singing a song in a language he didn't understand, but he recognized the tune as Onward, Christian Soldiers! Later he learned that he had stumbled on the only Christian village in the area, and that every other tribe was either loyal to the Japanese or were headhunters.

The leader of the natives was a solid little man with curly black hair who produced a note that identified him as the chief named Lauo. An Australian coastwatcher named John Stokie had signed the note, which also certified Lauo loyal to the Allies.

Hargesheimer nearly broke down and cried when he realized that the uncertainies and perils of the past month were virtually over. He was given fruit and some meat to replenish his depleted and ravaged body. However, he was still desperately ill and found it difficult to keep down the exotic food. The natives quickly took him in their canoe to the safety of their village of grass huts by a lagoon, and kept him hidden from occasional Japanese patrols and aircraft flying overhead. Even his bootprints were brushed over by the children of the village, who followed behind him to cover his trail from the Japanese.

With all the care that his new friends were lavishing on him, Hargesheimer was nevertheless becoming weaker and developed malaria. He was bedridden for a time, but Lauo and his people stood vigil and prayed over him. When it was apparent that he needed more nutritious food the natives provided mother's milk to keep the American flyer alive.

Gradually he began to recover and was able to sit up and take other nourishment. Under the care of the natives he survived and eventually began to take steps under his own power. By this time it was near the end of 1943 and word had reached the 8th Squadron that Hargesheimer was alive but in a badly weakened condition.

One day an unfamiliar native came to the village and reported that three Australians had just landed fairly nearby and had a wireless set. Even in his less than healthy condition, Hargesheimer set out with some of the natives to find the Australians. When he did find them they turned out to be coastwatchers sent to report on air activity between Rabaul and New Guinea.

Hargesheimer took his turn on radio watch during the next few months, and once when he was on duty heard the report that airmen on New Britain could be evacuated. He was delirious with joy at the news, and preparations were made to take him and a number of other Allied flyers off the island.

The next morning he set off with two Australian airmen who had been shot down and made their way to the same post to find the rendezvous point where the submarine USS *Gato* would stand by to pick them up. A few days later they found ten other Allied airmen at the rendezvous, and on the night of February 5, 1944, Fred Hargesheimer boarded the *Gato* and was on his way home. After eight months in the perilous New Britain jungle the first thing Fred heard when he was hauled aboard the submarine was one of the crewmen asking, "where the hell have you guys been? You were supposed to have been here yesterday!"

Hargesheimer was sent homeward to recuperate and didn't see much of the Pacific until the end of the war. Years later he began to feel a longing to meet his native benefactors once again and to do something in repayment of his debt to their kindness and bravery in risking their lives for his sake. From time to time he would send small sums of money through the Methodist mission at Rabaul.

There was yet a restlessness in Fred Hargesheimer to find and renew friendship with the natives to whom he literally owed his life. He scraped together enough finances to fly to New Guinea in 1960 and joined Matt Foley, one of the coastwatchers who participated in his rescue. Taking a launch to New Britain, Hargesheimer landed at the spot on New Britain where he found the village, and Lauo and all his other friends of seventeen years before.

After the joyous reunion, Hargesheimer returned home and was even more determined to do something permanent for his friends. Somehow, he gathered up the resources and returned with his son in 1963 to begin work on a school to be staffed by an Australian and two native teachers. The school opened in February 1964—just twenty years after Hargesheimer was picked up by the submarine.

Sgt Bissett of the 8th PRS. (McDowell)

Tom Farmer at Nadzab, of the 6th PRG. (Farmer)

Max Blank by his F5-F.

Major McCoy of the 25th PRS at Nadzab. (McDowell)

Wally Kennedy by F5-E and F5-G (McDowell)

The Admiralties Invasion on February 29, 1944. 17th RBS Photo.

Pilot Richard Monroe by the squadron sign at Nadzab. (McDowell)

8th PRS F5 #81 at Nadzab. (Kimbrough)

8PRS F5E at Nadzab. (National Archives Fred Pernell)

Major Dick Shipway at Nadzab. (McDowell)

20th Combat Mapping Squadron F-7 at Nadzab.

8th Photo Recon Officers at Nadzab. (McDowell)

Above, Left: Allen Blum on his F-5 around May 1, 1944.

Right: Supposedly this F5D #561 was the one flown by Art Post and Sgt Mendenhall when they were lost in a lagoon off Biak on August 25, 1944. The record states that Post was flying a F5A.

822nd Bomb Squadron of the B-25 equipped 38th Bomb Group dropping food, water, ammunition, and medical supplies to the 6th Army's 24th and 41st Division around the end of April or beginning of May 1944 at Hollandia. (John Miller)

Allen Blum and Tom Farmer being briefed by pilot Lloyd Daniels for a mission. (Farmer)

Moe Dmochowski and Curtis Dell sometime in 1944.

8PRS Flightline crew at Nadzab. (Bugai)

Unpainted F5A at Nadzab Drome. 8PRS began receiving natural metal F5 aircraft early in 1944. (McEwan)

8PRS F-5 at Mokmer Drome, Biak. (National Archives Kate Flaherty)

Bombed out Japanese Helen bombers at Hollandia. (Davis)

F5D of the 8PRS at Biak. (National Archives Dale Connelly)

Sgt Carl Squibb, an assistant crew chief of the 8th PRS near the 8-Ball on a F-5.

8PRS LST landing on Leyte Island in the Philippines. (McDowell)

8PRS pilot Wally "Screwball Wall" Kennedy on Dulag Strip. (McDowell)

Pilot Putnam McDowell on Dulag Strip. (McDowell)

The first three pilots on the ground from left to right are McDowell, Grey, and Jones at Dulag Strip.

Pilot Howard Belon on Dulag.

Pilot George Frankforter was a friend of Putnam McDowell at Harvard. They went into the LTSAAF together and both wound up in the 8th Photo Recon by accident.

Pilot Richard Boyer at Dulag. (McDowell)

McDowell by another F-5 Lightning at Dulag. (McDowell)

Pilot Richard "Junior" Monroe.

McDowell by a F-5 Lightning at Dulag. (McDowell)

8PRS #381 on its nose. (Bugai)

Engine change on a F-5. (Bugai)

Morotai Island with 13th AF B-24s on the revetments. (National Archives via Rocker)

8th Photo area on Leyte. (McDowell)

Changing a propeller at Dulag. (McDowell)

8th Photo jeep at Dulag Strip (McDowell)

8th Photo officers at Dulag around the end of 1944. (McDowell)

8th Photo pilots on a squadron F5. Commander Dick Shipway is standing on the pilot gondola, Dulag late in 1944. (Dmochowski)

Engine change at Dulag.

Pilots and officers at Dulag in December 1944.

8PRS enlisted men at Dulag.

8th Photo Camera Repair personnel at Dulag. (Hilliard)

Top, L to R: Matthews, Prince, and Merrill. Kneeling: Campbell, McKenzie, and Russ. Crew Chiefs for Monroe and Farmer.

8th PRS L-4 at Dulag. (Andrew J. Kappel)

Down on the 8th PRS line at Dulag

Just after #381 nosed over on the pierced steel mat.

Working on a F-5 engine at Leyte.

#275 taxiing onto the runway at Leyte.

SSgt. Glen Headley by a wrecked Ki-49 Helen at Wakde. (Headley, 17 R.B.S.)

#381 after its nose gear collapsed on Dulag. (Bugai)

Curtis Dell and Richard Boyer at Leyte. (Dell)

Richard Erickson at Dulag a few days before he was shot down in November 1944 over Leyte. (Dell)

8th PRS pilot Monroe beaming with pride at his F-5. (Carl Prince)

8PRS F-5 "LITTLE LORRAINE" at Dulag with different pilots Frankforter and Carmen. (Jeff Ethell/Jack Carmen)

8PRS F-5 at Dulag.

Another view of Lt. Richard Erickson, who was killed off Tacloban on a tactical photo mission in November 1944. (Dmochowski)

Pilot "Moe" Dmochowski before a flight. (Dmochowski)

8PRS F5E on Nadzab. (National Archives Mary Ilario)

Chapel on Biak in November 1944. (McDowell)

F-5E on Mindoro. Earl Lee's airplane. (Lee)

Pilot Byron Dobbs and crew chief near F-5C on Nadzab. (Dobbs)

Sgt. Frank Bissett, instrument specialist in the Philippines. (Earl Lee)

8PRS F-5Es on Mindoro. (Lee)

Rear: Earl Lee, Carl Squibb, Andy Kappel; Front: Frank Bissett, John Miller. All Sergeants in the Aviation Specialist Section at Nadzab ((Andrew Kappel)

8PRS pilot Byron Dobbs by F-5C at Nadzab. (Dobbs)

Carl Prince working on a L-4 at Dulag. (Lee)

Street in Tacloban. (Lee)

8PRS line at Tacloban. (Lee)

8PRS camp at Uleta, Philippines, around the time that Japanese paratroopers were dropped on Leyte on the evening of December 6. (Lee)

RAAF P-40N damaged in crashlanding of 8th Photo Recon F-5B at Tadji, New Guinea, on April 30, 1944. Hewitt Clark was the F-5 pilot. (Dale Connelly)

F5B #83 lies in a Sago Palm swamp at Tadji after crashing into the Australian P-40. (Kate Flaherty)

Three F-5s returning to base at Dulag, Leyte. (A. Faranda)

8PRS F5E being serviced at Dulag, Leyte. (A. Faranda)

8PRS F5Fs on the flight line, Mindoro Island. (A. Faranda)

Pilot Tad Dmochowski on the Dulag strip. (Rocker)

The bar in the officers' club at Dulag was constructed from the tail of a P-38. (Rocker)

The B-25 at Dulag. (Thureen/Rocker)

8PRS F5E at Dulag. (Rocker)

View South of Middleburg island. (Rocker)

Flight line at Dulag. (Rocker)

Leo Schoman, Flight Engineer and a pilot, is 4th from the left. (Rocker)

Lt. Col. Alex Guerry. (Rocker)

F5E at Dulag, with the ground crew hard at work. (Rocker)

Lt. Bernard Walzak next to his pair of wings. (Rocker)

San Fernando harbor on Luzon near Lingayen Gulf's northeast corner, photographed on January 5, 1945. (McDowell)

Manila bomb damage photographed by the 26th PRS on February 15, 1945. (McDowell)

Malogo Drome on Negros Island, two miles south of Alicante, photographed on Feb 20, 1945 (McDowell)

Lipa Drome concrete runway, 40 miles south of Manila. (National Archives Fred Pernell)

Bacolod Drome on northwestern Negros Island. (McDowell)

Grace Park Airdrome, Manila, on January 7, 1945. (McDowell)

Pilot Harold Southard finds a treasure in one of the bunkers in the Philippines (Southard)

8PRS squadron painter Sgt. Carl Hankey putting touches on the unit logo. (McDowell)

Bridges at Calumpit in central Luzon. These bridges carried the main lines of supply through the central portion of the island and were destroyed just prior to the landings on Lingayen. Vertical photo taken on January 7, 1945. Low angle photo of the same bridges taken in July 1945. (McDowell)

Pilot McDowell near one of the nipa huts on Dulag. (McDowell)

Richard Bailey and William Grey somewhere in the 8th PRS area around the middle of 1945. (McDowell)

Sgt T Looker and "The Beast" (Looker)

Clyde McConnell (McDowell)

Pilot George Frankforter and Sgt. Vaughn on Dulag. (McDowell)

Pilot Putnam McDowell on Mindoro Island. (McDowell)

Pilot David Alleman was killed during a flight in July 1945. (McDowell)

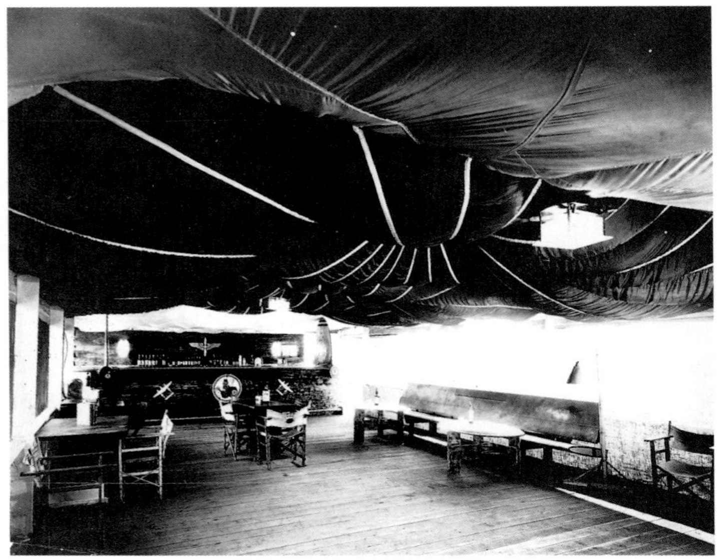

Two views the 8th Photo Squadron's bar on Leyte. The bar was a F-5 horizontal stabilizer. (McDowell)

Left: Insignia on 8PRS F-5. (McDowell) *Top:* 8PRS photo of the 503rd Parachute Regiment on Corregidor in February 1945. (McDowell)

Pilot Max Blank at Dulag.

Insignia on a squadron F-5. (McDowell)

Showers at Clark Field, Luzon, in the spring of 1945. (McDowell)

6PRG photo of the 475th Fighter Group dropping napalm near the Ipo Dam in south central Luzon during the sping of 1945. (McDowell)

8th PRS showers on Leyte. (National Archives Kevin Morrow)

8PRS F5-E undergoing repairs at Dulag. (Thureen)

Dick Shipway about the time he assumed command of the squadron.

Tad "Moe" Dmochowski by a F5-E on Dulag. (Dmochowski)

Left: Boyer and Dell back from a mission at Dulag. (Dell)

Squadron cub brought out of the jungle by crew chiefs. Commander Dick Bailey is at the right. (Connie Bailey)

Curtis Dell on a mission to Manila in January 1945. Photo taken by Putt McDowell. (Dell)

Essex class carier USS *Randolph*, which was struck by the F5 flown by 8PRS pilot Lewis Gillespie on June 7, 1945. (Lt. Cdr. Walter Timmons)

Ben Armstrong with crew chief Meicher. (Armstrong)

Lewis Gillespie was on his last flight before going home when his F5 went out of control and crashed on the deck of the Randolph in Tacloban harbor. Several sailors were killed or injured. (McDowell)

Luxury escort in the form of P-51s and even Navy F4U Corsairs late in the war. (Dell/Rocker)

8PRS F-5s on Dulag.

C.O. of the 8th Photo Recon Squadron, Dick Shipway.

Last wartime C.O. of the 8PRS, Major Richard Bailey.

Frank Lloyd, Dick Bailey, and Ben Armstrong socializing with Red Cross nurse. (Bailey)

LST landing on Okinawa. (McDowell)

Left: Motobu Field on Okinawa, last wartime home of the 8PRS, photographed on September 6, 1945. (McDowell)

8PRS tent on Okinawa.

Above, Below: Various views of the 8PRS line on Okinawa. (McDowell)

Japanese peace envoys in the surrender Bettys. (Thureen/Mattila)

Jack Lamdin, "A Great Guy and Pilot," 8th Photo Operations Officer at the time of his death in an accident on Mindoro Island in February 1945. (Dmochowski)

Japanese airfield on Honshu with Ki.84 Franks on the revetments. (McDowell)

Pilot Max Blank. Killed testing jet after WWII. (McDowell)

8PRS photo of Inchon Railyard on August 25, 1945. Note people below looking up at Lightning just passing over the yard. (McDowell)

8PRS pilot Wally Kennedy by F5G at Chofu, Japan. (McDowell)

Japanese trainer biplane at Chofu, Japan. (McDowell)

Pilot Richard Boyer in Japan. (McDowell)

8PRS at Motubu Drome, Okinawa.

Flightline at Johnson AFB. (Mattila)

Curtis Dell's groundcrew. (Dell)

8PRS F-5 flightline at Johnson AFB in Japan.

8PRS F6Ds at Johnson AFB. (Mattila)

P-51 s in Japan after the end of the war. (Mattila)

F6Ds at Johnson AFB. (Mattila)

F6 runup at Johnson AFB. (Mattila)

Another F6 at Johnson AFB.

Jack Mattila and crewman by an AT-6 at Johnson AFB.

Pilot Heller with his F6 after the war. (Mattila)

F5 late in 1945 or early 1946 at Johnson AFB, Japan. (Mattila)

8PRS pilots at Johnson AFB, Japan. (DuRant)

F-5F and 8PRS pilots, Johnson AFB, Japan. (DuRant)

F-5F and 8PRS pilots, Johnson AFB, Japan. (DuRant)

8PRS F-6s fly past Mt. Fuji in Japan. (DuRant)

Pilot Frank DuRant, left, and friend on the wing of a F6D Mustang. (DuRant)

8PRS F-6 in Japan. (DuRant)

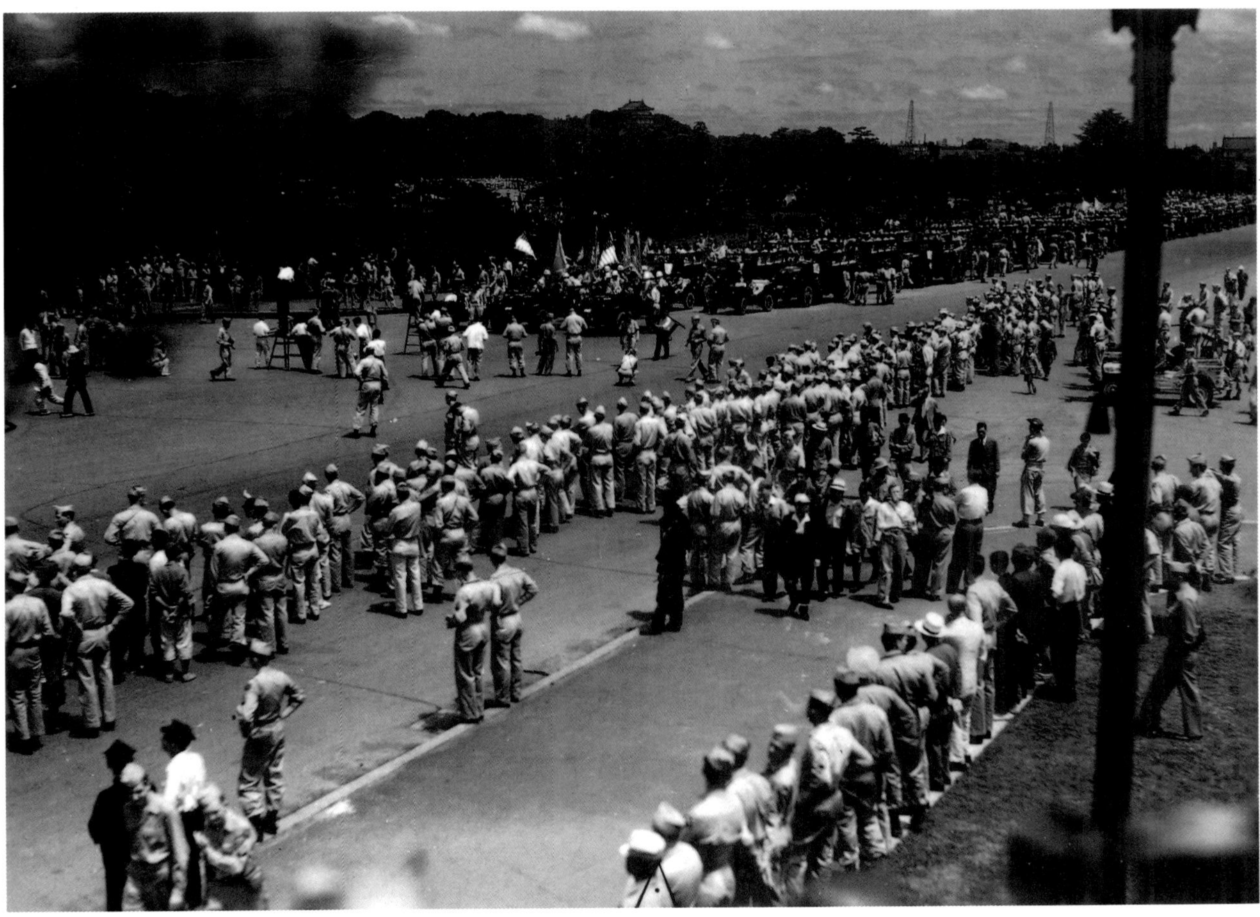

MacArthur's entrance into Tokyo. (Mattila)

F5E being serviced and fueled at Dulag in the Philippines. Bill Kumik leaning on the gas truck, John Miller on engine stand and Art Kreider on ground. (Faranda)

USS *Randolph* (CV-15) was struck by 8PRS F-5 on June 7, 1945. The crash killed a number of seamen and injured others. (Sharon Culley)

Color Gallery

432nd Fighter Squadron Lightning taking off from Dulag.

Wrecked Ki-21 Sally on Wakde. (Thureen)

Queen Mae, 20th Combat Mapping Squadron F-7 at Dulag. (Heller)

Jack Lamdin's crash in an 8PRS F5E on Mindoro during a courier flight.

Other views of P-38 taking off from Dulag. (Heller)

Major Tom McGuire, Operations officer of the 475th Fighter Group, former commander of the 431st Fighter Squadron and number 2 American ace with 38 confirmed victories, in his P-38, PUDGY V on Dulag strip. (Thureen)

17th Recon Bomb Squadron B25 on Dulag Strip. (Thureen)

8PRS F5E Camera Repair. (Susko via Thureen)

Navy TBM Avenger on Tacloban Strip. (Thureen)

Tacloban Strip from the south and from the southwest. (Thureen)

Clark Field in 1945.

B-25 (17-10) of the 19th Tactical Recon Squadron.

P-40N of the 110th Tactical Reconnaissance Squadron. (Thureen)

8PRS Lightning taking off in the Philippines.

F5 come to grief.

B-24 taking off, probably in the Philippines.

8th PRS F5E taking off from Motobu Drome, Okinawa. (Thureen)

8th PRS F5 at Dulag.

P-38 under the wing of a B-24 at Biak. (National Archives Fred Pernell)

The chowline at 14-Mile Drome, Port Moresby (Heller)

C-46 Commando at Dulag.

Following: **Wrecked Japanese aircraft on Lae and Hollandia dromes.** ***Left:*** **Note red primer on Japanese aircraft and scrapped B-24 in background. (Kirby)**

Note 9th Fighter Squadron P-38 in background. (Cooper via Tilley)

Tom McGuire and Frank Nichols examine wrecked Tony. (Tilley)

Wrecked Japanese aircraft at Hollandia. (John Babel)

39th Squadron P-38s and 40th Squadron P-39s on the Tsili Tsili Alert flight line in August 1943.

Alert tent at Tsili Tsili Drome in September 1943. The P-39s belong to the 40th Fighter Squadron. (Jeff Ethell)

Tsili Tsili Drome in August 1943.

Curtis Dell in the cockpit of his F-5 at Dulag. (Dell)

Oro Bay in August 1943.

12-Mile strip. (National Archives Kate Flaherty)

Appendix I: Losses in Action - Men and Machines Commanders of the 8th

Name	Aircraft	Location and Circumstance
Louis J. Connely		MIA, Lae, 2 May 42
Paul O. Staller		MIA 19 Aug 42, later found Misiama Island, fatally injured.
Andrew W. Peterson		MIA Buna, 9 Sep 42
Phillip D. Lissner		KIA, Crash on SW New Guinea coast, 28 Nov 42
Stephen Humenchick	B-24 Air Photog	Crash Wards Drome 7 Feb 43
Wm W. Morton		MIA, Ramu-Markham Valley 16 Mar 1943
Robt. M. Blackard	F4, Ser. 412177	MIA, Markham Valley 21 May 1943
Kenneth J. Murphy		MIA, Rabaul 26 Jun 1943
Clifford D. Taylor	F5A, Ser. 4213088	Missing on C/C flight, 10 Sep 43
C. E. Bateson		MIA, Madang 8 0ct 43
Fred W. Cross		25th Squadron pilot lost in 8th Sq. plane at Hood Point, 5 Dec 43
Philip J. Lynch		Enlisted men killed in B-17 crash at 14-Mile Drome, 26 Dec 43
Robert C. McGee		B-17 crash at 14-Mile Drome, 26 Dec 43
Charles K. Erb	F-4, Ser. 412209	MIA, Coral Sea, 30 Dec 43
	P-39Q, Ser. 4219949	Lost, 1 Jan 1944
Andrew Y. Davis	F5A, Ser. 4213090	MIA, Salamaua, 9 Feb 44
Sheldon P. Hallett	F5B, Ser. 42267384	Shot down over Tadji, 29 Feb 44
	F5B, Ser. 4267360	5 Mar 44
	F5B, Ser. 4267363	5 Mar 44
	B-17E, Ser. 41-2464	8 Ju 44
Arthur Post		KIFA in crash off Biak lagoon
Delbert Mendenhall	F5A, Ser. 4213093	25 Aug 44
	F7B, Ser. 4440422	30 Sep 44
	F5B, Ser. 4268247	24 0ct 44
Richard E. Erickson		24 Nov44
Clyde McConnell	F5E, Ser. 4328953	13 Dec 44 reported picked up by guerrilla forces on Luzon
	F6D, Ser. 4414621	1 Dec 44
	F5E, Ser. 4328970	28 Dec 44
W. J. Brunhaver	F5B, Ser. 4268270	KIA, 10 Jan 45
	F5B, Ser. 4423279	19 Feb 45
Jack F. Lamdin	F5E, Ser. 4328334	Crashed on takeoff on courier mission 20 Feb 45. Died of wounds 21 Feb 45.
	F5B, Ser. 4268249	4 April 45
	F5E, Ser. 4329034	10 May 45
David Alleman	F5E, Ser. 4423275	Killed in crash north of Subic Bay, 1 July 45.

Commanders

The seven wartime commanders of the 8th PRS were:

Capt. Karl Polifka	11 Feb 42 - 11 Nov 42	Capt. DeLasso Loos	9 Dec 43 - 25 Mar 44
Capt. Frank Savage	11 Nov 42 - 4 Jun 43	Maj. Richard Shipway	21 Apr 44 - 25 Mar 45
Capt. Arthur L. Post	4 Jun 43 - 20 Jun 43	Maj. Richard Balley	25 Mar 45 - ?
Capt. John G. Foster	20 Jun 43 - 9 Dec 43		

Appendix II: Celebrities Supporting the 8PRS

Some famous entertainment figures at one time or another gave support to the 8th Photo Squadron and lifted the morale of the unit considerably. During the latter part of 1943 Bob Hope took his USO troupe, including Frances Langford and Patti Thomas, to the Pactfic and made a stop at New Guinea. The 8th PRS was delighted to receive the show of solid backing from the home front.

Following: **Pinups dedicated to the 8th Photo Squadron.** ***Top:*** **Anne Baxter.** ***Right:*** **Gale Robbins (Hilliard)**

Top: **Carole Landis.** ***Right:*** **Trudy Marshall. (Hilliard)**

Sonja Henie. (Hilliard)

Patti Thomas and Frances Langford at Dobodura with the Bob Hope show. (McEwan)

Patti Thomas was a dancer with the USO and was highly popular with her G. I. audiences. She always represented the intangible girl back home to the airmen and soldiers in New Guinea.

Appendix III: Aerial Photos and Aircraft

Dobodura's Strip #7. (National Archives Sharon Culley)

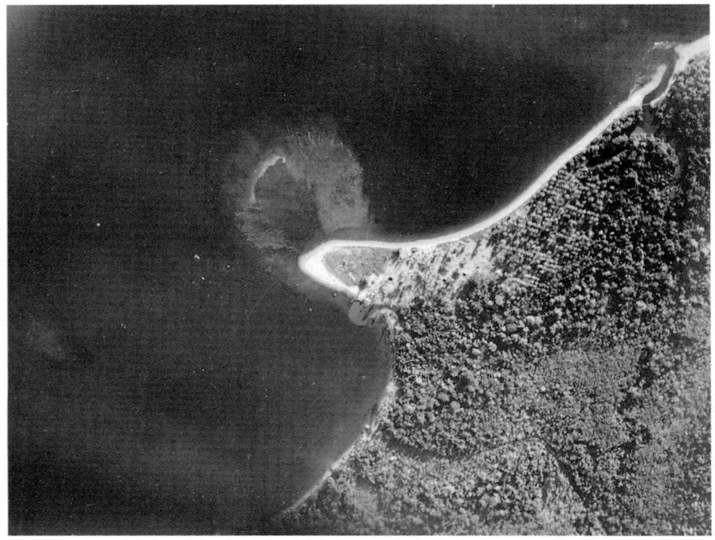

Buna's Sananandа Point, the center of focus for Allied operations at the end of 1942.

14-Mile Strip with 12-Mile in the background. (McEwan)

Lae, New Guinea, in June 1942. (Sowers)

Nadzab Strip #1 used by the 8PRS. (National Archives Mary Ilario)

Hansa Bay on August 28, 1943. Photographed by the 8th Bomb Squadron of the 3rd Bomb Group. (Andy Weigel 8 B.S.)

Nadzab Strip # 1 from the South/Southeast (Walter Benz via Larry Hickey)

Dagua Strip photographed on August 17, 1943, by the 822nd Bomb Squadron of the 38th Bomb Group. (Jim Kendall)

Dagua under attack on February 3, 1944. (Vic Tatelman)

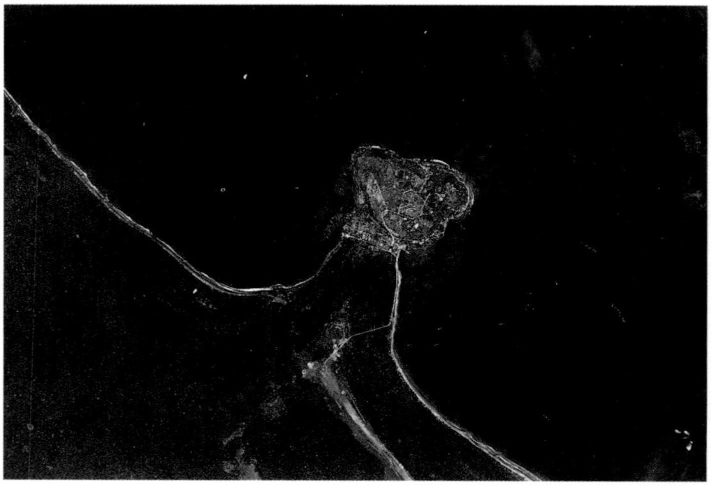

43rd Bomb Group photo taken on March 15, 1943, of Wewak Harbor and town. (Dieffenderfer)

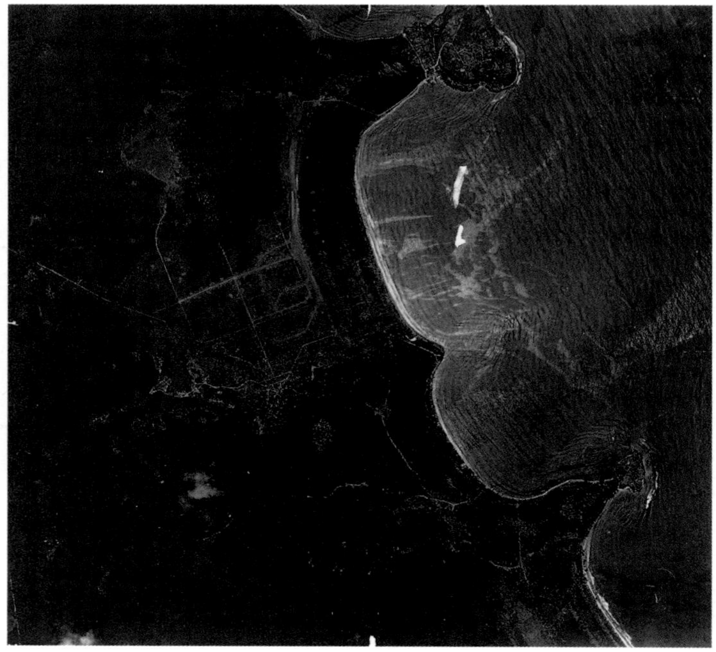

Wewak Harbor area early in 1943. (Dieffenderfer)

Wewak photographed in 1942. (Dieffenderfer)

Rabaul's Simpson Harbor with Lakunai Drome at the right. (National Archives Fred Pernell)

8PRS photos of Wewak Drome, town, and harbor taken on 30 August 1943. (Sowers)

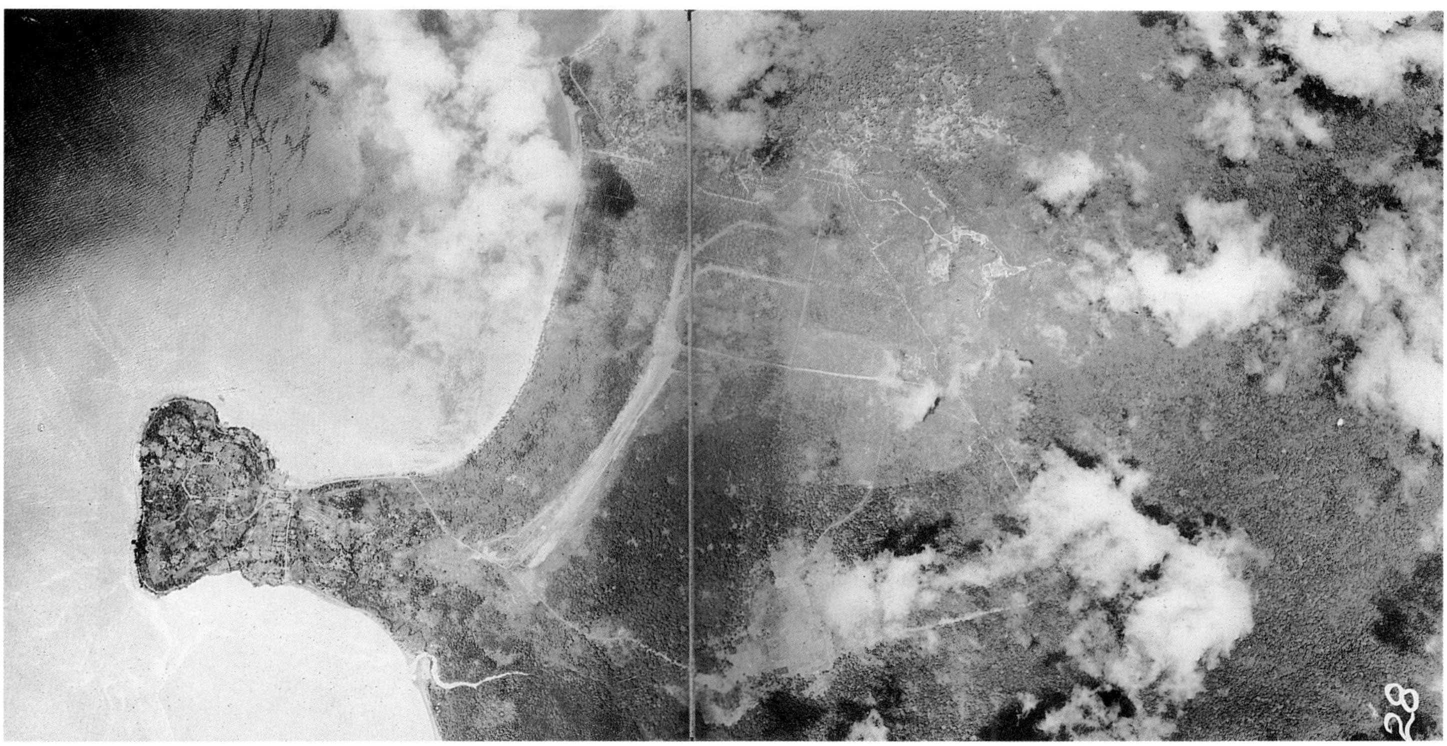

Oblique view of Rabaul town and Simpson Harbor. (Royal New Zealand Air Force)

1st Sentai Ki-43 Oscars and 68th Sentai Tonys on Rabaul's Vunakanau Drome. Northwest dispersal area. (National Archives Kate Flaherty)

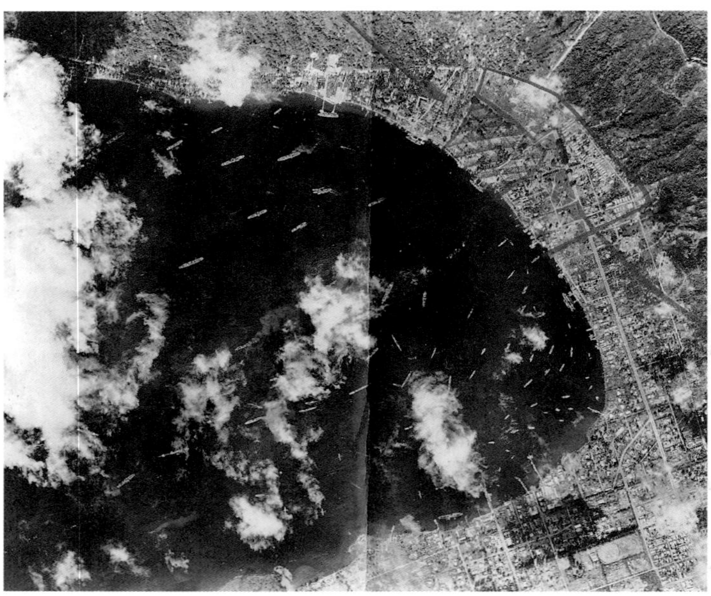

43rd Bomb Group vertical of Rabaul. (Dieffenderfer)

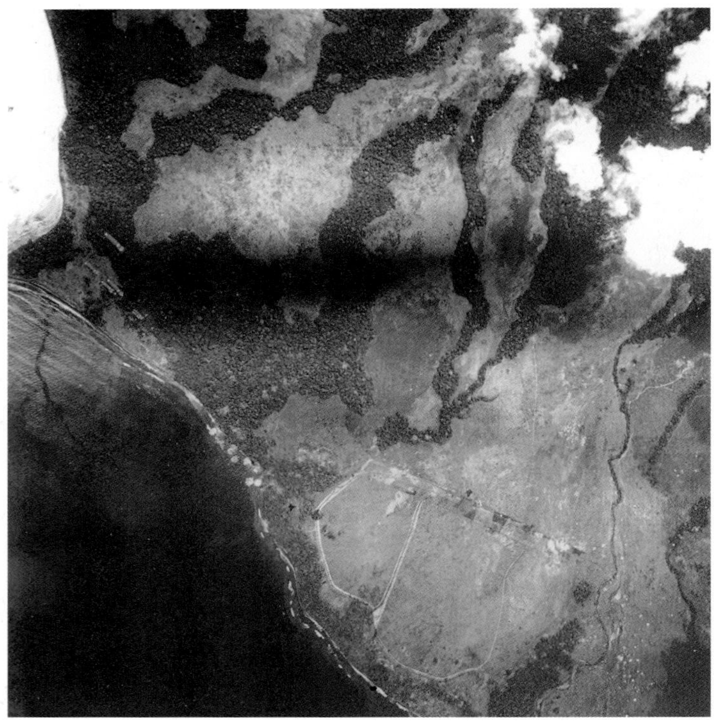

90th Bomb Group photo of Cape Gloucester taken on November 22, 1943. (Wiley Woods, 90 B.G.)

Japanese strips at Tadji. (Tatelman)

Puerto Princessa, Palawan Island. (Wiley Woods, 90 B.G. via Rocker)

Hollandia's Sentani and Cyclops Dromes. Ki.43 Oscars are visible on Cyclops. (National Archives via Jack Fellows)

Hollandia Strip, view east. (National Archives Fred Pernell)

25th PRS photo Inagahuan to Tagburos Palawan.

Tanguingui Island and lighthouse in the Visayan Sea. (Armstrong)

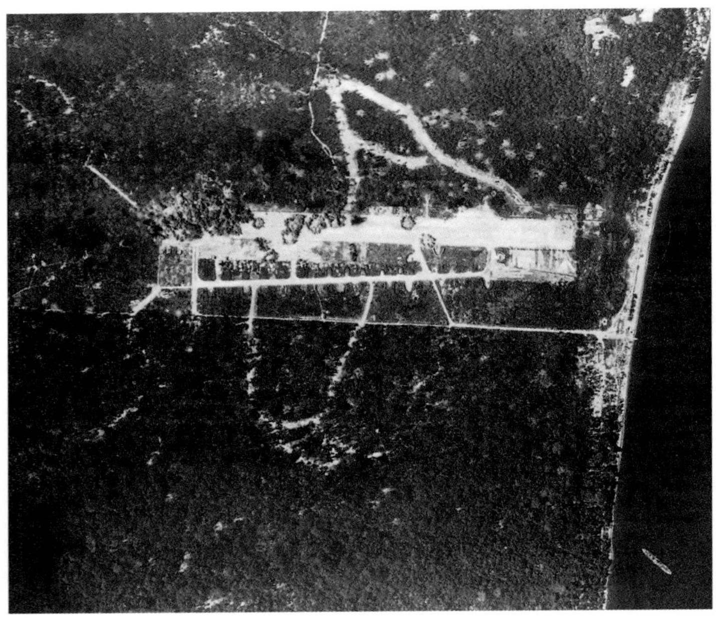

Kahili drome on Bougainville. (Jim Kendall, 307 B.G.)

Left: **Wakde Island attacked by 38 Bomb Group B25s on April 28, 1944. (Hal Wirlfrey)**

Manus Island in the Admiralties.

Momote Airstrip on the first day of the Admiralties invasion, February 29, 1944. Photographed by the 17th RBS. (Sgt Zock)

Kavieng Drome on 16 March 1944. (Dieffenderfer)

500 Bomb Squadron, 345th Bomb Group attack on Samah Drome, Hainan Island in the South China Sea (Armstrong)

A view of Gasmata on New Britain photographed on Mar 13, 1943. (Diefenderfer)

Aircraft of the Southwcst Pacific.

F4 and F-5 aircraft:

Pilot Belon by his F-5F, LOVELY LUCILLE the 4th. (Bugai)

8PRS flightline crew by F-5 #371. (Bugai)

8PRS F-4s at 14 Mile. (Davis/Cobb)

F-5Fs later in the war. (DuRant/Bugai)

Maintenance on #248. (Carl Prince)

Lightning over Dobodura. 433rd Fighter Squadron, 475th Fighter Group. (John Tilley)

A-20 Havoc

A20A over Papua on October 24, 1942.

Mike III of the 89BS, 3BG at 3 Mile.

Another 89Bomb Squadron A20 at 3 Mile.

A20 also photographed over Port Moresby on October 24, 1942. (Hilliard)

B-17

The 8PRS B-17E RFD TOJO. (Rogers/Sowers/Williams/Reindl/Melman)

The 8PRS B-17E RFD TOJO. (Rogers/Sowers/Williams/Reindl/Melman)

B-17 at Papua on October 24, 1942.

General Kenney's B-17E (Martha Cobb)

B-24

20th Combat Mapping Squadron F-7(B-24)

B-25

B-25 on a mission over New Guinea on October 21, 1942. (Hilliard)

8PRS B-25 REDHEADED GAL. Trimetragon cameras at 14 Mile on 20 August 1943. (Reindl)

90th Bomb Squadron's EARLY BIRD at 17 Mile. (McKinney)

6th Photo Group B-25 at Nadzab. (Ted Hanks 475 F.G.)

Another view of the B-25 on a mission over New Guinea on October 21, 1942. (Hilliard)

17 Recon Bomb Sq B-25s (F-10) in the Philippines.

B-26

B-26 used by 8PRS being serviced at 14 Mile Strip about October 1943. (John Neilson)

A B-26 of the 22nd Bomb Group's "Great Silver Fleet." (Lawrence Wulf, 22 B.G.)

Others

A B-29 photographed on Ie Shima around the end of the war. (Bill Wallisch, 35 F.S.)

C-47 at Nadzab. (McEwan)

41st FS P-39s. (Sowers)

Above and Following: F-4 and F-5 aircraft of the 8PRS. (McDowell/Cobb/Gerhard/Sowers)

U.S. ARMY
AIR FORCES

5926
826

22

8

142

Aircraft of the RAAF

Spitfire (452 Squadron)

Boomerang (4 Squadron)

Beaufighter (Delbert Wagenecht)

Mosquitos

Beaufort at Tadji in June 1944.

Lockheed Hudson on November 21, 1942. (Hilliard)

Surrender Betty on Ie Shima. (Davis)

35th FS P-40Ns and 80th FS P-38 on Cape Gloucester. (National Archives Dick West, 35th F.S.)

P-51s passing Mt. Fuji. (Gerhard)

82nd Tactical Recon Squadron P-51.